Introduction to
Computer-Assisted Reporting

Introduction to Computer-Assisted Reporting

A JOURNALIST'S GUIDE

Matthew M. Reavy
University of Scranton

Mayfield Publishing Company
Mountain View, California
London • Toronto

Library of Congress Cataloging-in-Publication Data
Reavy, Matthew.
    Introduction to computer-assisted reporting : a journalist's guide / Matthew Reavy.
      p. cm.
    Includes index.
    ISBN 0-7674-1155-2
    1. Electronic news gathering.   2. Journalism—Computer network resources.   I. Title.

PN4784.E53 R43 2001
070.4'3'0285—dc21

                                  00-065378

Manufactured in the United States of America
10   9   8   7   6   5   4   3   2   1

Mayfield Publishing Company
1280 Villa Street
Mountain View, California 94041

Sponsoring editor, Holly Allen; *production editor,* Carla White Kirschenbaum; *manuscript editor,* Karen Dorman; *text designer,* Michael Warrell; *design manager and cover designer,* Violeta Diaz; *art editor,* Rennie Evans; *illustrator,* Emma Ghiselli; *manufacturing manager,* Randy Hurst. The text was set in 10.5/12 Goudy by Thompson Type and printed on 50# Finch Opaque by Malloy Lithographing, Inc.

Cover image: Arthur S. Aubry/PhotoDisc, Inc.

Credits Netscape Communicator browser window. Copyright © 1999 Netscape Communications Corporation. Used with permission. Netscape Communications has not authorized, sponsored, endorsed, or approved this publication and is not responsible for its content. **Chapter 4** P. 33 With permission from Jules Siegel. P. 34 With permission from Lee Hickling. **Chapter 6** Figs. 6.1, 6.2 Reproduced with permission of Yahoo! Inc. Copyright © 1999 by Yahoo! Inc. Yahoo! Inc. Yahoo! And the Yahoo! Logo are trademarks of Yahoo! Inc. P. 64 With permission from Neil Reisner. **Chapter 7** Figs. 7.1, 7.2 Reprinted with permission. *http://www.ipswitch.com.* Fig. 7.3 Copyright © 1991–2000 WinZip Computing, Inc. WinZip® is a registered trademark of WinZip Computing, Inc. WinZip is available from www.winzip.com. WinZip screen images reproduced with permission of WinZip Computing, Inc. **Chapter 8** Figs. 8.1, 8.2, 8.8 Reprinted by permission from Microsoft Corporation. **Chapter 10** Fig. 10.1 Reprinted by permission from Microsoft Corporation. **Chapter 13** Fig. 13.1 Reprinted by permission from Microsoft Corporation. **Appendix I** Figs. I.1, I.2, I.3 Reprinted by permission from Microsoft Corporation. **Appendix II** P. 198 From *Tactics For Writing and Editing CAR Stories.* With permission from Jeffrey C. Kummer. P. 200 From "Detroit Cops Are Deadliest in the U.S.," May 15, 2000 by David Ashenfelter and Joe Swickard, *Detroit Free Press.* Reprinted with permission. P. 201 Reprinted with permission from the *New York Daily News.* P. 202 With permission from Richard Galant.

In memory of Jean Howatt

PREFACE

Computer-assisted reporting represents one of the most exciting advances in journalism since the advent of desktop publishing. News organizations are scrambling to find employees who have the ability to use computers to locate, gather and analyze electronic records for the purpose of creating news stories. Colleges and universities are striving to train more students to meet these needs. As a result, computer-assisted reporting is currently one of the fastest growing areas in journalism.

This text is intended primarily for use in the growing number of courses that concentrate on computer-assisted reporting; however, it can also serve as a supplement in classes aimed at introductory, advanced or investigative reporting, as well as in specialty courses such as medical, environmental, business or science journalism.

The goal of *Introduction to Computer-Assisted Reporting* is to demystify the use of the computer as a tool in reporting methods. By emphasizing the process of developing a computer-assisted story, students learn that a computer is only supplemental to the traditional values of good journalism. Chapter 2 provides a detailed case study of the development of a computer-assisted story allowing students to see the big picture as well as to better understand the process.

FEATURES

- **Numerous examples** taken from working journalists and published computer-assisted reporting (CAR) stories found throughout the text.
- **Internet Coverage:** Extensive coverage (five chapters) on how journalists use the Internet and the World Wide Web for reporting purposes.
- **Spreadsheet and Database Coverage:** Extensive coverage of using spreadsheets in CAR (5 chapters) as well as using databases in CAR (4 chapters).
- **Comparing Databases:** Provides coverage of joining databases (relational databases) for developing CAR stories. Uses a real-life example of a published article outlining a match comparison of the database for employees of the Georgia Public School system to a database of those convicted of crimes in the state of Georgia.
- **Writing the Story:** Complete appendix provides tips for writing the CAR story.

- **Glossary:** Complete glossary helps students understand the more specialized language in computer use.

Instruction focuses on the universal aspects of each tool discussed, without dwelling on the details of individual software packages. Because computer-assisted reporting remains a relatively technical enterprise, the text makes extensive use of definitions and lists to provide structure and help ensure that students do not become overburdened by complicated computer terminology. Emphasis is split between providing instruction on the skills of computer-assisted reporting and supplying a context that permits students to understand the value of what they learn.

ACKNOWLEDGMENTS

No work of this length is done without the help and support of many individuals. The list of people who deserve my thanks for this book is too long to recount here. However, a number of people deserve special mention. Foremost, I would like to thank Holly Allen, senior editor at Mayfield Publishing, who found me when this book was little more than an idea and shepherded me through the entire project. A host of other Mayfield editors have extended their expertise in producing this work. I owe particular thanks to Senior Production Editor Carla Kirschenbaum and Permissions Editor Marty Granahan for their patience with the project. I would also like to thank the following reviewers, who provided excellent feedback that resulted in substantial improvement to this book: Fred Blevens, Southwest Texas State University; Fred Endres, Kent State University; Daniel Foley, University of Tennessee; Bob Gassaway, University of New Mexico; Kent Middleton, University of Georgia; Steve Ross, Columbia University; Jeff South, Virginia Commonwealth University; Kim Walsh-Childers, University of Florida.

This work grew over the years, and so I would like to break my acknowledgments down by those who helped me as I moved from place to place:

NICAR/IRE/University of Missouri: Andy Scott, former head of the Missouri Institute of Computer-Assisted Reporting, who taught me the basics of CAR and gave me my first opportunity to teach professional seminars; Brant Houston, former managing director of the National Institute for Computer-Assisted Reporting and current executive director of Investigative Reporters and Editors, who helped me continue to learn through teaching and doing CAR; Dean Mills, Esther Thorson and Zoe Smith of the University of Missouri who gave me my first chance at teaching CAR in the classroom; Drew Sullivan, Richard Mullins, Andy Lehren, Gwen Carleton, Wally Winfrey, Jan Colbert and the rest of the NICAR gang, each of whom taught me something new at one time or another.

Manship School of Mass Communication: Jack Hamilton, dean of the Manship School, who gave me my first full-time teaching job and provided more support than any faculty member has a right to even hope for; Richard Nelson and Ron Garay, associate deans while I taught at the Manship School, who mentored me through stages of the book; David Perlmutter, Lou Day and the other faculty and staff at LSU who were always there when I needed help or advice; the Manship family, who graciously provided me with an endowed professorship so that I could complete the bulk of this work while I continued on the faculty at Louisiana State.

University of Scranton: Joseph Dreisbach, dean of the College of Arts and Sciences, who has gone to great lengths to grant me the time needed to complete this work; the faculty and staff of the communication department, who put up with me when the deadline pressure was on; and my old friend G. Donald Pantle, S.J., who helped take the pressure off.

On a more personal note, I would like to thank my parents, George C. Reavy and Antoinette Halas, whose enduring patience and sacrifice I can only hope to someday reward. Finally, I would like to thank my wonderful wife Susan and my stepson, Sam. When I needed time alone to work, they gave it. Yet, they always seemed to know when I needed to play as well. Together, they keep me in the "real" world.

CONTENTS

CHAPTER 14

Searching for the Expected and the Unexpected:
Linking Databases   175

APPENDIX I

Computer Basics   186

APPENDIX II

Tips for Writing the Computer-Assisted Reporting Story   198

What Is Computer-Assisted Reporting?

The business of making a newspaper is in a state of constant growth and change. You might almost say that it is revolutionized once every 10 years. The veteran returns to find the old weapons out of date, the old plans of action out of relation to the present arrangement of the forces. . . . The history of journalism, for 50 years, has been a rapid succession of revolutions and no man knows as well as the hardworking editor that perfection has not yet been evolved.[1]

In this chapter you will learn:

- What computer-assisted reporting is and what it is not

- The difference between data and information

- How computer-assisted reporting developed as a trend in journalism

- What precision journalism is and how it relates to computer-assisted reporting

- The meaning of some basic computer terms such as *mainframe* and *hardware*

Many journalists today can sympathize with those words, penned by pioneer reporter Whitelaw Reid in 1879. Journalism does appear to be in a constant state of flux, its weapons forever falling out of date. The manual typewriter goes electric, and then gives way to the VDT, or visual display terminal. The VDT and mainframe computers make way for stand-alone microcomputers. These personal computers, or PCs, are subsequently linked to create local or even wide area networks and, finally, to the Internet itself. It is no wonder journalists occasionally feel that technology threatens to pass them by.

Technology powers the modern news organization. Personal computers serve the functions formerly performed by typewriters, copyboys and composing room personnel. Programs help the copydesk by checking spelling, grammar and readability. Editors no longer count headline spacing by hand; they simply examine their work on-screen. Television producers edit copy, change production schedules and even converse with reporters entirely on-line. Indeed, computers are now so commonplace that they have become like telephones, hardly noticed except when they are absent.

Yet, computers have not changed the basic function of the journalist. Arville Schaleben, managing editor of the Milwaukee *Journal*, described the role of journalism more than 35 years ago: "News, information and more information—these are what [the media] exist for."[2] That description remains as true today as it was in Schaleben's time. Then, as now, the primary duty of the journalist is to gather, analyze and disseminate information. Computers do not change that duty. They simply provide a tool that enables journalists to fulfill that duty more easily, quickly and thoroughly than before.

A DEFINITION OF COMPUTER-ASSISTED REPORTING

Journalists use computers all the time. But does that mean that nearly all engage in computer-assisted reporting? If the term is taken literally, the an-swer must be yes. Some journalists have even argued that using the term *computer-assisted reporting* is as ludicrous as suggesting that there should be such a thing as "telephone-assisted reporting."[3] After all, as I have already noted in this chapter, computers are nearly as common as telephones in some newsrooms. Why should they be treated any differently?

The answer, of course, lies in the level of expertise required to effectively use each tool. A four-year-old child can pick up a telephone receiver and dial a number. A slightly older youngster knows how to use a phone book or call an operator for assistance. That is essentially all a person needs to operate a telephone. But while those same children might be able to turn on a com-puter and operate a word processor or a few simple games, it is unlikely they possess the ability to master the vast array of programs a typical journalist might use on the job. To state it plainly, computers require far more time and education to operate than a telephone does. Until that gap narrows, the term *computer-assisted reporting* remains a valid means of identifying a specific jour-nalistic skill.

So what is computer-assisted reporting? Broadly defined, **computer-assisted reporting,** or **CAR,** is the use of computers to gather or analyze data for the purpose of transforming that data into information used as part of a narrative to be transmitted via a medium of mass communication. It is possi-ble to break that description down into its constituent parts. By definition, computer-assisted reporting involves the use of a computer. Journalists can use the computer to gather data, as is the case when they connect to the Internet or a database for the purpose of retrieving a specific item. Or jour-nalists can use it to analyze data, as when they use a spreadsheet program or database manager to look for patterns in a specific group of data.

The term **data** refers to isolated facts. By themselves, they might reveal nothing. However, jornalists can use them to derive **information**—one or more facts placed in a context that gives them meaning. Remember that information, not newspapers or broadcast signals, is the business of journalism. Every modern journalist gathers data, such as that which arises from crime reports, press releases or public meetings. And every modern journalist analyzes that data, either internally or with the aid of experts who are interviewed to provide context. The journalist then transmits the resulting information to the public, usually through some kind of narrative—a news story. Therefore, computer-assisted reporting represents nothing more than a new technique for journalists to do the same thing they have been doing for hundreds of years, that is, gather facts and weave them into a story.

Some journalists employ computer-assisted reporting in their everyday routine. Others limit it to special projects. Still others have never used it. Computer-assisted reporting can be as simple as using the Internet to locate a phone number or examining a budget with a spreadsheet program. It can be as involved as analyzing multiple nationwide databases to uncover the causes of and solutions to crime. But computer-assisted reporting is more than just running programs. Effective CAR practitioners need to know something about the computer itself, how it operates and how it handles data. They must be able to identify potential applications of CAR techniques to routine as well as in-depth stories. They require an understanding of data—how to locate it, how to negotiate for it, how to move it from one computer to another and how to import it from one program to another. They must also know how to turn that data into a story through more traditional reporting skills. In the end, good computer-assisted reporters are just good reporters with the benefit of a new tool that helps them do their job more effectively.

A BRIEF HISTORY OF COMPUTER-ASSISTED REPORTING

Although we often think of computers as a new phenomenon, particularly in the media, journalists have been using the machines since the fall of 1951 when Remington Rand released the first commercially available computer— the Universal Access Computer, more popularly known as UNIVAC I. Just a few months after UNIVAC I went on the market, a representative of CBS approached the business machine maker with a proposal. The network would grant the Rand free commercial airtime in exchange for use of the company's typewriters and adding machines during presidential election coverage.

Rand offered a counterproposal. It would grant CBS use of all the machines it needed if the network let UNIVAC I play an active role election night by predicting the winner based on early poll results. The company's publicist, Harry Wulforst, suggested that viewers would stay tuned in throughout the night just to see whether the computer turned out to be right or wrong. CBS agreed and at 8:30 P.M. on Election Day, November 4, 1952,

Walter Cronkite appeared on air telling viewers, "It's awfully early, but I'll go out on a limb." He presented UNIVAC's prediction that Dwight D. Eisenhower would win the White House by a slim margin, a prediction that turned out to be off by only one percentage point. In so doing, Cronkite became the nation's first "computer-assisted" journalist.[4]

Early computers like UNIVAC I were known as **mainframes,** very large and expensive computers designed to be used by hundreds or thousands of users either simultaneously or in batches. To get an idea of just how big these computers were, consider that the fictionalized Jim Lovell, played by Tom Hanks in the film *Apollo 13,* bragged to visitors that NASA had a computer "small enough to fit in a single room." Mainframes had another problem besides their size and cost. Although the machines were physically capable of running programs, a person could not simply go out and purchase a program. Instead, companies had to employ computer programmers to create and maintain programs designed to perform specific functions for a specific company on a specific computer. A program that ran on a UNIVAC I would not necessarily run on any other mainframe, and many other mainframes were soon available.

Although some media outlets did purchase mainframes, the machines were usually reserved for business functions, such as billing and customer service, or for electronic typesetting at newspapers and magazines. It took nearly 15 years before a journalist once again began using computers to assist in reporting the news. That journalist was Philip Meyer, sometimes referred to as the Father of Computer-Assisted Reporting. In 1967, fresh from a year as a Niemann Fellow at Harvard University, Meyer found himself temporarily assigned to the *Detroit Free Press* during the height of that city's summer riots. In an effort to explore what caused the riots and who had been involved, Meyer conducted a survey of Detroit residents. With the assistance of John Robinson and Nathan Kaplan at the University of Michigan, he used a mainframe computer to analyze the survey results and generate information that could strengthen the paper's articles.[5] Meyer's work helped the paper win a Pulitzer Prize that year for its coverage of the riots and their aftermath.

Meyer pioneered the field of **precision journalism,** the use of social science techniques, particularly quantitative methods such as surveys, as an aid in reporting the news. Precision journalism usually makes use of computers to analyze data gathered by researchers. It therefore falls under the umbrella term of computer-assisted reporting. Because of precision journalism's reliance on computers, Meyer became a natural resource for journalists nationwide who wanted to explore using the machines in their work. For example, in 1973 Meyer helped *Philadelphia Inquirer* reporters Don Barlett and James Steele use a government-owned computer to analyze sentencing trends in the city's court system. That analysis formed the basis of the paper's first computer-assisted reporting series, "Unequal Justice." Later, at the *Miami Herald,* Meyer worked with reporter Rich Morin to secure and analyze real estate assessments stored on a magnetic computer tape reel, one of the first instances in which a journalist obtained government records that had been stored by a computer.

Although computer-assisted reporting powered a number of important investigations during the 1970s, it was often tedious. Getting data into a computer was no easy process. First, records had to be obtained from the appropriate government agencies. If the work had not been stored by a computer, workers had to translate the data into computer format by punching holes into paper cards that were organized and fed into the computer by hand. The cards had to be checked and rechecked for errors, especially those caused by inadvertently bending or tearing the paper. Because most newspapers did not have mainframe computers, journalists often were forced to rent time on other computers, which cost anywhere from $75 to $500 per hour. They also had to wait, often for days, while technicians manipulated the data. During the entire course of this process the journalists rarely, if ever, saw the actual data. Obviously, many were discouraged.

If mainframes had prevailed as the standard, computer-assisted reporting would likely have remained a field limited only to those journalists with the time and financial backing to undertake in-depth investigations. Fortunately, changes already under way within the computer industry would soon take computer-assisted reporting to its next level. Those changes had begun in 1971 with the invention of the **microprocessor,** a tiny silicon chip containing miniaturized circuits that comprise most of the computer's functions in a fraction of the space. By the mid-1970s handheld calculators were performing the same functions that large mainframes had less than two decades earlier. And they were doing it faster.

Calculators were obviously a boon to any journalist who had to deal with numbers, but an even greater advance were the new **microcomputers,** also known as **personal computers,** or **PCs,** desktop-sized computers designed to be purchased by individuals or small businesses. While some people tend to view microcomputers as mainframes in miniature, they are actually based on an entirely different concept. Mainframes were designed for multiple users and required programs specifically written for each type of machine. By contrast, microcomputers were intended to be used by one person at a time. More important, they were created so that they could use generic programs that could be purchased separately. Thus, a program written for an Apple II computer could be sold "off the shelf" and used in any Apple II. Computer users now spoke of computers in two terms: **hardware,** the physical components of the computer and the machines attached to it; and **software,** programmed instructions that tell the computer what to do. Microcomputers represented a revolution in the computer industry and a blessing for journalists.

As computers became more affordable in the 1980s, more journalists began using them. Perhaps the most successful of the decade was Bill Dedman of the *Atlanta Journal-Constitution.* Working with database specialist Dwight Morris, Dedman examined U.S. census data and Federal Reserve System records to explore lending patterns among Atlanta banks. The resulting series, which detailed discrimination in housing loans to African Americans, won the 1989 Pulitzer Prize for investigative reporting. Since that time a computer-assisted reporting project has won at least one Pulitzer Prize every year.

Up to this point, the history of computer-assisted reporting had been marked by individual successes. Although journalists had been talking about using computers, the industry had no focus. Information was not being exchanged quickly enough. That changed in 1989 when former *Providence Journal* reporter Elliott Jaspin founded the Missouri Institute for Computer-Assisted Reporting (MICAR), a joint effort of the University of Missouri–Columbia and the professional organization Investigative Reporters and Editors (IRE). Jaspin had been working with hardware that allowed microcomputers to handle data stored on magnetic tapes originally designed for use on mainframes. This breakthrough opened a new world of government data to journalists, data that could now be analyzed by individual reporters without assistance from computer technicians. MICAR became Jaspin's tool for spreading information about these new techniques. The institute served as a centralized knowledge bank for all information dealing with electronic government records, from negotiating for data to purchasing and maintaining equipment. Computer-assisted reporting had arrived.

Today MICAR lives on as NICAR, the National Institute for Computer-Assisted Reporting, which was renamed and rededicated with a new purpose under managing director Brant Houston in 1993.[6] The institute conducts training seminars in computer-assisted reporting, serves as a warehouse for certain government records, hosts an annual conference of journalists and consults on CAR projects with media outlets throughout the world.

SUMMARY

Envision these scenarios:

- A newspaper reporter checks assertions made about a government official's voting record in time to ask questions while the press conference is still in session.

- A television producer gains access to the complete history of a specific airplane only moments after it has crashed, and in time for the next breaking news update.

- A magazine editor compares national teacher certifications to a database of convicted child molesters and uncovers a list of pedofiles in elementary school classrooms throughout the country.

The future of computer-assisted reporting is the future of the computer. As the machines increase in power and portability, they become more useful to the everyday reporter. Advances such as cellular modems, satellite technology, voice recognition and so-called expert systems already aid many journalists by providing instant access to resources that in the not-too-distant past might have taken days to locate. It is happening now, and today's journalist needs to keep up or risk returning "to find the old weapons out of date, the old plans of action out of relation to the present arrangement of the forces."

NOTES

1. Whitelaw Reid, 1879. Quoted in Frank W. Rucker and Herbert Lee Williams, *Newspaper Organization and Management*, 4th ed. (Ames: Iowa State University Press, 1974), 89.

2. Arville Schaleben, "The News and You," in *The Citizen and the News*, ed. David Host (Milwaukee, Wis.: Marquette University Press, 1962), 91. Although Schaleben referred specifically to the role of newspapers, the pervasive nature of television today supports extending his remarks to the media in general.

3. For example, Bill Dedman, Computer-Assisted Reporting (presentation made to the annual meeting of the Association for Education in Journalism and Mass Communication, Kansas City, Mo., August 1993).

4. The event is detailed by Harry Wulforst, *Breakthrough to the Computer Age* (New York: Charles Scribner's and Sons, 1984).

5. Philip Meyer, personal interview, March 1, 1994.

6. Houston later took over as executive director of Investigative Reporters and Editors, which now operates NICAR.

2

The Computer-Assisted Reporting Story

START TO FINISH

In this chapter you will learn:

■ How a typical computer-assisted reporting story evolves

■ The seven phases of the computer-assisted reporting process

■ What is meant by the term *data mining*

■ The centralized and decentralized approaches to computer-assisted reporting in the newsroom

When the *New York Times* was presented with the opportunity to get involved in computer-assisted reporting in the 1980s, management initially rejected the concept. This was not traditional journalism, the paper said. Reporters were not simply covering the news, they were creating it.[1] The *Times* has since reversed its opinion and risen to become a leader in the field; however, management's early criticism retains some validity. Although computer-assisted reporting does not change the basic role of journalists—to gather, analyze and disseminate information—it does give them the flexibility to select and report stories based on their own judgment rather than on the whims and wishes of external sources. It allows journalists to take the lead in determining what is news and how that news should be reported.

Consider the role journalists have played throughout much of this century:

We ask only *whowhatwherewhenhowandwhy*, confident that people will tell us the truth and tell it completely. If there is a conflict, we only get quotes from the "other side," seriously endeavoring all the while to make the story somehow balanced. Let the reader decide which side is truthful, it's not our job; we are recorders, not reporters.[2]

Computer-assisted reporting helps transform recorders back into reporters. Every journalist becomes an investigative reporter capable of independently exploring claims made by sources. No longer do reporters need to rely on a police commissioner's statement that crime has decreased. They can check the data themselves. No longer do they need to wait for auditors to assess the local school board's spending during the previous year. They can perform their own analysis. Although computer-assisted reporters still interview sources to help provide a context for the data, they no longer need to depend on those sources to analyze and summarize the data for them.

ONE REPORTER'S STORY

When television reporter Kalleen Capps of Columbia, Mo., decided to get involved in computer-assisted reporting, she did what many journalists exploring the field do—she looked over computer-assisted reporting stories that had been done by journalists in other communities and searched for electronic records in Columbia that matched those in the stories. After some research, Capps contacted a few experienced CAR journalists, who recommended analyzing pet license records as a first-time project. Pet licenses have the advantage of being easy to obtain, easy to analyze and generally less worrisome than weightier investigative projects.

Capps's next task was to locate and obtain the records. A few phone calls to the city's administration revealed that dog and cat license records were maintained by the local health inspector. She called the inspector and arranged to stop by his office to pick up the records, which were stored on a single 3.5-inch computer diskette. Because the records were already in the proper format, Capps had simply to return to her office and begin her analysis.

Following the lead of journalists who had examined these records in other cities, Capps used her computer to answer some basic questions. How many dogs and cats were licensed in the city of Columbia? Who owned the most licensed cats in the city of Columbia? What was the most popular name of dogs? When was the most common time for people to license their pets? Which neighborhoods had the highest dog populations? When Capps completed her analysis of the records, her story was far from finished. While the records provided many answers to *who*, *what*, *when* and *where*, they shed little light on *how* and *why*. How did the person with the most cats in Columbia deal with so many pets around the house? What was it like to live in the neighborhood with the most dogs? Why did people choose particular names for their pets? Did the health department feel overwhelmed by licenses at certain times of the year?

Capps generated a list of pet owners whom she needed to contact in order to provide a context for her story. She interviewed the owners, a few veterinarians and the health inspector in order to flesh out the piece. She also gathered plenty of video of the pets themselves. Within a couple days, her story was edited and ready to run.

THE COMPUTER-ASSISTED REPORTING PROCESS

Computer-assisted reporting projects can range from relatively small features like Capps's pet story to large, involved investigative series. But whether large or small, most computer-assisted reporting stories generally proceed through seven phases: conception, location, acquisition, transformation, examination, exposition and composition. This section illustrates the seven phases of a CAR project by looking at the *Peoria Journal Star*'s yearlong investigation of bankruptcy and its impact on the local community—"The Bankruptcy Burden: Not Paying in Peoria."[3]

When reading through these various phases, do not look at them from the perspective that each phase must be encountered in order. No journalist looks at a project and says, "Now we have to enter the transformation phase." This presentation is not intended to be a blueprint for a project. Rather, look upon it as an aid in understanding the computer-assisted reporting process.

The Conception Phase

The **conception phase** is the phase during which the reporter generates the actual story idea. Every news story begins with either a question or an observation. The *Peoria Journal Star*'s investigative series began with both. During a newsroom brainstorming session, journalists at the paper observed that although the local economy was booming, bankruptcy filings were on the rise. The obvious question was, why? This question naturally led to a variety of other questions. Who is filing for bankruptcy? What types of creditors suffer when an individual or business declares bankruptcy? Where do the debtors live? How much do the debtors owe and how much do they earn? But it was one question that finally launched the computer-assisted reporting project, according to Valerie Lilley, the newspaper's high-tech and finance reporter. "Why do we have to rely on some government or industry-backed, potentially biased study to come along and feed us the answers?" she asked. "Why not do it on our own?"

Sources of most news stories traditionally fall into two categories: people sources and document sources. **People sources** represent any individual or individuals who might provide journalists with a story idea, from family and friends to government officials and whistle-blowers. People sources provide ideas in a variety of ways. A journalist whose friend recently witnessed an accident and blamed it on poor road conditions might decide to look into safety records for area thoroughfares. A school secretary might suggest that examining payroll records would show that relatives of some district board members were doubling their salaries with overtime pay. Journalists encounter dozens of people sources each day, most with their own agendas. It requires good imagination and well-developed news judgment to determine which stories are worth following and which, for one reason or another, are best left alone.

Document sources, on the other hand, represent written records that are either historical (e.g., government reports) or topical (e.g., press releases, advertisements, other news stories). Again, these sources can take many forms. For example, most government bodies publish an annual budget. Reporters can often request the budget in electronic format, which gives them the ability to read it directly onto their computer and analyze the data from a variety of angles rather than limiting themselves to the viewpoint provided by the print copy. In general, if a document created within the past decade exists in typewritten format, it will also exist somewhere in electronic format. If a government agency has a form to be filled out, the data on that form is likely stored on a computer. It is simply a matter of finding it.

The Location Phase

Once the reporter has an idea for a story, he or she enters the **location phase,** during which the appropriate data is located. If a reporter has a specific bit of data in mind, locating that data can simply be a matter of making a few telephone calls. In the example earlier in this chapter, television reporter Kalleen Capps knew she wanted to obtain electronic records of pet licenses. It took her only a few phone calls to learn that the local health inspector kept such records.

Of course, research is not always that easy, particularly when the journalist has a more general idea for a story and little or no idea what data are available. In the example of the reporter whose friend recently witnessed a car accident on a poorly maintained road, the journalist has a vague idea of trying to locate highway safety records. Does he or she want to locate records for local, state or federal roads? The records will likely be maintained by separate agencies. Moreover, the Federal Highway Administration might keep records that supplement state or local records. What types of records are available from each governmental agency? It is likely that records of injuries or fatalities might be separate from those related to property damage. Certainly they would be separate from records of road conditions and repairs. Locating the appropriate data can be quite challenging.

It fell to the *Journal Star*'s high-tech reporter, Lilley, to explore the existence of electronic records to support a bankruptcy investigation. Her first instinct was to visit the federal bankruptcy court and see what could be found on the public access computer. Although the computer had the records that the paper was looking for, it seemed that not all bankruptcies were listed. In many cases, the data was incomplete. In fact, it appeared that no one collected complete data in electronic format. As a result, the newspaper decided to collect the data on its own.

The Acquisition Phase

Once electronic records are located, the reporter enters the **acquisition phase,** during which the data is actually obtained. For most journalists, this phase is the most onerous aspect of the computer-assisted reporting process. Although some government officials encourage access to public records, others can be quite protective of "their" data. Reporters must often be prepared to file formal requests under the Freedom of Information Act in order to gain access to the records. Occasionally, access requires a court order.

Even if the official in charge of maintaining the records agrees to release them, the cost of obtaining the data can be absurd. For example, when the *Hartford Courant* sought driver's license records from the state of Connecticut, government officials originally quoted a price of $3 million. It took three years of negotiations before the state finally agreed to sell those records to the *Courant* at a far more reasonable price of one dollar.[4]

In some instances, the data may simply not be available, or it may be available but not in electronic format. In such cases, journalists must create their own electronic records. This was the problem that faced the *Journal Star*. The decision to collect data by hand should not be made lightly. Transferring printed records to electronic format often requires extensive planning and a good deal of time. How will the records be used? Will you need to compare these records to others in the future? Do you need all the information that appears on the printed record or just a portion of it? How much time will it take to input a single record? Accuracy is also a factor. Data is valuable only to the extent that it is accurate. Misspelling even one out of every 100 names can render a collection of electronic records virtually useless. Journalists creating an electronic record must devise a system for ensuring the accuracy of their records.

Lilley and features reporter Pam Adams quickly discovered the problems associated with entering the data by hand. The two journalists took a pair of laptop computers down to the courthouse and began inputting the data. Each case had 28 separate pieces of data to be recorded, as well as the name of each creditor in the case and the amount that creditor was owed. Some cases had as many as 200 creditors who were due money. After a week's work, Lilley and Adams had input just 90 of the estimated 2,000 bankruptcy cases on file. Having the reporters enter the data themselves proved too time-consuming and expensive for the newspaper to bear.

But the time was not necessarily misspent. As Lilley observed, "I think we could have learned later, but actually going down there and rifling through each file gave us a crash course on bankruptcy. We also couldn't help but read each file and wonder about the story behind it." Even in cases in which reporters can obtain data electronically, it is good practice for them to lay hands on a few paper records. Indeed, comparing the paper records to the electronic version can sometimes yield interesting information, such as the fact that the agency providing the data has arbitrarily removed a few categories before turning it over to the newspaper or television station.

In the case of the *Journal Star*, actually visiting the courthouse proved beneficial in another way. The two reporters met a group of women who came to the courthouse daily to enter data for information companies such as Dun and Bradstreet. The journalists ended up contracting with one of these women, a bankruptcy specialist, to enter the data for slightly more than a dollar per case. Over the next six months she provided the newspaper with roughly 2,800 cases in electronic form. *Journal Star* reporters checked a random sample of the records against the print counterparts and found no data entry errors. They were ready to enter the next phase of the process.

The Transformation Phase

The journalist has located and obtained electronic records, but those records may still not be ready to be used. The **transformation phase** involves moving the data to a usable storage medium, usually CDs or floppy disks, and translating it into a readable format. In an ideal world, a journalist could connect to a government computer over the Internet and simply download data directly to his or her computer. But most government agencies do not store their data on the Internet. Instead, many keep their electronic records exclusively on high-volume magnetic cartridges or tapes. Unfortunately, many journalists lack the resources needed to use data in this format. The data must be transferred to a more usable medium. The transferal process can usually be handled rather easily by any competent individual with access to the appropriate equipment. If the data is stored on a nine-track tape, for example, a knowledgeable journalist with a tape reader could transfer the data to a computer's hard drive within a matter of minutes.

The process does not end once the journalist has the data on an appropriate medium. The files themselves must often be translated into a usable format. Government agencies generally store information in generic text files. These files must be translated into a format that is readable by the program being used to analyze the data. For example, a journalist interested in examining data from the local school board might obtain a file stored in generic text format. He or she could then use a database program such as Foxpro or Access to translate the data into readable format.

The *Journal Star* had a simpler task at hand. The newspaper loaned its data contractor a laptop computer that contained Microsoft Works, an integrated software package that includes a spreadsheet program. She input the data directly into a Works spreadsheet file. Every few days the data contractor would drop a diskette off at the newsroom and pick up an empty one. (The same two diskettes were used repeatedly in order to reduce the chance that a virus would be introduced to the system.) Lilley would then open the Works file using the Excel spreadsheet program, which allowed her to easily save the file in Excel format. Excel also allowed Lilley to later save the file in database format so that it could be read by her Foxpro database management program.

The Examination Phase

With the data in proper format, a reporter can begin the **examination phase,** during which one or more computer programs are utilized to filter, sort, group and otherwise analyze records. The examination phase is what most people think of when they use the term *computer-assisted reporting*. This phase is when journalists do their number crunching—using the computer to answer the questions that they already have laid out as well as to explore new questions that might arise during the analysis. Usually, reporters have some ideas about what they are looking for, such as racial discrimination in mortgage lending or sentencing trends among male and female judges. However, it is also possible to engage in **data mining,** a process whereby reporters look at data from a number of different angles in search of patterns that suggest potential news stories. For example, a reporter on the police beat might wish to examine crime reports for an entire year with the idea that some kind of story will emerge from the data itself. The final product might be as interesting as a full-color map showing which neighborhoods were the most violent, or as simple as a list of the number of crimes by type. The results depend on the quality of the data and the ingenuity and expertise of the reporter.

The *Journal Star*'s first examination of the data produced an inch-thick packet of lists, statistics, definitions and the like. Lilley circulated copies of this packet among those working on the project, but she worried that few people would want to wade through all the numbers. "I'm not sure anyone read it or sorted through the readouts," she observed. "I don't think that I would've read it now that I think back." Lilley decided to sift through the data once more in order to generate a more concise document. She took each major piece of data and described it in sentence format. The final two-page report answered the most basic questions and later served as a "cheat sheet" for journalists working on the project.

The Exposition Phase

When the bulk of the data analysis is finished, it is time to begin the **exposition phase,** the traditional telephone line and shoe leather process of journalism. Often this phase begins with a brainstorming session within the newsroom. Various story angles emerge and need to be discussed. Then journalists go out in search of the material that will form the bulk of the story that finally appears. Documents need to be checked to provide more history and depth. Individuals need to be interviewed to give the story a human face. Sometimes the electronic records will need to be reexamined in light of new information provided by sources.

The *Journal Star* began its analysis by approaching its own cheat sheet as though it were a press release. Lilley explored the losers and the winners in local bankruptcies. She interviewed corporate CEOs, financial officers, vice presidents and other spokespeople. Pam Adams took on the task of locating and interviewing these debtors. She used computer records to isolate those who filed with the largest amount of debt as well as those who carried comparatively little debt when they filed. Contrary to expectations, most of those who had filed for bankruptcy were not living a wealthy lifestyle. In fact, most were living at or below the poverty level when they filed. Many tended to be transient, which made the task of locating them all the more difficult. Reporters used the newspaper's electronic library to sift through old bankruptcy announcements in an effort to track down those who had filed for bankruptcy.

Given the sensitivity of the issue, it should come as no surprise that the *Journal Star* had some difficulty getting people to go on the record. "The biggest problem was getting people to talk about their filing," Lilley explained. "Some didn't want to rehash sour memories. Others didn't want to have their names published in the newspaper . . . again." Despite the difficulties, *Journal Star* reporters were able to gather enough commentary to flesh out their project.

The Composition Phase

Finally, the project enters the **composition phase,** when the actual writing and editing takes place. It is all too easy to become distracted by the technological aspects of computer-assisted reporting and underestimate the task of writing the story. Don't. Data-driven news stories require some special consideration, particularly in broadcast news where the viewer can easily be overwhelmed by the numbers. In the case of the *Journal Star*'s bankruptcy project, the biggest difficulty was simply organizing everything. "We had so much data that we could easily have bombarded the readers with stat-packed stories," Lilley explained. It was a team effort to create the package that readers eventually would see. Chief photographer Larry Brooks, who handled most of the artwork for the team, suggested that the project run as a week-long series. Columnist Terry Bibo worked the series into a rough outline. The *Journal Star*'s Washington correspondents, Toby Eckert and Dori Meinert, wrote about related legislation brewing in Congress.

The *Journal Star* debuted its seven-part series on a Sunday with an examination of the elements of bankruptcy within the Peoria area. Monday's articles focused on examining bankruptcy itself and the myths associated with it. On Tuesday the paper focused on federal legislation and the ongoing battles within Congress. The paper explored the causes of bankruptcy on Wednesday, pinpointing credit cards as the root of most debt. Articles on Thursday and Friday examined the winners and losers in bankruptcy, while Saturday's wrap-up featured a discussion of what might be done to correct the problem.

The *Journal Star* series generated a great deal of response from readers, many of whom were surprised by what the newspaper had uncovered. A district bankruptcy trustee even sent the staff an azalea bush along with a note of congratulations. The response was not lost on *Journal Star* managing editor Jack Brimeyer, who was quick to praise those involved with the series both individually and as a group. The series also raised the standing of computer-assisted reporting in the newsroom, opening the door for staff members to incorporate use of the computer into more projects.

It should be noted that not every computer-assisted reporting project involves all these phases. Remember that CAR techniques might be used to do a five-minute search of the Internet to background a business—conception, location and acquisition. A reporter trained to use computers might call up a voter registration database to find the mayor's unlisted telephone number, which might involve only conception and analysis because the database has already been located and acquired. Consider the various CAR phases a road map rather than a specific set of directions.

COMPUTER-ASSISTED REPORTING IN THE NEWSROOM

Computer-assisted reporting is a dynamic process. The previous section outlines the various phases through which a typical story progresses. Of course, other factors will come into play. Foremost among these is the character of the newsroom in which the journalist operates. In general, newsrooms take either a centralized or decentralized approach to computer-assisted reporting.

In a **centralized approach,** computer-assisted reporting is confined to a specific person or group of people within the newsroom. Individual reporters who want to examine electronic records work with CAR specialists—news librarians, researchers, or special projects and investigative reporting units— to locate, obtain and analyze the appropriate data. The centralized approach has the benefit of saving short-term costs in computer training. Some managers also feel that it allows reporters to concentrate on story exposition rather than data analysis. However, the centralized approach to varying degrees removes reporters from an important part of the reporting process. It can also create bottlenecks if there are not enough resources to handle the influx of requests. While a centralized approach makes sense for many large-scale projects, it prohibits individual reporters from routinely employing computer skills in their everyday work—such as analyzing budgets and backgrounding individuals or businesses.

The **decentralized approach** emphasizes universal access to computer-assisted reporting tools. All reporters have access to the Internet and a variety of computer software either at their desks or at a specific location or locations within the building. Management must invest more time and money into computer training, but the decentralized approach gives reporters the freedom to direct the data analysis, using their expertise to identify and explore a variety of potential angles to their story. It also allows them to save time and effort in their more routine work.

In general, newsrooms taking a centralized approach to computer-assisted reporting are in a transitional stage. As journalists without computer skills see their CAR counterparts doing better stories in less time, they quickly gain an interest in developing these skills themselves. Many CAR specialists soon begin to proselytize their colleagues, often taking it on themselves to conduct impromptu training seminars. The time may not be far off when nearly every newsroom can boast a decentralized approach to computer-assisted reporting.

SUMMARY

Now that we know what computer-assisted reporting is and how a story evolves, let's take a look at some of the specific tools of computer-assisted reporting, beginning with the Internet and the World Wide Web.

NOTES

1. Dwight Morris, personal communication, November 14, 1993.
2. John Ullmann and Jan Colbert, *The Reporter's Handbook: An Investigator's Guide to Documents and Techniques* (New York: St. Martin's Press, 1991), 3.
3. The complete series can be found through the newspaper's Web site at <http://www.pjstar.com>.
4. Brant Houston, *Computer-Assisted Reporting: A Practical Guide* (New York: St. Martin's Press, 1996), 165–66.

3

Journalism and the Internet

AN INTRODUCTION

In this chapter you will learn:

- Four ways the Internet has had an impact on journalism

- What the Internet is and how it has developed

- How the Internet works

- The difference between online service providers and Internet service providers.

A Louisiana newspaper reporter returns from a suburban township meeting during which officials have decided to investigate charges that a local solid waste facility's containers are leaking onto neighboring property. With little time to spare before deadline the reporter decides to do a quick search on the Internet. Less than two minutes later the search uncovers a press release from the state's Department of Environmental Quality naming the firm's compliance manager "Solid Waste Operator of the Year." It is exactly one year since the award was announced.

Computer-assisted reporting does not necessarily involve a yearlong investigation requiring the effort of several reporters. It can sometimes be as simple as spending a couple minutes searching the Internet. Indeed, the Net has become an important weapon in any reporter's arsenal. With it a reporter can locate sources, conduct interviews, access press releases and perform a host of other routines of the job that previously relied on some combination of the telephone and shoe leather. The Internet does not replace the telephone or a trip to the office of some local government official. It augments them by providing additional avenues of approach that can sometimes be faster and more comprehensive than traditional methods.

This chapter focuses on the Internet as a tool for journalism. It provides an overview of the Internet and a brief history of its development as well as information on how the Internet actually works. Specific attention will be given to why journalists should care about the Internet and what it means to the practice of journalism. This information is useful for several reasons. First, anyone interested in computer-assisted reporting needs to understand the Internet in all its many facets. Perhaps more important, computer-assisted reporters often become Internet experts within their newsrooms. Their input is sought on everything from arranging the company's Web site to putting up a database that readers can read online to helping create an intranet for the newsroom. In these situations, a little understanding about the Internet and journalism serves us well.

THE INTERNET AND JOURNALISM

When terrorists struck a federal building in Oklahoma City on April 19, 1995, Americans reacted the way most people do during times of crisis—they looked to the media for information and help in understanding events. But, perhaps for the first time in history, a large percentage of them turned to a new medium for answers. They turned to the Internet. Just minutes after the blast, one site in Oklahoma offered a brief sketch of the explosion and a list of government offices located in the building. Later that day, an organization titled Social Workers Advocating Network Technologies set up a site devoted to providing information about the incident. Traditional news media soon followed with sites of their own. Electronic discussion groups sprang up overnight as individuals shared their thoughts on the implications of the terrorist attack.

The Oklahoma City bombing helped illustrate four ways that the Internet has had an impact on the practice of journalism: as news source, news subject, news medium, and news forum.

The Internet as News Source

Many reporters faced with deadline pressures now turn to online resources for answers, as *Rapid City Journal* reporter Mark Anderson did in 1993 when South Dakota governor George Mickelson's plane crashed in Iowa.[1] Anderson logged onto CompuServe, a provider of online services and Internet access. Once there he entered the service's Aviation Forum and asked pilots and aviation aficionados whether they knew of any special problems with the type of plane that crashed, a Mitsubishi MU-2. Anderson quickly learned that the National Transportation Safety Board had months earlier asked the Federal Aviation Administration to ground all MU-2s because of systematic problems in the planes. After a few phone calls to confirm his facts, Anderson ran the story.

Contacting experts and eyewitnesses represents only one small benefit of online resources. Journalists frequently cruise electronic discussion groups in order to locate potential story ideas. They use electronic mail (e-mail) to track down and interview hard-to-reach sources. They check out what the competition has been doing by reviewing online newspapers. They use government computers to background individuals or locate information about publicly held companies. They search through online databanks covering everything from congressional bills to the nationwide Yellow Pages. They access technical reports and survey data that help explain economic trends. The possibilities are seemingly endless.

Internet research raises some interesting questions, chief among them—how reliable is the data? The answer is that what journalists find online is no more or less reliable than what they might find offline. No good journalist would run a press release without making a phone call to ensure its reliability, especially if there were questions regarding its authenticity. The same is true when one receives a press release by e-mail. But just as a journalist might expect fairly accurate information when contacting a government office, he or she should have a reasonable expectation of accuracy from a government site (i.e., one that ends in .gov).

Of course, it is still possible to fall victim to people pretending to be someone or something they are not—a practice known as spoofing. "BClinton" at America Online is not the president of the United States. Neither is <www.whitehouse.com> the White House's address on the World Wide Web. Rather, it is a pornography site that once featured doctored, seminude photos of President and Mrs. Clinton. Even an official government site can sometimes be spoofed. The CIA found that out in September 1996 when Swedish computer saboteurs changed the site's name to the "Central Stupidity Agency" and added a variety of vulgarities. The page remained up for more than 12 hours before site administrators removed it. Just one month earlier, the U.S. Department of Justice suffered a similar attack in which saboteurs dubbed it the "Department of Injustice." However, despite these occasional problems, most government sites offer consistently reliable data.

The Internet as News Subject

What happens on the Internet is often itself worth a story. Indeed, an analysis of the three major U.S. newsmagazines—*Time, Newsweek,* and *U.S. News and World Report*—shows that coverage of the Internet rose steadily during the 1990s. The three magazines ran only two articles dealing with the Internet in 1992. By 1996, the publications devoted nearly 400 articles to Internet issues.[2] Articles about the Internet initially tended to focus on its positive aspects. News media proclaimed the arrival of the "information superhighway," which promised universal access to information. But after a brief honeymoon period, journalists began reporting about the seedier side of the Internet. Pornography, sexual predators, saboteurs and other criminals commanded the headlines. Eventually this period of negative coverage wore off as well, to be replaced by the more balanced reporting we see today.

Depending on how a newsroom is organized, a computer-assisted reporter may double as a technology writer covering the computer beat. More likely, a reporter pursuing a story using the Internet may stumble on other stories during his or her time there. For example, after the Oklahoma City bombing, Internet-savvy journalists uncovered how antigovernment militia groups were using the Web to organize themselves. Most recently, journalists have been covering music piracy online. Stories such as these often develop out of the journalist's simply "being" online.

The Internet as News Medium

The *San Jose Mercury News*, generally considered the first true online newspaper, debuted its America Online site May 10, 1993.[3] Today there are thousands of online newspapers in the United States alone.[4] These developments have prompted struggles within the industry to create new online story forms and to simply understand the future of online publishing.

The Internet offers the immediacy of television and the depth of newspapers. That might sound like a perfect match, but some observers fear that Internet media struggling to provide abundant detail quickly do so at the expense of accuracy. These weaknesses were spotlighted in online media coverage of allegations regarding the affair between President Bill Clinton and White House intern Monica Lewinsky in early 1998. *Editor and Publisher* columnist Steve Outing argued that in the need to keep up with coverage provided by smaller online publications, traditional media were drawn into what amounted to little more than rumormongering. Whether the story turned out to be true or not, Outing said, the media were reporting allegations without the facts in hand.[5] Illustrating the point, the *Dallas Morning News* was forced to withdraw an article from its Web site, saying that it could not find any support for the article's accusations.

For the computer-assisted journalist, the Internet offers a way to share data with the audience. A good "numbers" story usually doesn't have all that many numbers in it. Instead, the writer works hard to turn those numbers into something more meaningful to the reader. But there is a balance to be made between too many numbers and too few. One solution is to write the story with few numbers, then refer readers to a searchable online database. Perhaps the most popular of these stories are the school guides. Newspapers such as the *Philadelphia Inquirer* and the *St. Louis Post-Dispatch* routinely publish online databases containing information about public schools. The idea is to help parents who are "shopping for a school."

In many ways, the jury is still out on the Internet as a news medium. Most publishers still have not found a way to make money in online media. Internet users do not seem interested in paying for news material they have received free of charge up to this point. Advertising has not filled the void. With most online sites actively losing money, how long will traditional news media continue their Internet ventures? But whether the Internet becomes the news delivery system of the future or eventually gives way to some other new medium, it certainly bears attention at the present time.

The Internet as News Forum

The Internet does more than give journalists a new way to reach the audience, it gives the audience a new way to reach journalists. It also gives journalists a good way to reach each other. Most modern journalists have access to e-mail, and some even correspond regularly with their readers or viewers. Others frequent electronic discussion groups where they discuss their work with colleagues and others. The quality of the discussion can range from an exchange of helpful reporting tips to allegations about who shot John F. Kennedy (more about this in chapter 4). However, with some experience, working journalists can determine which groups can help them and which serve merely to waste time.

A BRIEF HISTORY OF THE INTERNET

People have a variety of metaphors for the Internet. Some call it a virtual community, others see it as a vast electronic library and still others view it as a kind of plaza where entrepreneurs and others can go to sell their wares. No matter what metaphor is used to describe its various functions, remember that the **Internet** is, in reality, nothing more than a global network of computer networks utilizing a common language to communicate with one another. Many of the terms that journalists now encounter while working on the Internet originated during the network's earliest days of operation.

The Internet got its start in the 1960s when U.S. military experts, still smarting from the Cuban Missile Crisis, expressed concern that the nation's telephone system could be rendered useless by a well-placed nuclear strike. In January of 1969 the Advanced Research Projects Administration (ARPA) authorized teams of scientists to begin experimenting with a more durable communications system. These researchers devised a system in which computer software breaks a chunk of data, like an electronic mail message, into **packets,** small pieces of data that include an origin and destination. A computer then sends these packets to a **router,** a piece of hardware that sends data in the general direction of its destination. If possible, the router sends each packet directly to its destination. If not, each packet goes to another router determined to be in the best position to see that the packet gets to its destination. If one portion of the communication system were to be destroyed in a nuclear strike, the packets would simply be routed around the damaged area.

The new data network, known as ARPANET, caught on with many researchers. Scientists enjoyed the ability to send data and electronic mail across the country much more rapidly and inexpensively than could be accomplished by courier. By 1983 traffic on the network had become large enough that military communication broke off into a separate network known as MILNET, while ARPANET remained for academic and other non-military uses. However, the two networks were still able to communicate with

TAKE TWO!

One way to demonstrate that you are a polished speaker is by waiting for the person you are introducing to approach the podium. Once the person arrives, step back, and welcome this individual with a warm smile and confident handshake.

ENCORE!

After the person has completed his/her part of the program, return to the podium promptly. Thank the person for what he/she presented with another warm smile and confident handshake.

ONE LAST "P & Q!"

If you are the person who is being introduced, be sure that your first words at the podium include thanking the person who introduced you. By doing this, you will be displaying your polish and podium protocol.

HOW TO FEEL AS COMFORTABLE ADDRESSING AN AUDIENCE OF 200 AS YOU ARE WHEN INTERACTING WITH TWO PEOPLE

[...]ey rule for being at ease when addressing a group is to speak in the same manner [...] you would address these people if you were having a conversation with them on a [...]-to-one basis. Make eye contact, smile, and be aware of what their body language [...] you. (i.e. Frequently, individuals who question something you say may lean forward, [...] a baffled look on their faces, etc. These nonverbals may be your cue to clarify what [...] said).

[...]ly, present your program with passion! Believe in what you have to say! By doing [...] your audience will be as comfortable with you as they are with the information that [...] are sharing with them.

TIPS FOR SPEAKING IN FRONT OF A CAMERA OR VIDEO MONITOR

[...]ts, camera, action!!! You have been asked to appear on television. What terrific [...]sure this will be for both you and the organization you represent!

[...] are four tips for speaking in front of the camera:

[...]SS FOR SUCCESS ON CAMERA.

[...]ure that both the colors of your clothing and your jewelry enhance your appearance [...]r than detracting from it. Stay away from bright reds, white, plaids, and checks. Make [...]nt of having your shirt/blouse lighter in color than the accompanying jacket. Finally, [...] shiny jewelry.

[...]AT THE CAMERA AS YOU WOULD ANOTHER PERSON.

[...]ourself. For example, if you are animated when talking to others face to face, be [...]way on camera.

[...]W YOUR MATERIAL.

[...]mber, one of the reasons that you have been asked to speak is because you are the [...]t. Become familiar with your material backwards and forwards, inside and out so [...]ou can be conversational in your approach.

[...]ICIPATE THE QUESTIONS YOU WILL BE ASKED.

[...]u were the interviewer, what questions would you ask? List the ones that you are [...] to be asked, and then practice answering these questions in 10 to 12 words.

FIRST IMPRESSION TIPS	HI-TECH ETIQUETTE
IMAGE TIPS FOR MEN	TELEPHONE ETIQUETTE TIPS
IMAGE TIPS FOR WOMEN	TIPS FOR CORRESPONDENCE
BODY LANGUAGE ETIQUETTE	MEETING MANNERS
ACCESSORY ETIQUETTE FOR MEN	JAPANESE ETIQUETTE TIPS
ACCESSORY ETIQUETTE FOR WOMEN	MEN AND WOMEN AS COLLEAGUES
BUSINESS INTRODUCTION TIPS	TRAVEL ETIQUETTE
CONVERSATION TIPS	SPECIAL OCCASION ETIQUETTE
MIXING & MINGLING	OFFICE ETIQUETTE
JOB INTERVIEW ETIQUETTE	TABLE MANNER TIPS
FIRST WEEK ON THE JOB ETIQUETTE	BUSINESS ENTERTAINING
✓ PRESENTATION TIPS	FORMAL DINING ETIQUETTE
BUSINESS ETIQUETTE TIP SHEETS	**BUSINESS ETIQUETTE TIP SHEETS**

Presentation Etiquette

By Ann Marie Sabath
Author, Business Etiquette In Brief

Did you know that one of the greatest fears that people encounter is speaking in front of groups? The "good news" is that it is really an unnecessary fear.

Speaking in front of both small and large groups should be considered an honor. The reason most people are asked to address others is to share their expertise. Giving a presentation should take no more effort than having a conversation with another person.

This PRESENTATION ETIQUETTE TIP SHEET will teach you:

- The Three Ways To Avoid Nervousness
- The Five Most Commonly-Made Presentation "Faux-Pas"
- The Three "Tricks Of The Trade" For Giving An Effective Presentation
- The Four Key Rules Of Podium Protocol
- How To Feel As Comfortable Addressing An Audience Of 200 As You Are When Interacting With Two People
- Tips For Speaking In Front Of A Camera Or Video Monitor

AT EASE INC. • 119 East Court Street • Cincinnati, Ohio 45202 • (513) 241-5216
©AT EASE INC. 1992 • Protected by the United States Copyright Laws
IT IS ILLEGAL TO DUPLICATE THIS MATERIAL

THE THREE WAYS TO AVOID NERVOUSNESS

Although being nervous has a "bad" connotation, experiencing a "positive" nervousness can be good for you, your audience, and the topic you're delivering. Why? Those last minute jitters can actually get your adrenalin flowing. Did you know that a positive nervousness can add a certain drama to your presentation and even make your eyes shine?

While you may not think you LOOK nervous, the individuals you are addressing may think so. Here are the three ways to avoid being perceived (or really being) nervous.

1. **BE PREPARED.**
   Whether you are "pitching" an idea to one person, or are addressing an audience of 200, live by the motto, "be prepared." A secret of some of the best speakers is to know the topic being addressed inside out. When possible, try to practice what you preach. In other words, choose a topic that you have experienced. By doing so, you will be able to integrate first-hand experiences into your presentation.

   Being prepared means knowing your topic. It also means becoming familiar with your audience and integrating that information into your presentation (i.e., when speaking to bankers, give examples relevant to that industry).

   Finally, being prepared means becoming familiar with the room in which you will be speaking. One way to do so is to arrive at the meeting location early enough to "walk the room", and test the audio-visual equipment.

2. **BELIEVE IN WHAT YOU HAVE TO SAY.**
   Unless you are truly convinced that what you have to say has value, why should the individuals listening to you think so?

3. **PRACTICE, PRACTICE, AND PRACTICE.**
   Stand in front of a mirror, video tape yourself, have others critique you. How would you rate yourself? If you watched yourself on tape, how well did you keep your own attention? Practice until you can give yourself an A class rating!

AVOIDING THE FIVE MOST COMMONLY-MADE PRESENTATION "FAUX PAS"

1. **NOT VIEWING YOUR "AUDIENCE" AS A GROUP OF INDIVIDUALS.**
   The people you are addressing may represent the same organization. However, since they are individuals with many different experiences, they will react differently to what you say and how you say it. Consider the group you are addressing as individuals rather than as a cluster of people.

2. **NOT RECOGNIZING THAT YOUR NONVERBALS ARE AS IMPORTANT AS THE WORDS YOU SPEAK.**
   Your nonverbals can either add or detract from the quality person you are. For example, a confident-looking person maintains eye contact, smiles, and has good posture.

3. **NOT TREATING YOUR PRESENTATION AS A "CONVERSATIO[N] BETWEEN YOU AND YOUR AUDIENCE.**
   Who wants to be TALKED AT rather than talked to? An effective pr[esentation] is characterized by involving the individuals you are addressing. (i.e., u[se] names, role-playing, encouraging questions.)

4. **NOT RECOGNIZING WHEN YOUR TIME IS UP.**
   What could be worse than overextending your stay? Rather than findin[g yourself] in this situation, have someone give you a "sign" when your time is [near the] end. By doing this, you will be in control of your time, and not be t[empted to] look at your watch during your presentation.

5. **NOT WANTING TO ENHANCE YOUR PRESENTATION THROUGH FEEDBACK.**
   To learn is to continue living. Learn from each program. One of the [ways] to do so is through evaluations.

THE THREE "TRICKS OF THE TRADE" FO[R] GIVING AN EFFECTIVE PRESENTATION

1. **MAKE YOUR PROGRAM INTERACTIVE.**
   A confident speaker is not afraid to share the stage with the audience [using] questions and role-playing when appropriate. Note: Most individual[s] interested in being "involved" in a program will CHOOSE to sit in f[ront of the] room. Those who choose to sit in back of the room typically prefer to b[e] participants.

2. **LET YOUR AUDIENCE KNOW WHAT THEY CAN EXPECT.**
   An age-old trick of the trade of an effective speaker is to tell the gro[up you are] addressing what you are going to tell them, do it, and then summariz[e what you] told them.

3. **OPEN THE DOOR TO FUTURE PROGRAMS THROUGH YOUR [PRESENT] ONE.**
   Frequently, an effective presenter gives the audience something to tak[e home] that is lasting. It could be a bookmark summarizing of the program[, or a] card giving participants access to the presenter's organization, etc. B[y being] of benefit to participants, you will find these giveaways the key to op[ening the door] for future programs.

THE FOUR KEY RULES OF PODIUM PROTO[COL]

1. **GET READY, GET SET, GET PREPARED!**
   Practice aloud what you are going to say. By doing so, your remarks [will sound] natural, extemporaneous and conversational.

one another using **Internet protocol,** the formal set of rules that govern how electronic messages are broken into packets, routed and reassembled. Internet protocol combines with transmission control protocol to form **TCP/IP,** the standard set of rules that all networks use to communicate over the Internet.

The system worked well enough that three years later, when the National Science Foundation (NSF) decided to make its multimillion-dollar super-computers available to researchers around the country, it selected ARPANET to handle communications. When a variety of problems prompted NSF to drop the idea of using ARPANET, it borrowed TCP/IP and other protocols to create its own computer network. The new NSFNET linked supercom-puters at five separate locations throughout the United States. These connections became known as the network **backbone**—the fast, top-level communication lines that handle most of the network's data traffic. NSFNET soon began linking with networks in Canada, Mexico and other nations, creating the global network of computer networks that we now know as the Internet. As researchers moved to the new NSFNET, ARPANET began a slow decline that ended when it was finally shut down in 1990. Today much of the traffic on the Internet has shifted to commercial computer sites run by companies such as Sprint and IBM.

INTERNET ADDRESSING

In order to properly route the data, the Internet requires that each piece of data have a source and a destination. This takes the form of an **IP ad-dress**—a series of four numbers, separated by periods, that uniquely identifies every computer connected to the Internet. For example, the IP address <198.137.240.91> identifies a specific public access computer at the White House.

While computers have no problem handling long strings of numbers, humans do not deal well with them. It is much easier for us to remember a company's name than its telephone number. With this in mind, network administrators involved in Internet development created the **domain name system (DNS),** a hierarchical scheme for converting a name to a numeric IP address. The domain name system allows people to specify an easier-to-remember Internet address. For example, two computers at the Vatican connect to the Internet using the IP addresses <194.91.153.2> and <194.91.153.249>. By registering the computers within the DNS, church leaders were able to give them more easily recognizable names—*michael.vatican.va* and *gabriel.vatican.va*. You might ask why the Vatican could not just name its computers *Michael* and *Gabriel* without putting *vatican.va* at the end. It was not that the names were already taken. Rather, the DNS requires that all computers fit within its organizational hierarchy. But once you know something about this system, Internet addressing schemes appear logical and easy to understand.

Remember that the domain name system is hierarchical, much like the post office system. But where a postal address relies on geographical groupings—state, city, street—an Internet address relies on logical groupings. To examine the DNS naming conventions, let's look at a typical Internet address, this one belonging to a documentation computer once jointly operated by the Bureau of Labor Statistics and the U.S. Census Bureau:

www.bls.census.gov

Just as a postal address is best analyzed from bottom to top, an Internet address is best analyzed from right to left, from the largest logical grouping to the smallest. To the far right is the **top-level domain,** a two- or three-digit extension that represents all those computers operated by organizations of a specific type. There are six typical three-digit top-level domains:

.com   Commercial organizations

.edu   Educational organizations

.gov   U.S. governmental organizations

.net   Network companies that handle administration of the Internet

.mil   U.S. military organizations

.org   Nonprofit, not-for-profit and other organizations

By the mid-1990s, computers in the commercial area far outnumbered those in any other top-level domain, accounting for 23 percent of all registered addresses. Computers registered in the educational domain made up the second largest portion, roughly 15 percent, followed by networks with approximately 11 percent. Looking at the three-digit extension confirms that our example is a government computer. Computers registered in the government domain make up slightly more than 2 percent of those on the Internet.[6]

In addition to the three-digit top-level domains, each nation has its own two-digit domain. Although the United States has a two-digit country code (.us), that code is used primarily by state government organizations (e.g., <www.state.pa.us>). Most other U.S. organizations utilize only a three-digit code. Some country codes can be easy to infer. For example, the two-digit code for Canada is .ca. Others are more difficult, often because the code represents the nation's name in its own language, such as .de for Germany (Deutschland) or .hr for Croatia (Hrvatska). The United States accounts for the vast majority of all computers registered on the Internet. The top five users outside the United States, and the percentage of registered names they represent, are: Japan (4.9 percent), the United Kingdom (4.5 percent), Germany (4.5 percent), Australia (3.6 percent), and Canada (3.5 percent).[7]

www.bls.census.gov

To the left of the top-level domain, just beyond the period, is the second-level domain. The **second-level domain** represents a shorthand name for the organization operating the computer. In most cases, these names are easy to guess (e.g., *.fsu* for Florida State University or *.whitehouse* for the White House). The second-level domain name confirms that our example represents a computer in the U.S. Census Bureau.

www.**bls**.census.gov

In some cases, there will be a **third-level domain,** which represents a subdomain within the organization. These subdomains can be local area networks or simply aliases that help the organization maintain a certain structure within its computer system. The *.bls* designation in our example indicates that the Census Bureau has earmarked the computer for use with the Bureau of Labor Statistics project.

Note that third-level domains are not nearly as easy to guess as second-level domains. Second-level domains usually bear the name of some organization we are familiar with. Third-level domains usually have meaning only to people within the organization. The third-level domain in <www.sncc.lsu.edu> has little meaning except to those people at Louisiana State University who know it represents the System Network Computer Center. Luckily, few organizations make use of third-level domains on their public access computers.

www.**bls**.census.gov

To the far left is the name of the computer. Computers on the Internet have a variety of names, from Greek gods (*Venus* is most popular) to characters on Star Trek (*Spock* remains the favorite), whatever the system administrators decide. However, most administrators designate public access computers according to their purpose. The most common computer names of interest to us here are:

www	Computers hosting pages on the World Wide Web
mail	Computers designated as electronic post offices
news	Computers serving up Usenet news
lists	Computers housing electronic mailing lists
ftp	Computers offering files via file transfer protocol

The address in our example tells us we are looking at a computer that has been designated as a host for pages on the World Wide Web.

Putting all these parts together allows us to make some fairly intelligent guesses concerning the address of certain computers on the Internet. For example, how could we contact the World Wide Web computer at America Online? We begin with the top-level domain. America Online is a commercial firm, so it would be in the commercial domain (*.com*). We then have to make a guess about how America Online would designate its organization in an Internet address. In general, most organizations want to make their names as short as possible while still guaranteeing that they can be recognized. America Online often goes by the acronym AOL, so let's guess *aol.com*. The last part is the easiest. We know we want to connect to the machine designated for the World Wide Web, and we know how to specify that computer. Thus, we know that America Online's World Wide Web site can be found at <www.aol.com>.

It is possible to build the addresses of many other sites with varying degrees of success. Consider the following examples:

University of Missouri's mailing list site	<lists.missouri.edu>
CompuServe's news site	<news.compuserve.com>
National Institute for Computer-Assisted Reporting's FTP site	<ftp.nicar.org>
Canadian Department of Energy's Web site	<www.doe.ca>
U.S. Department of Education's mail server	<mail.ed.gov>

Guessing at an Internet address may be the fastest way to locate a computer on the Internet, but there are other options. The chapters to follow will explore a few of the more advanced methods for finding specific Internet addresses.

E-mail addresses work much the same as other Internet addresses, except that they add a way to find a specific user on a system. Take, for example, this e-mail address:

auser@mail.ed.gov

Working right to left, we can see that the address belongs to someone in the government domain, at the U.S. Department of Education and on the department's *mail* computer. The at sign (@) indicates that this address is an e-mail address.[8] The portion to the left of the at sign is the individual's user name—how they log on to the system and identify themselves to the host computer.

CONNECTING TO THE INTERNET

Accessing the Internet is a relatively simple process assuming you have the right equipment. At a minimum you need a computer, communications hardware and an IP address. If you are working at a university or a reasonably large news outlet, all these tools will likely be provided. If your computer is connected to a network, it utilizes communications hardware known as a **network interface card,** a circuit board installed in the computer with ports for wires that physically connect it with the rest of the network. If the network has Internet access, your computer probably will too. This situation is often called a "live" connection because the Internet remains constantly available to the machine.

FIRST IMPRESSION TIPS		HI-TECH ETIQUETTE
IMAGE TIPS FOR MEN		TELEPHONE ETIQUETTE TIPS
IMAGE TIPS FOR WOMEN	**Presentation**	TIPS FOR CORRESPONDENCE
BODY LANGUAGE ETIQUETTE		MEETING MANNERS
ACCESSORY ETIQUETTE FOR MEN	**Etiquette**	JAPANESE ETIQUETTE TIPS
ACCESSORY ETIQUETTE FOR WOMEN	By Ann Marie Sabath Author, *Business Etiquette In Brief*	MEN AND WOMEN AS COLLEAGUES
BUSINESS INTRODUCTION TIPS		TRAVEL ETIQUETTE
CONVERSATION TIPS		SPECIAL OCCASION ETIQUETTE
MIXING & MINGLING		OFFICE ETIQUETTE
JOB INTERVIEW ETIQUETTE		TABLE MANNER TIPS
FIRST WEEK ON THE JOB ETIQUETTE		BUSINESS ENTERTAINING
✓ PRESENTATION TIPS		FORMAL DINING ETIQUETTE
BUSINESS ETIQUETTE TIP SHEETS		BUSINESS ETIQUETTE TIP SHEETS

Did you know that one of the greatest fears that people encounter is speaking in front of groups? The "good news" is that it is really an unnecessary fear.

Speaking in front of both small and large groups should be considered an honor. The reason most people are asked to address others is to share their expertise. Giving a presentation should take no more effort than having a conversation with another person.

This PRESENTATION ETIQUETTE TIP SHEET will teach you:

- The Three Ways To Avoid Nervousness
- The Five Most Commonly-Made Presentation "Faux-Pas"
- The Three "Tricks Of The Trade" For Giving An Effective Presentation
- The Four Key Rules Of Podium Protocol
- How To Feel As Comfortable Addressing An Audience Of 200 As You Are When Interacting With Two People
- Tips For Speaking In Front Of A Camera Or Video Monitor

THE THREE WAYS TO AVOID NERVOUSNESS

Although being nervous has a "bad" connotation, experiencing a "positive" nervousness can be good for you, your audience, and the topic you're delivering. Why? Those last minute jitters can actually get your adrenalin flowing. Did you know that a positive nervousness can add a certain drama to your presentation and even make your eyes shine?

While you may not think you LOOK nervous, the individuals you are addressing may think so. Here are the three ways to avoid being perceived (or really being) nervous.

1. **BE PREPARED.**
    Whether you are "pitching" an idea to one person, or are addressing an audience of 200, live by the motto, "be prepared." A secret of some of the best speakers is to know the topic being addressed inside out. When possible, try to practice what you preach. In other words, choose a topic that you have experienced. By doing so, you will be able to integrate first-hand experiences into your presentation.

    Being prepared means knowing your topic. It also means becoming familiar with your audience and integrating that information into your presentation (i.e., when speaking to bankers, give examples relevant to that industry).

    Finally, being prepared means becoming familiar with the room in which you will be speaking. One way to do so is to arrive at the meeting location early enough to "walk the room", and test the audio-visual equipment.

2. **BELIEVE IN WHAT YOU HAVE TO SAY.**
    Unless you are truly convinced that what you have to say has value, why should the individuals listening to you think so?

3. **PRACTICE, PRACTICE, AND PRACTICE.**
    Stand in front of a mirror, video tape yourself, have others critique you. How would you rate yourself? If you watched yourself on tape, how well did you keep your own attention? Practice until you can give yourself an A class rating!

AVOIDING THE FIVE MOST COMMONLY-MADE PRESENTATION "FAUX PAS"

1. **NOT VIEWING YOUR "AUDIENCE" AS A GROUP OF INDIVIDUALS.**
    The people you are addressing may represent the same organization. However, since they are individuals with many different experiences, they will react differently to what you say and how you say it. Consider the group you are addressing as individuals rather than as a cluster of people.

2. **NOT RECOGNIZING THAT YOUR NONVERBALS ARE AS IMPORTANT AS THE WORDS YOU SPEAK.**
    Your nonverbals can either add or detract from the quality person you are. For example, a confident-looking person maintains eye contact, smiles, and has good posture.

3. **NOT TREATING YOUR PRESENTATION AS A "CONVERSATION" BETWEEN YOU AND YOUR AUDIENCE.**
Who wants to be TALKED AT rather than talked to? An effective presentation is characterized by involving the individuals you are addressing. (i.e., using their names, role-playing, encouraging questions.)

4. **NOT RECOGNIZING WHEN YOUR TIME IS UP.**
What could be worse than overextending your stay? Rather than finding yourself in this situation, have someone give you a "sign" when your time is nearing an end. By doing this, you will be in control of your time, and not be tempted to look at your watch during your presentation.

5. **NOT WANTING TO ENHANCE YOUR PRESENTATION SKILLS THROUGH FEEDBACK.**
To learn is to continue living. Learn from each program. One of the best ways to do so is through evaluations.

THE THREE "TRICKS OF THE TRADE" FOR GIVING AN EFFECTIVE PRESENTATION

1. **MAKE YOUR PROGRAM INTERACTIVE.**
A confident speaker is not afraid to share the stage with the audience. Welcome questions and role-playing when appropriate. Note: Most individuals who are interested in being "involved" in a program will CHOOSE to sit in front of the room. Those who choose to sit in back of the room typically prefer to be "passive" participants.

2. **LET YOUR AUDIENCE KNOW WHAT THEY CAN EXPECT.**
An age-old trick of the trade of an effective speaker is to tell the group you are addressing what you are going to tell them, do it, and then summarize what you told them.

3. **OPEN THE DOOR TO FUTURE PROGRAMS THROUGH YOUR PRESENT ONE.**
Frequently, an effective presenter gives the audience something to take with them that is lasting. It could be a bookmark summarizing of the program, a hotline card giving participants access to the presenter's organization, etc. Besides being of benefit to participants, you will find these giveaways the key to opening doors for future programs.

THE FOUR KEY RULES OF PODIUM PROTOCOL

1. **GET READY, GET SET, GET PREPARED!**
Practice aloud what you are going to say. By doing so, your remarks will appear natural, extemporaneous and conversational.

2. **TAKE TWO!**
   One way to demonstrate that you are a polished speaker is by waiting for the person you are introducing to approach the podium. Once the person arrives, step back, and welcome this individual with a warm smile and confident handshake.

3. **ENCORE!**
   After the person has completed his/her part of the program, return to the podium promptly. Thank the person for what he/she presented with another warm smile and confident handshake.

4. **ONE LAST "P & Q!"**
   If you are the person who is being introduced, be sure that your first words at the podium include thanking the person who introduced you. By doing this, you will be displaying your polish and podium protocol.

HOW TO FEEL AS COMFORTABLE ADDRESSING AN AUDIENCE OF 200 AS YOU ARE WHEN INTERACTING WITH TWO PEOPLE

A key rule for being at ease when addressing a group is to speak in the same manner that you would address these people if you were having a conversation with them on a one-to-one basis. Make eye contact, smile, and be aware of what their body language tells you. (i.e. Frequently, individuals who question something you say may lean forward, have a baffled look on their faces, etc. These nonverbals may be your cue to clarify what you said).

Finally, present your program with passion! Believe in what you have to say! By doing so, your audience will be as comfortable with you as they are with the information that you are sharing with them.

TIPS FOR SPEAKING IN FRONT OF A CAMERA OR VIDEO MONITOR

Lights, camera, action!!! You have been asked to appear on television. What terrific exposure this will be for both you and the organization you represent!

Here are four tips for speaking in front of the camera:

DRESS FOR SUCCESS ON CAMERA.
Be sure that both the colors of your clothing and your jewelry enhance your appearance rather than detracting from it. Stay away from bright reds, white, plaids, and checks. Make a point of having your shirt/blouse lighter in color than the accompanying jacket. Finally, avoid shiny jewelry.

TREAT THE CAMERA AS YOU WOULD ANOTHER PERSON.
Be yourself. For example, if you are animated when talking to others face to face, be that way on camera.

KNOW YOUR MATERIAL.
Remember, one of the reasons that you have been asked to speak is because you are the expert. Become familiar with your material backwards and forwards, inside and out so that you can be conversational in your approach.

ANTICIPATE THE QUESTIONS YOU WILL BE ASKED.
If you were the interviewer, what questions would you ask? List the ones that you are likely to be asked, and then practice answering these questions in 10 to 12 words.

one another using **Internet protocol,** the formal set of rules that govern how electronic messages are broken into packets, routed and reassembled. Internet protocol combines with transmission control protocol to form **TCP/IP,** the standard set of rules that all networks use to communicate over the Internet.

The system worked well enough that three years later, when the National Science Foundation (NSF) decided to make its multimillion-dollar super-computers available to researchers around the country, it selected ARPANET to handle communications. When a variety of problems prompted NSF to drop the idea of using ARPANET, it borrowed TCP/IP and other protocols to create its own computer network. The new NSFNET linked supercom-puters at five separate locations throughout the United States. These con-nections became known as the network **backbone**—the fast, top-level communication lines that handle most of the network's data traffic. NSFNET soon began linking with networks in Canada, Mexico and other nations, creating the global network of computer networks that we now know as the Internet. As researchers moved to the new NSFNET, ARPANET began a slow decline that ended when it was finally shut down in 1990. Today much of the traffic on the Internet has shifted to commercial computer sites run by companies such as Sprint and IBM.

INTERNET ADDRESSING

In order to properly route the data, the Internet requires that each piece of data have a source and a destination. This takes the form of an **IP ad-dress**—a series of four numbers, separated by periods, that uniquely identifies every computer connected to the Internet. For example, the IP address <198.137.240.91> identifies a specific public access computer at the White House.

While computers have no problem handling long strings of numbers, humans do not deal well with them. It is much easier for us to remember a company's name than its telephone number. With this in mind, network administrators involved in Internet development created the **domain name system (DNS),** a hierarchical scheme for converting a name to a numeric IP address. The domain name system allows people to specify an easier-to-remember Internet address. For example, two computers at the Vatican connect to the Internet using the IP addresses <194.91.153.2> and <194.91.153.249>. By registering the computers within the DNS, church leaders were able to give them more easily recognizable names—*michael.vatican.va* and *gabriel.vatican.va*. You might ask why the Vatican could not just name its computers *Michael* and *Gabriel* without putting *vatican.va* at the end. It was not that the names were already taken. Rather, the DNS requires that all computers fit within its organizational hierarchy. But once you know something about this system, Internet addressing schemes appear logical and easy to understand.

Remember that the domain name system is hierarchical, much like the post office system. But where a postal address relies on geographical groupings—state, city, street—an Internet address relies on logical groupings. To examine the DNS naming conventions, let's look at a typical Internet address, this one belonging to a documentation computer once jointly operated by the Bureau of Labor Statistics and the U.S. Census Bureau:

www.bls.census.gov

Just as a postal address is best analyzed from bottom to top, an Internet address is best analyzed from right to left, from the largest logical grouping to the smallest. To the far right is the **top-level domain,** a two- or three-digit extension that represents all those computers operated by organizations of a specific type. There are six typical three-digit top-level domains:

.com   Commercial organizations

.edu   Educational organizations

.gov   U.S. governmental organizations

.net   Network companies that handle administration of the Internet

.mil   U.S. military organizations

.org   Nonprofit, not-for-profit and other organizations

By the mid-1990s, computers in the commercial area far outnumbered those in any other top-level domain, accounting for 23 percent of all registered addresses. Computers registered in the educational domain made up the second largest portion, roughly 15 percent, followed by networks with approximately 11 percent. Looking at the three-digit extension confirms that our example is a government computer. Computers registered in the government domain make up slightly more than 2 percent of those on the Internet.[6]

In addition to the three-digit top-level domains, each nation has its own two-digit domain. Although the United States has a two-digit country code (.us), that code is used primarily by state government organizations (e.g., <www.state.pa.us>). Most other U.S. organizations utilize only a three-digit code. Some country codes can be easy to infer. For example, the two-digit code for Canada is .ca. Others are more difficult, often because the code represents the nation's name in its own language, such as .de for Germany (Deutschland) or .hr for Croatia (Hrvatska). The United States accounts for the vast majority of all computers registered on the Internet. The top five users outside the United States, and the percentage of registered names they represent, are: Japan (4.9 percent), the United Kingdom (4.5 percent), Germany (4.5 percent), Australia (3.6 percent), and Canada (3.5 percent).[7]

www.bls.census.gov

To the left of the top-level domain, just beyond the period, is the second-level domain. The **second-level domain** represents a shorthand name for the organization operating the computer. In most cases, these names are easy to guess (e.g., *.fsu* for Florida State University or *.whitehouse* for the White House). The second-level domain name confirms that our example represents a computer in the U.S. Census Bureau.

www.**bls**.census.gov

In some cases, there will be a **third-level domain,** which represents a subdomain within the organization. These subdomains can be local area networks or simply aliases that help the organization maintain a certain structure within its computer system. The *.bls* designation in our example indicates that the Census Bureau has earmarked the computer for use with the Bureau of Labor Statistics project.

Note that third-level domains are not nearly as easy to guess as second-level domains. Second-level domains usually bear the name of some organization we are familiar with. Third-level domains usually have meaning only to people within the organization. The third-level domain in <www.sncc.lsu.edu> has little meaning except to those people at Louisiana State University who know it represents the System Network Computer Center. Luckily, few organizations make use of third-level domains on their public access computers.

www.**bls**.census.gov

To the far left is the name of the computer. Computers on the Internet have a variety of names, from Greek gods (*Venus* is most popular) to characters on Star Trek (*Spock* remains the favorite), whatever the system administrators decide. However, most administrators designate public access computers according to their purpose. The most common computer names of interest to us here are:

www   Computers hosting pages on the World Wide Web
mail   Computers designated as electronic post offices
news   Computers serving up Usenet news
lists   Computers housing electronic mailing lists
ftp   Computers offering files via file transfer protocol

The address in our example tells us we are looking at a computer that has been designated as a host for pages on the World Wide Web.

Putting all these parts together allows us to make some fairly intelligent guesses concerning the address of certain computers on the Internet. For example, how could we contact the World Wide Web computer at America Online? We begin with the top-level domain. America Online is a commercial firm, so it would be in the commercial domain (*.com*). We then have to make a guess about how America Online would designate its organization in an Internet address. In general, most organizations want to make their names as short as possible while still guaranteeing that they can be recognized. America Online often goes by the acronym AOL, so let's guess *aol.com*. The last part is the easiest. We know we want to connect to the machine designated for the World Wide Web, and we know how to specify that computer. Thus, we know that America Online's World Wide Web site can be found at <www.aol.com>.

It is possible to build the addresses of many other sites with varying degrees of success. Consider the following examples:

University of Missouri's mailing list site	<lists.missouri.edu>
CompuServe's news site	<news.compuserve.com>
National Institute for Computer-Assisted Reporting's FTP site	<ftp.nicar.org>
Canadian Department of Energy's Web site	<www.doe.ca>
U.S. Department of Education's mail server	<mail.ed.gov>

Guessing at an Internet address may be the fastest way to locate a computer on the Internet, but there are other options. The chapters to follow will explore a few of the more advanced methods for finding specific Internet addresses.

E-mail addresses work much the same as other Internet addresses, except that they add a way to find a specific user on a system. Take, for example, this e-mail address:

auser@mail.ed.gov

Working right to left, we can see that the address belongs to someone in the government domain, at the U.S. Department of Education and on the department's *mail* computer. The at sign (@) indicates that this address is an e-mail address.[8] The portion to the left of the at sign is the individual's user name—how they log on to the system and identify themselves to the host computer.

CONNECTING TO THE INTERNET

Accessing the Internet is a relatively simple process assuming you have the right equipment. At a minimum you need a computer, communications hardware and an IP address. If you are working at a university or a reasonably large news outlet, all these tools will likely be provided. If your computer is connected to a network, it utilizes communications hardware known as a **network interface card,** a circuit board installed in the computer with ports for wires that physically connect it with the rest of the network. If the network has Internet access, your computer probably will too. This situation is often called a "live" connection because the Internet remains constantly available to the machine.

If you are working at home or in a smaller news outlet, you will probably not have a live connection. Instead, you will have to create a temporary connection with the Internet each time you use it. For that you will need an open telephone line and a **modem,** a piece of hardware that allows a computer to send and receive signals over a telephone line. The modem, short for *modulator/demodulator*, converts digital (computer) signals into analog (telephone) signals and vice versa. Anytime computers use telephone lines to transmit data, there must be a modem at each end of the line.

Most modern personal computers come with modems already installed. Early Internet users frequently used 300 bps modems. A modem's **bps rate** refers to its speed—the number of *bits per second* that it can move over the line. At 300 bps, a modem requires more than a minute-and-a-half to transmit one page of single-spaced text. By comparison, a modern 56K bps modem can send that same page in under a second.

In addition to the hardware necessary for accessing the Internet, you must have some agency willing to grant you a temporary Internet connection. The two most common forms of obtaining a temporary connection are online service providers and Internet service providers. An **online service provider (OSP)** concentrates on connecting its subscribers to a variety of services located on its own site. One of these services may be Internet access, especially with larger providers; however, not every OSP offers a full range of Internet capabilities. Major OSPs include America Online, CompuServe, Prodigy, and the Microsoft Network. By contrast, an **Internet service provider (ISP)** concentrates on connecting its subscribers directly to the Internet. ISPs may offer their customers special services, but they focus on serving as a gateway to the Internet. Major ISPs include Netcom, Mindspring, and Concentric.

Choosing between an OSP and an ISP depends on an individual user's expectations. OSPs focus on being easy to set up and operate. They supply free proprietary software and usually can get even inexperienced users up and running within a short time. They also furnish subscribers with a wealth of information not available to the general Internet audience. For example, America Online offers access to a variety of newspapers and magazines that nonsubscribers cannot receive. CompuServe provides areas for journalists to get together and exchange information and files with one another. But with so many new people connecting at once, subscribers often encounter busy signals during peak evening hours and on weekends. Internet connections tend to run a bit more slowly as well. Moreover, OSPs frequently permit only a limited array of programs for accessing information on the Internet.

ISPs emphasize supplying fast Internet connections that permit the use of a much wider range of Internet-related software. As a result, users often find the learning curve a bit steep initially. This difficulty is compounded by the fact that most ISPs do not offer much information that could not be found free elsewhere on the Internet. While most major OSPs tend to offer similar products and services, the quality of ISPs can vary greatly. The less expensive ones run the gamut from highly reliable and efficient enterprises to one teenager trying to make some extra money with a few modems in the parents' basement. Users need to plan accordingly when making their selection.

THE CLIENT-SERVER RELATIONSHIP

In order to communicate, two computers usually adopt a client-server relationship. One computer, the **server,** runs software that provides some type of service to other computers able to connect with it. Because they provide useful services to a variety of other computers, servers are sometimes referred to as **hosts.** Many people regard servers as large, powerful mainframes, but that is not necessarily true. An aging personal computer worth a few hundred dollars can act as a server—provided it has a live Internet connection.

Most server software runs continuously, just waiting for requests to arrive. Those requests come from **clients,** computers running software that requests services from a server. Although the term *client* is often used to refer to the computer, it actually relates to the computer's function at a given point in time. A single computer might act simultaneously as a client, requesting data from other computers on the Internet, and as a server, making its data available to other computers. However, for our purposes, it is perhaps best to think of your own computer as a client that connects with servers elsewhere on the Internet.

One of the oldest means for connecting one computer to another over the Internet is **telnet,** a protocol that allows a user to create a text-based link to a remote host and utilize its programs. If you are working in a lab or on a network and your computer allows you to log on to another computer, it probably uses a telnet client to do so. Users normally log on to a text-based **shell account,** an interface that allows the user to input text commands in order to access the server's programs. Telnet can also be used to log on to a server running some type of program, typically an information server or some type of game. Telnet allows the user's computer to act as though it were a terminal directly connected to the server. This mimic ability classifies telnet as a type of terminal emulation software.

Terminal emulation has its limitations. First, you can only use programs on the computer that you are connected to. The only program running on your computer is the telnet program itself. Second, transfers between the server and your computer are mostly limited to simple text. Although you can usually capture text that appears on your computer screen, any operations performed by the server remain on the server. Finally, you have to live within the boundaries set by whoever operates the server you are connected to. You may be given strict limits on the amount of data you can store on the computer. For example, some servers limit you to no more than one megabyte of disk space. If you attempt to store more than the specified amount of data, your account may lock up, which prevents further access until a system administrator can fix the problem.

Remember that the term *telnet* describes an entire class of software, much like the term *word processing*. This terminology often appears confusing because Unix operating systems come with a program called "telnet," which is like Windows operating systems that carry a program called "word processor." But just as there are a variety of word processors, there are also a variety of telnet programs. The more popular Winsock-compatible telnet clients include Trumpet Telnet, CRT, NetTerm, CommNet and EWAN. These clients all provide the basic function of connecting your computer to a remote host on the Internet. However, some offer additional features such as address books and screen capturing capabilities.

Journalists generally use telnet for the same reason as most other Internet users, to log on to their Unix-based shell accounts in order to check their e-mail while on the road. Some Internet hosts do offer a variety of resources via telnet, but they are fading quickly as many move their information to other media, including the World Wide Web.

SUMMARY

This chapter discussed how the Internet came to be and how journalists have staked out their own territory online. We looked superficially at how the Internet works and, more important for our purposes, how it is organized. Now we are ready to start looking at some of the specific ways computer-assisted reporters use the Internet.

NOTES

1. The incident is detailed in Tom Koch, "Computers vs. Community: A Call for Bridging the Gap between Two Camps, Two Tools," *The Quill*, May 1994, 18–22.

2. Matthew M. Reavy, "Trends in Magazine Coverage of the Internet" (paper presented at the annual conference of Association for Education in Journalism and Mass Communication, New Orleans, La., August 1999).

3. Christopher Harper, "Online Newspapers: Going Somewhere or Going Nowhere?" *Newspaper Research Journal*, summer/fall 1996, 2–13.

4. *Editor and Publisher*, "Online Newspaper Statistics," November 5, 1997, available at <http://www.mediainfo.com/ephome/npaper/nphtm/stats.htm>.

5. Steve Outing, "The Internet Is Influencing News Coverage—for the Rest," *Editor and Publisher Interactive*, January 30, 1998, <http://www.mediainfo.com>.

6. Figures are based on the Internet Domain Survey of July 1997 compiled by Network Wizards. The data is available online at <http://www.nw.com/zone/WWW/dist-bynum.html>.

7. Ibid.

8. The @ symbol is generally referred to as the at sign. For an interesting discussion of its representation in English and other languages, see <http://www.sfs.nphil.uni-tuebingen.de/linguist/issues/7/7-968.html>.

CHAPTER 4

Two-Way Communication
ELECTRONIC MAIL AND DISCUSSION GROUPS

Stephen Miller had a problem. Coming up on deadline for an article about computer financial software, he found himself unable to land a crucial interview with Andrew Tobias, whose book *Managing Your Money* had recently come out on computer disk. "I had been trying for a couple of weeks to get an interview," said Miller, who is now assistant to the technology editor at the *New York Times*. "I had done all of the traditional things. I had called the publisher. I had called his PR people. Nobody was

In this chapter you will learn:

■ Why and how to use e-mail

■ The difference between server-based and POP e-mail clients

■ How to send and receive files attached to an e-mail message

■ The ins and outs of electronic mailing lists

getting back to me." While doing some research for the upcoming article, Miller found an online forum for people who had bought the product. "I went into the service and lo and behold, there was Andy Tobias answering questions, and there was his e-mail address. So I sent him a note." About an hour later, Miller received a phone call from Tobias. No one had informed the author about any attempts to contact him for an interview. He indicated that he was busy at the moment, but if Miller wanted to forward his comments via e-mail, he would answer them as soon as possible. That evening, the reporter received a 1,500-word response full of details about the financial software business.[1]

E-mail is the least sexy but most important tool on the Internet. It allows journalists to conduct interviews, participate in online discussions and even publish their own newsletters. This chapter examines the power of e-mail and some other basic tools to create an environment for two-way communication on the Internet. It also explores the e-mail's capacity for sending commands to distant computers and building cheap and easy online publications.

TALKING ONE-ON-ONE: E-MAIL

E-mail is rapidly becoming the communication medium of choice for the United States. In one decade it has sprung from obscurity to rival the telephone for long-distance communication.

There are many advantages to using e-mail:

- *Speed*. Messages can often be sent and received in the time it might take to walk to the nearest mailbox. This speed has prompted Internet users to jokingly refer to the postal service as "snail mail."
- *Cost*. Most service providers give their subscribers free, unlimited e-mail access. Without the need to purchase paper, envelopes or stamps, users pay virtually nothing to send one e-mail message or 100,000.
- *Convenience*. A message can be sent at 2 A.M. on a Sunday and be accessible on the recipient's home computer whenever he or she wakes up. Messages can be easily checked at home, at the office or on the road.
- *Flexibility*. Users can forward messages they receive, easily copy specific sections into a new document or even store their mail electronically.
- *Power*. E-mail can handle data attached to messages in the form of electronic records, word processing documents or even picture files. It can also deliver commands to remote computers over the Internet.
- *Security*. With current encryption technology, e-mail communications are more secure than most overland mail delivery services, not to mention cellular or cordless telephones.

E-mail offers many advantages over more traditional forms of communication. Unfortunately, not everyone can embrace these benefits. A number of barriers stand in the way of universal access:

- *Equipment*. Although sending an individual piece of e-mail does not cost much, obtaining the commonly used hardware remains beyond the means of many individuals in the United States and elsewhere.
- *Education*. Computer technology presents a major hurdle for some people. Operating the equipment continues to require more training than does more traditional forms of communication.
- *Language*. E-mail favors languages that rely on Latin-based characters. Messages written in Chinese, Japanese, Arabic and other languages based on cursive alphabets are difficult to communicate via e-mail.
- *Geography*. Internet access is not available in all cities or nations. The use of such technology may be culturally unacceptable. A country's telephone system also plays an important role in its ability to handle e-mail. Nations with few telephones or low technology lines have more difficulty accessing e-mail. Even in the United States, some Internet users must make a long-distance phone call in order to gain access.

When you consider these advantages and disadvantages, it becomes easy to see how e-mail benefits the modern journalist.

E-Mail: The Pros

If you are interested in getting information or expert opinion, the e-mail interview is ideal, especially if you are dealing with a subject who writes well. I've been on the subject side of this on occasion and I much prefer it to a personal interview. It's much more accurate.

There's a tendency to see the interview as a confrontational situation, but that makes people tense and guarded—or nervously voluble (my reaction). I always feel like a fool after a telephone or face-to-face interview, often with good reason. Embarrassing statements do not guarantee a good interview or a good story.

Spontaneity is limited, of course, but if you get a real exchange going, you might be surprised at how people open up, perhaps even more so because of the absence of personal contact, which can be perceived as threatening by some people.

—Jules Siegel
writer/graphic designer

E-Mail and the Journalist

Just a few years ago, if you had asked a group of journalists whether they had access to e-mail, few would have said yes. Now e-mail has become commonplace. Nearly every staff member at larger media outlets has an e-mail address. Freelancers and journalists working at smaller companies frequently have access to e-mail as well, even if they have to provide it themselves. Why? Because it is so useful. The following sections describe the various uses that a typical journalist might have for e-mail.

Reaching Hard-to-Find Sources   Stephen Miller's story, which launched this chapter, is a typical example of a journalist using e-mail to reach a difficult source. Sometimes it's easier to contact an individual by e-mail than it is to reach that person by telephone. Once the source is reached, you can either conduct the interview by e-mail or schedule an in-person interview—particularly if the story is for television.

Time-Shifting an Interview   Sometimes sources don't have time to answer questions when you have the time to ask them. E-mail allows the interview to fit into both schedules. This benefit is especially important if the two people do not share the same time zone, says *Peoria Journal Star* reporter Valerie Lilley. "E-mail is great for interviewing people on the other side of the world. Even if I could get approval to call Geneva, I'd have to come back to the newsroom in the middle of the night to make the call."

Contacting Multiple Sources   There are times when you want to ask the same questions to several different people, either because you want differing opinions on the same issues or because you are hoping that at least one of

E-Mail: The Cons

E-mail is a wonderful time-saver for a reporter and for her or his sources, but I would be uncomfortable relying on it as a primary method. I write health and medical news for a web site, from an office in my house in an exurban area.

My sources, mostly researchers in the fields of science and medicine, seem to be quite comfortable with e-mail, and even like it because it saves them valuable time. I feel, though, that the first contact with a source is best made by phone, after which follow-up questions—an occasional need for them is a point no one has raised in this thread—can be handled quickly and economically by e-mail. It often happens that when I start writing, I have questions that did not occur to me, or to the source, which need to be answered. I use e-mail then if I can, rather than to call back.

Nothing will ever substitute for direct person-to-person contact. Face to face is best, telephoning is second best. E-mail does not feel safe to me until I have built some kind of rapport with persons to whom I need to talk, so that I have an idea of what they are like and how much they are to be trusted, and they have reached the same level of qualified trust with me.

—Lee Hickling
drkoop.com
former national science and medicine reporter in the Gannett Newspapers' Washington bureau

your sources will respond before deadline. E-mail allows you to write a list of questions once and then use the blind carbon copy feature to distribute that list to several possible sources at the same time.

Freelance writer Carole Ashkinaze used this feature for a story about electronic commerce: "With just two days to pull a whole story together, and my principal sources already interviewed in person and by phone, I set my search engines loose and found a dozen sites from Australia to Ireland that I thought might be good sources of secondary information. That is, corroborating/confirming/anecdotal info. and quotes. . . . Since they were in wildly divergent time zones, and in some cases I didn't have phone listings or individuals' names, only e-mail addresses, the only practical way to do this was to send them each the three questions I wanted addressed, and hope for responses.

"If I hadn't gotten any, I still would have had my story. But I did—in fact, I heard from eight out of the 12 within 24 hours—and though some were less forthcoming than others, and I only got a paragraph out of all that for the main story, it really helped to flesh my story out."

Interacting with Readers   The previous chapter noted that many online newspapers provide e-mail addresses so that readers may contact reporters directly. An increasing number of newspapers and television stations are following suit by either providing the addresses online or in their traditional news offerings. Readers offer everything from corrections to tips that further the story.

Asking Precise Questions   E-mail allows you to ask very precise questions and allows the subject to give very precise responses. It gives the subject time for reflection. Of course, the reverse is also true. Because of the lack of immediate feedback, you can never "surprise" the subject in an e-mail interview. Jonathan Sweet of the *Stevens Point Journal* uses e-mail for interviews, but only in specific circumstances: "My preference is to use e-mail only for technical, expert-type interviews that require long answers. I don't like to use it for anything local or where I think they may be trying to hide something from me. My preference for anything like that is obviously face-to-face, although a telephone will do in a pinch. I've also found e-mail is useful for things where someone needs to do some research before they can answer the questions."

Following Up on a Personal Interview   No matter how thorough your interview is, you will likely come up with additional questions when you start writing the story. E-mail is a great way to ask these fact-based questions. That's how freelance writer Brian Robinson uses it: "I prefer a personal interview if I can get it, because my experience is that first interviews tend to be wide-ranging, searching for information types (unless it's for a personality profile). Then the more specific follow-up questions, where the focus is much tighter, can be made by e-mail. Interestingly, I'm finding more and more that interviewees prefer it this way."

How E-Mail Works

If you are going to use e-mail, it pays to have some knowledge of how it works. E-mail involves passing a message from one person to another through a computer system. A user composes the message on an e-mail client. **E-mail clients** allow users to read, write, send, receive and manage e-mail. Clients send and receive messages from servers. These servers run programs that examine e-mail messages and either deliver them locally or forward them to another server. Computers handle all these transfers using **simple mail transfer protocol (SMTP),** a set of rules governing the exchange of electronic messages between servers.

Most Internet users do not operate mail servers on their desktop machines. Instead, their e-mail clients make use of a remote server for all the transfer operations. Users can check e-mail on the server in accordance with **Post Office Protocol (POP),** a set of rules governing the exchange of electronic messages between a client and a server. The client sends a log-on ID, a password and a request to download any of its mail currently waiting on the server. Some clients can be set to check mail on the server every few minutes and then notify the user if new mail arrives. To send mail, the client contacts the server and passes the log-on ID, a password and a request to send mail that the client has identified as outgoing.

Parts of an E-Mail Message

E-mail messages consist of three parts: the header, the body and the signature. The **header** consists of the first few lines of an e-mail message, those that handle information regarding the source, destination and contents of the message. In general, the header contains the e-mail address of one or more recipients and information regarding who might receive a carbon copy (cc) or a blind carbon copy (bcc). Addresses under both cc and bcc will receive copies of the message; however, the names and addresses of those who receive a bcc will be hidden from other recipients. The header also contains the address of the sender, which is generally supplied by the e-mail client, and a subject, which allows the sender to provide recipients with a few words that identify the message's contents. The **body** contains the actual content of the message. Users may also specify a **signature,** a short text file tacked onto the end of all outgoing messages, usually providing details about the sender and his or her company. Signature files can be created using standard text editors such as Pico on a Unix system or Notepad for Windows. Some POP e-mail clients, such as Eudora Light, allow users to create and edit signature files within the program itself.

The amount of information appropriate for a signature depends on the purpose of the message or messages being sent; however, signature files of more than six lines tend to draw rebukes from other Internet users. In general, a signature includes the name, e-mail address and, if applicable, the Web site address of the sender. In business or professional correspondence, senders often include the name of their employer as well as telephone and fax numbers. (Figure 4.1) Some senders also tack on a brief quote. Such quotes range from the legalistic (e.g., "This message reflects the views of the sender and not his or her company.") to the comical (e.g., "I'm not a complete idiot, some parts are missing!").

Attaching Files to E-Mail Messages

One of the more interesting developments in e-mail is the ability to attach files to messages, allowing users to send those files through the Internet. For example, a reporter working on a story in Tokyo could send an e-mail message back to his newspaper in California. The message might say not only that he had finished an article on financial markets there, but that he had attached a copy of the article in Word format along with the spreadsheet file he had used to derive his figures and a graphics file containing a picture of the Tokyo Stock Exchange at closing bell that afternoon. His editor could read the message at her computer, then pull the attached files off her hard drive and send them to others in the news and graphics departments for processing.

```
===========================================================
```
I. M. Encharge, Editor   The Local Paper
editor@TheLocalPaper.com   Ph: (666) 555-4444

"I feel no falsehood and fear no truth." -- Thomas Jefferson
```
===========================================================
```

Figure 4.1

A typical e-mail signature contains the author's name, e-mail address, business name and telephone number. Many also contain a brief quote.

Sending an attachment works much like sending a basic e-mail message. The e-mail message contains all the appropriate routing information, such as where the message originated and where it should be going. Most e-mail systems allow users to append files to the end of their messages. When it comes to plain text files, computers have no trouble. E-mail systems were designed to handle these kinds of messages—messages coded in ASCII, the generic coding scheme used by personal computers. A document coded in ASCII format on one computer can be read by any other computer that "knows" that code. Because every computer on the Internet uses the code, they can all read ASCII documents. But spreadsheets and graphics files consist of codes other than text. Even commercial word processing documents such as those created by Word and WordPerfect can contain, in addition to plain text, codes for underlining, italics, page layout, and the like. As a result, such files remain in their original binary format—unintelligible to the ASCII-based e-mail systems.

In order to send attachments, e-mail systems must translate the files' binary codes into ASCII. The attachments can then be sent across the Internet to their destination, where a program decodes them and places them back into their original binary format. Although a number of binary/ASCII coding systems exist, two have come to dominate most e-mail traffic: UUencoding and MIME. **UUencode** is an older, Unix-based program used to translate binary data into ASCII format. In order to read files created by UUencode, a user must have access to **UUdecode,** the program that translates UUencoded ASCII files back into binary data. Generally UUencode and UUdecode come packaged together, either as basic network utilities on a Unix system or as part of a software package such as MacUUcode or UUTool. Although once a mainstay of binary (nontext) file transfers, UUencode had several difficulties, including some compatibility problems when transferring files between different versions of the program. As a result, UUencode has given up much of its territory to **MIME,** or **multipurpose Internet mail extensions,** the current standard for transferring multimedia e-mail messages, binary attachments and other nontext data. MIME's dominance in the field of ASCII/binary translation has eased the burden on end users considerably. PINE, Eudora Light and most other e-mail programs are MIME compliant, meaning that they use the coding scheme to handle message attachments. As a result, users no longer need to worry as much about whether messages can be decoded properly.

When attaching a file to an e-mail message, you need to be concerned about two things: (1) does the recipient have the program necessary to view or use the file you are sending? and (2) does the recipient use the same type of coding scheme you do? The best procedure is to try sending the attachment first. If it doesn't work, then you can contact the other user directly by phone or e-mail to figure out how to correct the problem. Documents created in one word processor, spreadsheet program or database manager can generally be read in most other software of that type. For example, if you create a file in WordPerfect and the recipient uses Word, he or she can easily open and edit the file. The decoding issue often proves more troublesome; however, it can usually be solved with two basic questions: (1) What e-mail program are you using? If the sender and recipient use the same program, the attachment can be translated easily. (2) Is your e-mail program MIME compliant? The documentation will usually say whether the software can handle MIME attachments. Most clients can. For example, MIME messages can be decoded by PINE, Eudora Light, Pegasus, Outlook and most other top e-mail programs.

Attaching a file to an e-mail message is much easier than it might sound. It involves three basic steps:

1. *Creating the message.* Start your e-mail program and create an e-mail message as you normally would.
2. *Attaching the file.* The file to be sent can be of any type, from word processing documents to the word processing program itself; however, the user needs to know the name of the file and its location. The file must also be accessible to the user at the time it is to be attached—it cannot be open in another program or on a drive to which the user does not have access.
3. *Sending the message.* Send the e-mail message and attachment the same way you would any other e-mail message.

THE INS AND OUTS OF ELECTRONIC MAILING LISTS

We normally think of e-mail as a means for one-to-one communication, much like mail sent through the postal service. But computers also give us the ability to use e-mail for a kind of mass communication through electronic mailing lists. A **mailing list** is an electronic discussion group consisting of computer users who register their addresses with a server that facilitates the exchange of e-mail on a specific subject or subjects. At the time of this writing roughly 85,000 mailing lists exist on the Internet. Several dozen lists relate to the practice of journalism, from the Agriculture Journalism Topics Forum to WRITE, a list for English and journalism faculty members. Mailing lists range in size from a few subscribers to several thousand.

Most mailing lists are actually programs running on servers throughout the Internet. A user can send a message to the server or to a human moderator asking to subscribe to a specific list. Once subscribed, he or she will receive a copy of every message sent to the list by users or by the list moderator. A subscriber could receive one message every couple of months or one message every couple of minutes, depending on the list. For example, you might sub-scribe to the IRE-L list, which devotes attention to issues of concern to members of the Investigative Reporters and Editors organization. Once the computer processes the subscription, the messages begin rolling in. A typical day's correspondence on IRE-L might include 34 messages with subjects such as "Federal Trade Commission FOIA Requests," "The Media Is Blind," and "Media/Court Relations."

Here is how a mailing list works. When a message comes in to the list's address, the list server accepts the message and sends copies to all subscribers. The message header shows who sent the e-mail, but replies are directed to the entire list. On most lists, subscribers can respond to any message. The previ-ous subject, preceded by the "regarding" (Re:) marker, appears in the header to help identify the discussions. The term **thread** refers to a single discussion consisting of the initial message and all subsequent replies. Conversations can continue over the course of several days, and most lists have several different conversations going at once.

Of course, not all posts turn into full-blown conversations. Most messages serve as alerts to list subscribers, such as "New Spanish journalism website" or "Editor opening." In fact, some lists act like newsletters, serving up infor-mation but not allowing users to reply directly to the entire list. BONG-L, the Burned-Out Newspapercreatures Guild list, is one such example. The mailing list serves as a distribution mechanism for the weekly BONG Bull newsletter, a collection of newspaper-related anecdotes. Subscribers can join the list and receive a free weekly copy of the newsletter in the form of an e-mail message. Other newsletters have also been made available through electronic mailing lists.

Those electronic mailing lists designed to facilitate two-way discussion expect their subscribers to observe proper **netiquette,** a loose code governing acceptable behavior for communication on the Internet. Most of the rules of netiquette center on the idea that the Internet represents a *public* forum for communication. A message posted by a mailing list subscriber might be seen by thousands of users around the world. Although most journalists have stud-ied ethics and law as part of their college coursework, many forget that mail-ing lists represent a kind of mass communication. If you approach mailing lists as media of mass communication, you may more easily remember the following basic rules of netiquette.

Remember your audience. Journalists working on a news story should never forget that they write for an audience. Subscribers to a mailing list constitute an audience as well. If you feel you must engage in personal conversation, particularly if you intend to hurl insults at an individual, use personal e-mail and not a mailing list.

Do not break the law. Although legal minds have been struggling to keep up with the Internet, most laws that pertain to journalism also pertain to mailing lists—particularly those laws regarding libel and privacy. Suggesting that someone has committed a crime could easily land you, and possibly your employer, a lawsuit. The same goes for posting a person's telephone number, address or other information.

Use proper grammar and spelling. I would hope that this rule comes as second nature to journalists. Capitalize and punctuate properly. Although you may use all capital letters for emphasis, typing an entire message in capitals makes it appear that you are shouting.

Follow the rules of the list. Nearly every mailing list has its own set of rules. Often these rules will be e-mailed to you when you join the list. The initial e-mail may also contain a list of answers to Frequently Asked Questions (FAQ) concerning the list. Read these documents. Most lists advise that you wait a week or two before posting your first message. If you saw a group of people having a discussion, you probably would not walk up and start asking questions. You would listen for a few minutes to hear what they were talking about. The same holds true for discussions on mailing lists. In most cases, it is also wise to avoid posting long messages to mailing lists unless absolutely necessary. Even so, the message's subject line should contain a warning concerning the message's size. File attachments should generally not be sent to mailing lists.

Handling Mailing Lists

A number of different types of mailing list servers exist on the Internet. The three most common types are listserv, Majordomo and listproc. Listserv, the oldest of the three, handles the bulk of the mailing lists on the Internet. Any of these three programs can be configured to allow various degrees of control to the **list owner,** the person responsible for administering a mailing list. Here are some of the options available:

Subscription control: Some list owners control who can sign on to their list, either because they want to restrict the list to certain individuals or because they want subscribers to provide certain bits of additional information. You can identify these lists by the word "request" in the address to which you are directed to send your subscription inquiry (e.g., jour-request@lists.ufl.edu).

Message control: Some lists are moderated, meaning that a human being reads over each message before allowing it to be sent to the entire list. Most are unmoderated. A moderated list has the advantage of reducing the off-topic conversations and mindless chatter that plague some discussions. However, this advantage comes at a price. Because moderated lists hold each message until a human can read it, they lack the immediacy of unmoderated lists.

Reply control: Most mailing lists allow users to reply to the entire list. These mailing lists serve as true electronic discussion groups. Other lists do not allow replies; they act more like electronic newsletters.

Most mailing list servers allow the use of a variety of commands. These commands vary slightly from one program to another. Therefore, it is important to know what kind of list program a server uses before you attempt to send any commands to it. You can determine the type of program used by simply looking at the address for the server (e.g., listproc@latech.edu, listserv@lists.missouri.edu, majordomo@mail.cyberwerks.com). Commands are sent to the program through e-mail messages.

It is imperative to remember that these commands are sent to the program address and not to the list address. Thus, a message containing commands pertaining to the NICAR-L list would be sent to listserv@lists.missouri.edu and not nicar-l@lists.missouri.edu. The listserv program processes commands. The NICAR-L address just forwards the message to the list's more than 1,000 subscribers—a rather embarrassing blunder.

The following commands cover the basic needs of most list subscribers. To send a command to a computer, simply send an e-mail addressed to the program. No subject is required. In the body of the message, simply type the appropriate command. Note that more than one command can be sent in a single message. Just hit the Return key after each command.

Joining a List   Once you obtain the name and address of the list that you want to join, you must send a message asking to be added to the list. In all cases, the command begins with the word *subscribe* followed by the name of the list. Some programs require you to supply your real name as well.

Program	Listserv	Majordomo	Listproc
Command	subscribe <list> <name>	subscribe <list>	join <list> <name>
Example	subscribe carr-l I.M. Encharge	subscribe cwd-l	join agjour-l I.M. Encharge

Leaving a List   Lists can generate a lot of messages, sometimes overwhelming your mailbox. Occasionally, you may simply become bored with a list. To stop the messages you will need to sign off or unsubscribe from the list.

Program	Listserv	Majordomo	Listproc
Command	unsubscribe <list>	unsubscribe <list>	signoff <list>
Example	unsubscribe carr-l	unsubscribe cwd-l	signoff agjour-l

Getting Subscriber Addresses   List programs allow you to request a roll call of the names and e-mail addresses of those people who subscribe to a given list. Because list owners have the option of removing this feature or limiting it to subscribers only, not every list will allow users to obtain the roll call. However, for those lists that permit it, getting a roll call of subscribers can serve as a quick way to locate someone's e-mail address.

Program	Listserv	Majordomo	Listproc
Command	review <list>	who <list>	statistics <list>
Example	review carr-l	who cwd-l	statistics agjour-l

Locating Files   Some mailing lists maintain an archive of files available to subscribers. Once you have subscribed to a list, you can send a command that shows all those files contained in the list's archive.

Program	Listserv	Majordomo	Listproc
Command	index <list>	index <list>	index <list>
Example	index carr-l	index cwd-l	index agjour-l

Retrieving Files   Once you know the name of a file, you can ask the server to send you a copy of that file.

Program	Listserv	Majordomo	Listproc
Command	get <list> <filename>	get <list> <filename>	get <list> <filename>
Example	get carr-l journ lists	get cwd-l journ lists	get agjour-l journ lists

Getting Help   List programs offer a wide range of additional capabilities; however, these capabilities vary. To get a list of additional commands that pertain to any list you are interested in, you can request a help file.

Program	Listserv	Majordomo	Listproc
Command	help	help	help
Example	help	help	help

Electronic Mailing Lists and Journalism

Electronic discussion lists serve a variety of purposes for journalists. Beat reporters can make use of lists related to their specific area of interest. For example, reporters covering cops and courts can find lists dealing with everything from law enforcement on college campuses to the problems faced by gay and lesbian police officers. Lists covering education, medicine and the environment abound as well. Reporters can cruise these lists looking for possible story ideas or use them to follow various trends. By following discussions over a period of time, reporters can usually identify individuals who would serve as good sources for future articles. Being able to reference discussions that have gone on for several days or weeks also lends the reporter a certain amount of credibility with potential sources.

In addition to discussion lists that cover traditional newspaper beats, dozens of journalism-related lists exist on the Internet. Later chapters will discuss how to locate these and other lists via the World Wide Web. However, the following "list of journalism lists" should be enough to get you started.

Name: Agriculture Journalism List
Abbreviation: AGJOUR-L
Program address: listproc@lists.missouri.edu

Name: Baltic States Journalism Discussion
Abbreviation: BALTJ-L
Program address: listproc@lists.missouri.edu

Name: Brock Meeks' CyberWire Dispatch
Abbreviation: CDW-L
Program address: majordomo@mail.cyberwerks.com

Name: Computer-Assisted Reporting and Research
Abbreviation: CARR-L
Program address: listserv@ulkyvm.louisville.edu

Name: Ethics in Journalism Forum
Abbreviation: JOURNETHICS
Program address: listproc@lists.missouri.edu

Name: Forum for European Journalism Students
Abbreviation: FEJS
Program address: listserv@gumncc.terena.nl

Name: High School Scholastic Journalism
Abbreviation: HSJOURN
Program address: listproc@latech.edu

Name: Investigative Reporters and Editors
Abbreviation: IRE-L
Program address: listserv@lists.missouri.edu

Name: Journalism Education Discussion List
Abbreviation: JOURNET-L
Program address: listserv@american.edu
Send subscription requests to: journet-l-request@american.edu

Name: Journalism History Group
Abbreviation: JHISTORY
Program address: listproc@lists.nyu.edu

Name: Journalism and Religion
Abbreviation: JREL-L
Program address: majordomo@iclnet93.iclnet.org

Name: National Institute for Computer-Assisted Reporting
Abbreviation: NICAR-L
Program address: listserv@lists.missouri.edu

Name: National Press Photographers Association
Abbreviation: NPPA-L
Program address: listserv@cmuvm.csv.cmich.edu

Name: Society of Professional Journalists
Abbreviation: SPJ-L
Program address: listserv@lists.psu.edu

Name: Student Journalism List
Abbreviation: SJ
Program address: majordomo@world.std.com

Name: Student Media
Abbreviation: STUMEDIA
Program address: listserv@uabdpo.dpo.uab.edu

Name: Union/Labor Issues Discussion
Abbreviation: GUILDNET-L
Program address: majordomo@acs.ryerson.ca

Name: WRITE: Discussion for English/Journalism Faculty
Abbreviation: WRITE
Program address: listproc@listserv.acns.nwu.edu

SUMMARY

E-mail is the most important tool for communication on the Internet. Today virtually no journalist works without an e-mail address. It may not be the perfect tool for every communication. But used properly, it is indispensable for gathering information.

NOTES

1. Stephen Miller, "Where We Are/How Did We Get Here?" *Journalism and the Internet*, C-SPAN, January 9, 1998. Available online in RealAudio format at <http://www.c-span.org/onak0198.htm>.

5

Putting It All Together
THE WORLD WIDE WEB

In this chapter you will learn:

- Why journalists use the Web

- Basic Web terminology

- How to use a browser to navigate the Web

- What bookmarks are and how to use them

In the past decade the Internet has evolved from a medium for exchanging highly specialized scientific information into one of the most important research tools available today. The main force behind that evolution has been the **World Wide Web,** a subsegment of the Internet that allows users to exchange graphical images, sound and hypertext. By allowing the use of graphics and sound, the Web has enabled information providers to create dynamic designs that allow the Internet to mimic more traditional media such as newspapers, radio and television. But the addition of hypertext allows the Internet to take on an entirely new face.

Hypertext, as the name implies, is a kind of "super" text. Whereas traditional English writing proceeds linearly—that is, in a line from left to right and top to bottom—hypertext allows readers to exercise some control over how they read a passage. Certain words within a hypertext document can be highlighted and logically connected to other documents. These connections, or **links,** allow users to jump from one hypertext document to another referenced by the link. You have probably read textbooks in which words were defined in the margins. A hypertext document would allow the page designer to simply highlight the difficult word, reference it to another document that defines the word and allow the reader the option of clicking on it to view the definition. Links are usually identified as such by being underlined or written in a different color than nonlinked text. On the Internet, a hypertext document on one computer can be linked to a document on another computer, creating the illusion that they form a continuous global "web" of information.

A journalist reading through a U.S. Department of Transportation analysis of changing traffic patterns at the turn of the century might be able to click on the hypertext phrase "census figures" and be connected to the U.S. Census Bureau's population projections for the next 10 years. Hypertext offers users the power to do more research for themselves, a power that good journalists cherish.

JOURNALISM AND THE WEB

When Russell Eugene Weston Jr. burst into the U.S. Capitol building and killed two guards with a revolver in July 1998, hundreds of journalists around the nation scrambled to find out everything they could about him. Most followed the usual routine of going to the suspect's house, calling his neighbors and talking with old friends and acquaintances. When it got too late at night for that, Bill Dedman of the *New York Times*'s Chicago bureau turned to the World Wide Web. What he found became the basis of an "exclusive" story that he says could have been had by any junior high school student with the right information.

An experienced Internet searcher, Dedman prowled the Web for anything he could find about the Capitol Police. He soon located the site of a private company that had sold "threat assessment" software to the department. On a hunch, Dedman sent an e-mail message to the head of the company, Gavin de Becker, requesting an interview. He was surprised by the response: "Late that night, I got an e-mail back from Mr. de Becker—in Fiji! He was on vacation. He sent his phone number and I called him. He was a great interview." De Becker talked about his best-selling book, which had two chapters on the subject of public-figure attacks. He also told the reporter how to get his hands on a new Secret Service report that detailed the cases of every person who has tried to kill a public figure since 1949.

Too many news directors and editors are frightened by the idea of computer-assisted reporting, imagining that it involves only large investigative projects that can last up to a year or more. But many newspaper reporters and television producers practice computer-assisted reporting nearly every day on the World Wide Web. "The Web is not just an electronic gizmo," says Joseph Schneider of the *San Diego Union-Tribune*. "It's a tool we used in workaday journalism." In that typical workday, a journalist might use the Web for some of the following activities.

Finding information for cutlines. Schneider's paper had a photo of a U.S. Navy SEAL member holding a strange-looking rifle. A quick Web search revealed that the rifle was a cut-down version of the standard M-16, especially modified for the SEALs.

Getting numbers to back up a story. Jeff Newell of the *Northwest Florida Daily News* says he uses census data for a wide variety of stories: "I recently helped an intern researching a piece on daycare to determine how many children ages 5 and under live in our county. We used the same source for a water resources project. We needed the 1960–90 (plus '97 estimate) numbers to work up a pop chart showing what's happened here in terms of population growth, comparing those numbers to aquifer levels that have steadily gone down over the same period. Nothing like good numbers to make the point."

Locating hard-to-find details. Hank Nuwer, author of *Broken Pledges: The Deadly Rites of Hazing,* relies on the Web for information that would be hard to obtain elsewhere: "Because many hazing incidents are noted only in the college press, I regularly check college on-line newspapers for incidents. I've found many incidents (and two deaths) that received sparing media attention locally and little, if any, nationally."

Saving time. While working with the *Daily Times* in Farmington, N. M., George E. Schwartz used the Web to examine all bills proposed by the state legislature: "It saved me a trip to the bill room, the cost of copying and me drowning in paper in the pressroom at the Capitol. In short, it was a life-saver."

Scanning for background information. Jonathan Oatis, an Internet specialist with the Reuters news service, found the Web to be invaluable during his investigation of the Heaven's Gate suicides in California: "Using information from other media outlets, most notably MSNBC, and confirming information from a former member of the cult, I was able to provide our Los Angeles bureau with all kinds of information on the cult's business, their beliefs and background."

Checking for accuracy. Carol Napolitano, then working at the *Omaha World-Herald,* ran into trouble while examining the locations of crimes in and around the city. Some of the locations provided by police were failing to show up in her computer mapping program, and she had to determine whether the addresses really existed: "We used the U.S. Postal Service's site on the Web to check the addresses and see if they were legitimate ones. We left the postal site running in the background so we could toggle back and forth between that and the mapping program. It helped speed up the work for us."

These activities are just a few examples of how journalists use the Web. The large number of media outlets, government agencies, nonprofit organizations and businesses on the Web today make it a terrific hunting ground for the modern journalist. All you need is an Internet connection, a Web browser and some time to become acquainted with what is out there.

BASIC WEB TERMINOLOGY

When you use a computer to write a news story, you generally need to have a special type of program, known as a word processor, in order to type and print.

Likewise, when you use the computer to access the World Wide Web, you also need a special type of program called a browser. The term **browser** refers generically to any program that allows users to connect with a Web server, access files and display those files on the computer. At present, the two most popular browsers on the market are Microsoft Internet Explorer and Netscape Navigator (often packaged with other programs as Netscape Communicator); these two browsers account for roughly 85 percent of all Web traffic.[1] Although experts debate which is the "better" browser, most agree that both do a good job of helping users access the World Wide Web. Moreover, both operate in a similar fashion. This book uses Netscape Navigator for illustration purposes; however, most of the material can easily be applied to Microsoft Internet Explorer as well.

Browsers communicate with Web servers using **hypertext transfer protocol,** or **HTTP,** a formal set of rules that allows computers to exchange Web documents. HTTP uses a rather detailed procedure to pass data over the Internet, but luckily, it all happens behind the scenes. It is enough for most of us to know that we must include *http://* when connecting with a server in order to let the computers know how they should communicate. In fact, it is so important that most modern Web browsers will put the *http://* in if the user forgets to.

Once a server transfers a requested document to the local computer, the browser needs to determine how to display that document on the screen. Most Web documents are simply text files. However, they contain hidden instructions that let the browser know how the file should be displayed on the screen. The instructions might tell the browser to make one piece of text appear as a title in the bar at the top of the screen or display another bit of text as a large, boldfaced headline. They could also tell the browser to retrieve a graphics file from the server and display it on the left side of the page near the top. These instructions are written in **Hypertext Markup Language,** or **HTML,** a specialized code that uses hidden tags to format documents that will be read by Web browsers. HTML documents can usually be identified by their *htm* or *html* file extensions (e.g., *contents.htm* or *contents.html*).

A **Web page** is nothing more than an HTML document placed on a Web server.[2] Every page on a Web server has its own distinct address. The term **uniform resource locator,** or **URL,** refers to the precise access address for a Web page. A URL (sounded out, as in "U-R-L," or pronounced as a word, "url") can appear somewhat imposing at first glance. For example, the URL for technical questions related to Netscape Navigator is <http://help. netscape.com/faqs/nav3x.html>. But it is not as confusing as it might appear. Remember that *http://* merely tells the server that you want to use hypertext transfer protocol. The *help.netscape.com* is the server's Internet address (discussed in chapter 3). The slashes after the Internet address indicate directories, and the *nav3x.html* segment simply states the name of the HTML file you want to look at. Thus, all we are telling the computer is that we want to use HTTP to transfer the file called nav3x.html, which can be found in the faqs directory at help.netscape.com.

HTML has its own set of advantages and disadvantages. Although the code scheme does a good job of transmitting data quickly, it was not intended to be graphically pleasing. Quite simply, HTML does not offer page designers a great deal of control over what the finished product actually looks like. While HTML will allow a designer to specify that Headline1 will be displayed larger than Headline2, it does not allow that designer to specify an exact size. The actual look of the headline will depend on a variety of other factors, such as the size of the user's screen, the number of colors the computer can display and the type of browser used to view the document. Thus, the same document may look subtly or even radically different from one machine to the next.

While HTML may limit the designer's flexibility in creating a page, it enhances the reader's flexibility in using it. Normal text proceeds linearly. In English, the reader starts at the upper left corner of the page and reads left to right and top to bottom. But HTML allows the designer to make use of hypertext, a kind of "super" text consisting of traditional, linear text together with links to other documents or to other places within the same document. An HTML document usually displays these links in a distinctive way, such as with an underline or in a different color from the regular text.

Most designers use the linking feature of hypertext to create **Web sites,** collections of related Web pages. A large newspaper such as the *New York Times* might have a site featuring thousands of Web pages. An individual reporter at that paper might have a personal site with only two or three pages. No matter how large it is, each Web site has its own **home page,** the site's front or opening page, which often acts both as a gateway and as a tool for organizing the site's contents. By convention, the home page is given the name "index" (i.e., *index.htm* or *index.html*). If you fail to specify a file name when connecting to a Web site, the browser automatically looks for a file called index and displays that file on your computer. That way individual users do not need to worry about how to find a site's front page.

NAVIGATING THE WEB

Making contact with a Web site is relatively simple once you have an Internet connection and a browser. You enter the URL of the Web site, and within a few seconds the site's index page appears on your screen. The browser handles all the details and provides you with updates of its progress. Still, it is worth taking a quick look at the process so that you can better understand what goes into making a Web connection. It works like this:

1. Using your browser, you enter the URL of the Web site that you would like to connect with (e.g., <http://www.whitehouse.gov>).
2. The browser looks up the site's IP address over the Internet using the domain name system distributed database.[3] You can tell this step is happening because you will generally see a message at the

bottom of your screen along the lines of "Connect: Looking up host: www.whitehouse.gov."

3. The browser tries to contact the server. Again, you can tell this step is happening by a message at the bottom of your screen saying "Contacting host www.whitehouse.gov."

4. Once the browser makes contact, it asks for the file you've re-quested. The message at the bottom of the screen will now read "Host www.whitehouse.gov contacted. Waiting for reply . . ."

5. The server sends along the file you have asked for. Now the message says "Reading file . . ." or "Transferring data," or it displays other information about how the transfer is proceeding (e.g., "66% of 8K transferred").

6. Once the transfer is complete, the server breaks the connection. You can then see a message such as "Document: Done."

Note that even though people often use the phrase "on the Web," you are not actually connected with anything when you are looking at Web pages. You simply send a request to a server and the server sends back a file. Your browser then stores the file temporarily on your computer. The page you are looking at could change or even disappear from the site and you would not know about it until you tried to access that page again or until the server automatically resends the page to you.

USING A BROWSER

A browser is nothing more than a computer program, like a word processor or a video game. Whereas a word processor allows users to type papers or stories, a browser allows users to navigate the Internet and read a variety of files, including HTML documents. Notice that a Web browser looks much like other Windows-based programs, with a menu bar and a toolbar at the top of the screen. Clicking on a word in the menu bar displays a pull-down menu that allows the user to select from among various options. Although these options vary from program to program, some key features are standard—such as the ability to create, open, save and print files. Figure 5.1 illustrates the Netscape Navigator browser with the File pull-down menu selected. Note that the browser displays the complete URL of the site.

There are only ten basic functions that you need to know in order to operate a Web browser:

Open Page: You can connect with Web sites and view the pages stored there by clicking on File in the menu bar and selecting Open Page. This opens a pop-up window that allows you to input the URL of a page you would like to connect with via the Web. An easier way to open a page is to simply type the URL in the white Location box at the top of the browser screen.

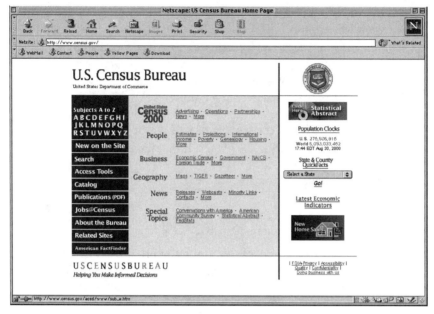

Figure 5.1

The Web browser allows users to navigate the Internet and read a variety of files, including HTML documents. Notice that it appears very similar to many other Windows-based programs, with a menu bar and a toolbar at the top of the screen. Users can connect with a Web site either by selecting Open Page from the File menu and entering the site's URL or by typing the URL directly into the white address box at the top of the screen. Here, Netscape Navigator is used to view the U.S. Census Bureau's Web site.

Print: You can choose to print the document that you are viewing by clicking on File in the menu bar and selecting Print.

Close: This function closes the document that you are looking at. If you have more than one document active, the browser will remain open. To close a document, click on File in the menu bar and select Close.

Exit: This function allows you to close all files and exit the browser. Click on File in the menu bar and select Exit.

Select All: You can select all the text in the document that you are viewing. This function is particularly useful when you want to copy text from an HTML document into a word processor. Click on Edit in the menu bar and select Select All.

Copy: This function copies the text onto the clipboard, a temporary memory location that holds data while the computer remains turned on. Text can then be moved from the clipboard to a document with the Paste command. Click on Edit in the menu bar and then select Copy.

Figure 5.2

The browser toolbar allows you to perform many of the most common navigation functions within the browser—Back, Forward, Reload and Stop. You can also choose to print the entire document that you are viewing, reload your designated home page or search the Web.

> *Find in Page:* This very useful command locates a specified bit of text within the document that you are viewing. Click on Edit in the menu bar and select Find in Page.
>
> *Reload:* This function reconnects with the Web server that delivered the page you are viewing and requests that the page be resent. This capability is useful when you are viewing pages that are updated continuously. Click on View in the menu bar and select Reload.
>
> *Back:* When you move from one Web page to another, your browser keeps the previous page stored in a temporary file on your drive. You can view the previous page by using the Back command. Click on Go in the menu bar and select Back.
>
> *Forward:* Think of the Web pages you have viewed as a chain of documents. Once you move back to a document that you have previously viewed, you can then move forward again. Click on Go in the menu bar and select Forward. (Note that the Go menu also allows you to jump directly to any of the documents most recently stored as temporary files on your hard drive.)

The most commonly used of these commands can also be found in the toolbar at the top of your screen (Figure 5.2).

USING BOOKMARKS

The World Wide Web comprises hundreds of millions of pages. A typical journalist might view hundreds or even thousands in a single week. Keeping track of which sites are most important to you can be quite a chore. Luckily, browsers offer a special tool called a bookmark that allows your browser to "remember" pages that you deem worth saving. A **bookmark** is a URL that your computer stores together with the title of the page to which the URL refers. The term *bookmark* is sometimes used as a verb meaning "to create a bookmark." The browser keeps bookmarks on the local computer as a special HTML document called *bookmarks.htm*. When you first start using your browser, or if you are using a browser on a school computer, some bookmarks will probably already be set up for you—such as those marking sites for searching the Internet or locating news on the Web. In all likelihood, they will be organized into a system of folders containing related bookmarks

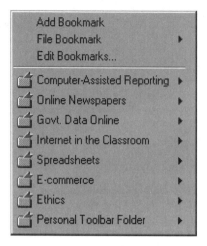

Add Bookmark
File Bookmark ▶
Edit Bookmarks...

▢ Computer-Assisted Reporting ▶
▢ Online Newspapers ▶
▢ Govt. Data Online ▶
▢ Internet in the Classroom ▶
▢ Spreadsheets ▶
▢ E-commerce ▶
▢ Ethics ▶
▢ Personal Toolbar Folder ▶

Figure 5.3

A typical list of bookmarks shows the folders into which they are categorized.

(Figure 5.3). You can then add, delete, rename or recategorize the bookmarks as you wish.

Adding Bookmarks

Adding a bookmark is easy. To do so, simply load the page that you want to remember by typing its URL either in the Open Page pop-up window or in the Location box at the top of the screen. Once you are viewing the page, you may click on Bookmarks—found either on your menu bar or next to the Location box at the top of the screen. This brings up the pull-down menu shown in figure 5.3. Select Add Bookmark and the page is automatically added to your bookmark list. Or you can select File Bookmark and place it directly into a folder.

Most browsers also have a faster way to add a bookmark; simply click on an icon in the toolbar and drag that icon onto your bookmark list.

Categorizing Bookmarks

When adding bookmarks, it is important to keep them well organized. The best way to do this is to plan out in advance what categories of Web sites you will be needing. For example, you will probably want to bookmark a few sites that allow you to search the Internet (these sites will be discussed in chapter 6). You might also want to bookmark a number of media sites, both local and national, so that you can keep up with the news. As a journalist, you will also want to bookmark sites devoted to the practice of journalism, various government sites that provide information of use to journalists and some sites offering basic reference materials. Creating categories or folders for these

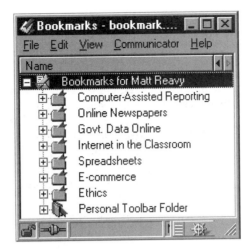

Figure 5.4

The Bookmarks window allows you to create folders, organize folders and bookmarks, delete bookmarks and change bookmark properties.

sites in advance helps you focus your search when you go looking for them on the Web.

Working with a Bookmark List

To work with your bookmark list directly, click on Bookmarks and select Edit Bookmarks from the pull-down menu. This launches a pop-up window that enables you to work with your bookmarks directly (Figure 5.4). The pop-up window offers a variety of options, many of which you will probably never use, such as creating bookmarks by hand. In fact, there are only four common uses of the bookmarks window: creating folders; organizing folders and bookmarks; deleting folders and bookmarks; and changing folder and bookmark properties.

Creating Folders   To create a bookmark folder:

1. Click once on the area where you want the new folder to go. With the top Bookmarks icon selected (see figure 5.4), the new folder would be created directly on the top level alongside Editing, Daily Items and the other main folders.
2. Click on File in the menu bar and select New Folder. A pop-up window will appear with the name New Folder highlighted.
3. Change the name New Folder to a more descriptive name and hit Enter. The new bookmark folder will appear on your list.

Note that folders can contain bookmarks or other folders. As an example, you can have a folder called News Media that contains other folders called

Newspapers, Magazines and Television Stations. Each of these folders can, in turn, contain bookmarks or additional folders.

Organizing Folders and Bookmarks   The bookmark window operates very much like **Windows Explorer,** the program that allows you to interact with your computer's various drives, directories and files. First, take a look at the Bookmark window (figure 5.4). The plus sign (+) to the left of a folder indicates that it contains bookmarks or other folders. Clicking on the plus sign will cause the folder to expand, revealing the contents. A minus sign (−) next to a folder indicates that it has already been expanded. Clicking on the minus sign will cause the folder to close, concealing the contents. If you clicked on the minus sign next to Bookmarks at the top of the window, all the main folders would vanish and the minus sign would change to a plus sign.

When organizing your bookmark list, you can pick up any bookmark or folder and drop it anywhere on the list. To do so:

1. Click on the folder or bookmark that you want to move and hold down the mouse button.
2. Drag the folder or bookmark to the location that you want.
3. Release the mouse button.

Deleting Folders and Bookmarks   It is good practice to update and reorganize your bookmarks on a regular basis, if for no other reason than to remind yourself what resources you have access to. You can also delete bookmarks to sites that are no longer available or a folder that you no longer have use for. To delete a bookmark or folder:

1. Click on the object once to highlight it.
2. Press the Delete key.

Changing Folder and Bookmark Properties   Some Web pages have no title. Others have a title that either is not descriptive or is too long to appear easily on your screen. In these cases, you will want to alter the properties of your bookmark for that site in order to make its description more useful to you. To do so:

1. Click once on the folder or bookmark whose properties you want to change.
2. Click on Edit in the menu bar.
3. Select Bookmark Properties (even if you are changing the name of a folder). A pop-up window will appear showing the name of the object. If the object is a bookmark, the window will also display the URL it refers to.
4. Alter the name of the bookmark or folder and hit the Enter key.

Bookmarks are an invaluable tool for journalists who use the Web frequently. It is well worth it for you to sit down and spend some time learning how to use them properly. The effort will pay off when you need to locate information quickly.

SITES WORTH BOOKMARKING

Every journalist working on the Web has his or her list of favorite sites. In most cases, the list depends on a number of factors. When creating your bookmark list, take into account the following questions.

Where are you located? Obviously journalists in different locations have different priorities. Most journalists in Uruguay often care little about what happens in the United States and vice versa. The same could be said of journalists in Pennsylvania and Louisiana. Nearly every state and nation has its own server. U.S. state servers usually use the URL <http://www.state.xx.us>, where *xx* is the two-letter state abbreviation. ISleuth and other sites feature lists of important state and regional servers. You will also want to scout out most servers in your county and municipality.

What beats do you cover? The bookmarks of a business writer and an education writer will have some overlap, but probably not much. There are a number of specialized sites out there that offer everything from news releases and speeches to in-depth background material. Spend some time seeking out information-packed sites related directly to the subjects you cover most.

What kinds of reference materials do you need access to? If you need to look up a word in a dictionary, you are better off keeping one on your desk than bookmarking it on your Web page. It is faster and easier *not* to use the computer for that purpose. But there are times when Web page reference materials can be extremely helpful. For example, the Web has pages that allow users to calculate interest rates, adjust for inflation, convert units of measurement, and so on. Whether you are looking up ZIP codes or checking out the latest sports scores, there is a site out there to help.

What is your competition? Chances are that the newspaper or television station across town has a Web site. So do similar media outlets around the world. Bookmark these sites so that you can check out the competition with the click of a button.

How do you like to search the Web? Chapter 6 deals with how to search the Web for information. Most journalists have one or two favorite search sites that they like to use for most of their information hunts. It is worth keeping these sites bookmarked, if for no other reason than to save you the effort of typing in a URL every time you use one.

As a rule of thumb, if you find yourself going back to a site more than once or twice, it is probably worth bookmarking. As a starting point, you may want to check out the following popular journalism sites.

Computer-Assisted Reporting Sites

The CAR/CARR Links Page   <http://www.ryerson.ca/~dtudor/carcarr. htm>   Dean Tudor's comprehensive list of links to sites dealing with computer-assisted reporting and research.

Computer-Assisted Research   <http://www.poynter.org/car/cg_chome. htm>   Nora Paul's online guide to using the Internet and other online resources.

Editor & Publisher Interactive   <http://www.mediainfo.com/>   E&P's site devoted to media in the age of technology.

The J-Files @ VCU   <http://saturn.vcu.edu/~jcsouth/>   A "21st Century News Center" maintained by Prof. Jeff South at Virginia Commonwealth University. It contains a variety of journalism-related files and links.

National Institute for Computer-Assisted Reporting   <http://www.nicar. org>   The nation's foremost resource for journalists interested in computer-assisted reporting.

The Poynter Institute   <http://www.poynter.org/>   A self-described "school for journalists," offering seminars and files aimed at students and professionals. The site also offers of wealth of articles on journalism. A particularly nice feature is the Hot News/Hot Research list of links pertaining to items currently in the news.

Ryerson Institute for Computer-Assisted Reporting in Canada   <http:// www.ryerson.ca/~ricarc/>   Promotes the growth of computer-assisted reporting in Canada with a Database of Databases among other features.

Journalism Organizations

American Copy Editors Society   <http://www.copydesk.org>
American Society of Newspaper Editors   <http://www.asne.org/>
Asian American Journalists Association   <http://www.aaja.org>
Canadian Association of Journalists   <http://www.eagle.ca/caj/>
Education Writers Association   <http://www.ewa.org>
The Freedom Forum   <http://www.freedomforum.org>
Investigative Reporters and Editors   <http://www.ire.org>
National Association of Black Journalists   <http://www.nabj.org>
National Association of Broadcasters   <http://www.nab.org>
National Association of Hispanic Journalists   <http://www.nahj.org>

National Association of Minorities in Communication
<http://www.namic.org>
National Association of Science Writers   <http://www.nasw.org>
National Conference of Editorial Writers   <http://www.ncew.org>
National Press Club   <http:// npc.press.org>
Native American Journalists Association   <http://www.medill.nwu.
edu/naja/>
Radio-Television News Directors Association   <http://www.rtnda.org>
Religion Newswriters Association   <http://www.rna.org>
Society of American Business Editors and Writers   <http://www.
sabew.org>
Society of Environmental Journalists   <http://www.sej.org>
Society of Professional Journalists   <http://www.spj.org>
Southern Newspaper Publishers' Association   <http://www.snpa.org>

SUMMARY

The World Wide Web has been a boon for journalists interested in gathering information from a broad array of sources. Now that you have a basic understanding of the Web, we can explore tools and techniques for finding information on the Web.

NOTES

1. According to BrowserWatch, <http://browserwatch.internet.com/stats/ stats.html>.
2. It is worth mentioning that Web pages can also be created on the fly using Common Gateway Interface scripting and other advanced mechanisms.
3. The DNS database, discussed in chapter 3, contains the registered Internet addresses of Internet servers cross-referenced with the machines' IP addresses. That way human users do not need to remember the numeric address (e.g., <208.34.222.1>) of machines on the Internet.

6

Locating Information Online
THE WORLD WIDE WEB REVISITED

In this chapter you will learn:

- The difference between Web directories and search engines

- What Booleans are and how you can use them to search the Web

- What metasearch engines do

- Which specialized search engines are useful to journalists

The helter-skelter nature of the Internet poses serious obstacles for reporters on deadline. You can spend hours searching for something and never find it, and never really know if it's on the Net or not. After becoming more familiar with the idiosyncrasies of cyberspace, you will be able to find information with relative ease, and feel comfortable relying on it for deadline. But it takes both time and patience—commodities often in short supply for reporters up against tight time constraints.

—Christopher Callahan, American Journalism Review, April 1997[1]

Raising a child in the United States today costs quite a bit of money. Raising twins even more. But what does it cost each year to feed, clothe and house a set of quadruplets? That was the question facing Neil Reisner, computer-assisted reporting specialist with the *Miami Herald*. The day a South Florida woman gave birth to quadruplets, Reisner's editor wondered whether the paper could do something other than rehash the same story and photos it did every time there was a multiple birth. Reisner thought it could. He got on the World Wide Web and searched for variations of the terms *child, care* and *costs*. As he explains,

> That led, oddly enough, to a college professor's classnotes, which took note of the U.S. Department of Agriculture's annual estimate of child-rearing cost. It was easy to search the USDA site and find the press release announcing the most recent estimate and a full report on the estimates.[2]

The *Herald* had its answer . . . almost. Reisner's research showed that the cost of raising one child cannot simply be multiplied by four in order to determine the cost of quadruplets. There are economies of scale involved. But a quick phone call to the person named on the USDA press release provided the formula that the paper needed to determine the cost of raising four new-borns—all with the Web and a little old-fashioned reporting.

The World Wide Web is made up of literally millions of pages. When a person creates a Web page, he or she is not required to register that page at any sort of central catalog. As a result, while the Web may indeed be the world's largest library, critics quip that all its "books" lie scattered on the floor. Internet developers have worked to create a variety of tools to catalog as well as to search the World Wide Web. These search mechanisms come in two basic forms: subject-oriented directories and keyword-oriented search engines. The Web provides a variety of directories and search engines, each with its own unique offerings. In addition, there exist an assortment of metasearch engines and specialized search engines. This chapter examines these various tools and discusses how they can be used to find what you are looking for on the Web.

WEB DIRECTORIES

A **Web directory** looks like a table of contents for the Web; it usually allows users to either browse through categories or conduct a subject-oriented search of its Web page database. Perhaps the most popular Web directory in existence is Yahoo![3] Launched in 1994 by two doctoral candidates in electrical engineering at Stanford University as a way of keeping track of its creators' own interests on the Web, Yahoo! posted $53.6 million in revenue and $16.7 million in net income during the third quarter of 1998.[4] Yahoo! is generally recognized as the best directory on the Web, earning *PC Magazine*'s Editor's Choice honors as well as dozens of other awards.

Yahoo! is organized into more than a dozen major categories (Figure 6.1). Each of these categories is further broken down into subcategories. News & Media contains several dozen subcategories ranging from Broadcasting to Weird News. Subcategories, in turn, consist of other subcategories and links to various Web sites.

The category system makes it very easy for journalists to browse Yahoo! in search of information related to a topic. An education reporter might select Education from the top-level directory, then pick and choose from the various subcategories. In this way, this reporter might find not only the items that he or she had been specifically looking for (e.g., educational statistics) but also some sites related to subtopics that might not have come to mind, such as online discussions devoted to education.

Most of the sites on Yahoo! are submitted by Web users, usually by each site's **webmaster,** the person who creates or maintains the Web site. If the

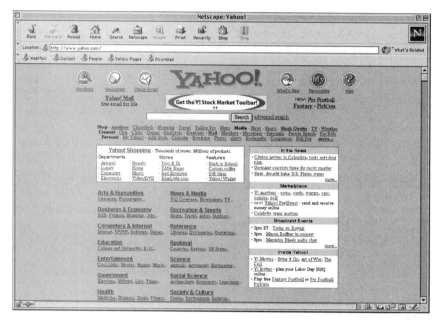

Figure 6.1

The Yahoo! Web directory is one of several that endeavor to serve as a table of contents for the Internet. The directory allows users to browse its contents by using links to its various categories or to search for a specific subject using the search box near the top of the page.

webmaster does not register the site with Yahoo!, it will usually not appear on the directory. Luckily, most webmasters, certainly those who work on large sites, know this and choose to register their sites. The registration process is free and relatively easy. A user goes to the Yahoo! home page, locates the appropriate category for his or her site, clicks the box titled Suggest a Site, and fills out a brief form. The form includes, among other things, a title for the site, the site's URL, and a brief description. In most cases, that description is then included with the site's link. Descriptions provide basic information about the site's contents, such as:

> **Pennsylvania Women's Press Association** professional association laboring on behalf of journalistic excellence, with information on programs, annual contest, scholarships, district, and membership info.[5]

These descriptions allow users to gain an understanding of what a site might contain before they decide whether to connect with it.

When someone submits a site to Yahoo!, the company assigns it to one or more categories and adds the site to its database.[6] In addition to finding the new site by browsing through the various categories, users can also attempt to

---

Sample Yahoo! Search:

1. Enter the word "journalism" in the white box below the Yahoo! logo.
2. Click on the gray Search button. You should see a list of more than a dozen categories followed by hundreds of individual sites.
3. Click on News Stories in the square bar above Category Matches. You should see a list of recent news stories that mention journalism.
4. Back up one page (using the Back button in your browser's toolbar).
5. Click on Net Events in the square bar above Category Matches. You should see a list of events on the Net pertaining to journalism.

---

locate it by using a special search mechanism located at the top of the front page. Users can enter the sought-after word or phrase in the white box below the Yahoo! logo and then click on the Search button next to it. Yahoo! then looks for the specified word or words in its category titles, Web site names and Web site descriptions as well as in its database of news stories and Net events.

The Yahoo! search engine then ranks the results according to how important it judges each match will be to the user. The judgment is based on three factors:

- *Multiple search word mentions:* Matches that mention the search word more than once will be judged more important that those that mention the word less frequently.

- *Document section weighting:* Matches that feature the search word in the title section will be ranked higher than those that mention it in the description.

- *Generality of category:* General categories that mention the search word will be ranked higher than more narrowly focused categories or individual Web sites.

The results first list matching categories, followed by matching sites. You can also get a listing of news stories or Net events that match your search criteria by clicking on the appropriate word in the bar at the top of the search page.

Directories like Yahoo! have a variety of uses when you are seeking information on the World Wide Web. They are of particular value when you want to obtain an overview of a very general topic. If you are covering business, you can browse through a number of categories related to business and the economy in order to locate specific sites that might interest you.

Web directories are also valuable when you want to locate entire Web sites devoted to your subject. Directories generally reference sites that are devoted entirely or primarily to a given subject. If you are looking for

Choosing a Search Engine

Neil Reisner, computer-assisted reporting specialist for the *Miami Herald*, uses the Web to help his reporting on a daily basis. Here is his advice on selecting a search engine:

When I'm on the Web, I just want to get the information I need. Fast. On deadline.

So, I'm not big on the debates about which search engine is best, which gives the most hits or cruises the most sites. Discussions like that are kind of like the debate between PC fans and Mac devotees. They're a matter of belief, of religion.

Give me what works.

What that means in practice is that I use only a couple of Web search sites. The way I figure it, any one of the search engines is likely to give me more hits than I can possibly review, so I'll just learn how to use one or two very well and assume that something they find will give me what I need.

I use Yahoo! some, because it's so well organized. And I like AltaVista, because it's real flexible and I've been using it so long that I can make it sing and dance; I can narrow my search from 10,000 hits of chaos to 17 really focused hits in a couple of minutes.

And that goes to a theory of using the Web I first heard about from Sarah Cohen of the National Institute for Computer-Assisted Reporting.

It's real simple: Treat the Web like you treat your beat. Just like you develop sources on a beat, get to know them and what they're good for, you should find the Web sites you are going to need often and learn them real, real well.

You'll be able to go directly to the U.S. Census Bureau or to Florida Secretary of State's site or to the site maintained by the city you cover—what site really depends on your beat—and get what you need.

information on Newt Gingrich, you will not have to waste time sifting through every document on the Web that mentions him. Yahoo! will only list sites that have his name in the title or description of the site.

SEARCH ENGINES

Web directories are a good place to start or to look for broad subjects. But when you are interested in narrowing your search to a very specific topic, you need to consult a search engine. A **search engine** is a server-based program that allows interaction with a searchable database of Web pages, a database that usually contains each page's title, URL and a brief excerpt or description. Search engines allow users to provide one or more **keywords,** words that the search engine attempts to match in documents within its database. If a keyword is found within a document, the search engine will list that document among the search results.

A number of good search engines exist on the Web, including:

AltaVista <http://www.altavista.com> Undoubtedly the most powerful search engine on the Web, AltaVista claims to index more than 140 million Web pages. However, the site generally receives lower marks in magazine reviews, which complain that it can be difficult to use properly. AltaVista also lacks some of the bells and whistles of other search engines, though the site's creators have been working to upgrade its offerings.

Excite <http://www.excite.com> Where AltaVista falters with its user interface, Excite picks up the slack. It also has plenty of extras, including e-mail and chat areas. The site has a nice feature that suggests words that might narrow down a user's search. Type in "cronkite" and the search engine suggests adding words like "anchorman," "newsman" and "cbs." It also boasts a unique concept-oriented search that allows users to locate pages devoted to similar concepts even if they fail to match the search words that the user has provided. The user simply runs a normal search, locates a document that he or she finds interesting and then clicks on the link titled Search for More Documents Like This One.

Google <http://www.google.com/> Google wins points for its next-generation technology, which uses the hyperlinks pointing *to* a page to help determine how highly that page should be ranked in your search. Launched in 1998, Google has won a very strong following among Web searchers.

HotBot <http://www.hotbot.com> HotBot claims to offer access to more than 110 million documents in its database. It also features a very user-friendly interface, though it lacks some of the extras that Excite and Infoseek provide. However, the easy interface and accurate results have been enough to keep HotBot at the top of most reviews.

Infoseek <http://www.infoseek.com> Infoseek has won the admiration of many Web searchers for its ability to provide fast, accurate search results. However, it falls short in its ability to allow users to conduct more powerful, in-depth searches of the Web. Infoseek gains back some of those lost points with its browseable directory of more than 500,000 Web sites.

How Search Engines Work

Unlike directories, which require webmasters to submit URLs manually, search engines can go out looking for Web sites. This task is accomplished through the use of **spiders,** programs that connect to Web pages and download the text to a database. Once a spider catalogs a specific Web page, it follows links from that Web page to other pages on the same or different sites. The spider returns to the site anywhere from a day to a month later to update the search engine database. On a typical day, AltaVista catalogs approximately 10 million Web pages in this manner.

Once the spider downloads a site's contents, the search engine must index those contents. Unlike directories, which index only the title and description of each site, the bigger search engines generally index the entire contents of every page on that site. As a result, they are more comprehensive than directories. If you search for the word "grinch" in a Web directory, you will likely find a number of sites devoted primarily or exclusively to people or things named Grinch. Look for "grinch" using a search engine and you will find any page that so much as mentions the word. A search for "grinch" in Yahoo! turned up 12 site matches. The same search in AltaVista resulted in 9,169 matches on pages throughout the Web.

Every major search engine on the Web allows users to simply type words in a box near the top of the screen and click on a button to search its contents. However, what you get back will not always be the same. A quick inquiry for "spj" (the Society of Professional Journalists) yields different results from each of the four search engines I mentioned earlier. AltaVista found 12,192 Web pages that mentioned the term "spj," nearly one-third more than the next best search engine—Google, which found 8,862—and more than five times the others (HotBot yielded 2,224, while Infoseek only turned up 1,892).

The number of results generated by a particular search engine can be impressive, but it should be remembered that some of these results can be duplicates. A recent review in C | Net magazine found that one of every five pages returned during an Excite search were duplicates.[7] The way that the various search engines rank their results can be important too. The "spj" search produced the Society of Professional Journalists home page at the top of the results generated by Excite, Hotbot and Infoseek. It was tops on Google as well. Yet that home page did not appear among the top 10 Web pages suggested by AltaVista, although a few other pages on SPJ's site did.

Combining Search Keywords

Because the bigger search engines can return thousands or even hundreds of thousands of Web pages in a given search, most search engines offer you some advanced options to narrow your search. These advanced options often include the use of **Booleans,** logical expressions that specify a set of conditions that Web documents must match in order to be deemed relevant. Boolean expressions on Web search engines make use of four basic operators:

> OR—The OR operator indicates that a document containing any of the words specified will be deemed relevant. (Example: Looking for *reporter* OR *producer* would call up all the documents that mention "reporter" as well as all the documents that mention "producer"). Another way of thinking about this operator is to consider it an ANY command, as in "any of these words."

AND—The AND operator indicates that a document must contain all the words specified in order to be deemed relevant. (Example: Looking for *journalism AND jobs* would call up only those documents that mention both terms.) You can think of this operator as an ALL command, as in "all of these words."

Note that when users of AltaVista, Excite and Infoseek want to make certain that a word appears in the document, they place a plus sign directly in front of the word. (Example: Using the search term *+reporter +producer* would generate a report of Web pages that mention both words.)

NOT—The NOT operator indicates that documents containing the specified word or words will not be deemed relevant. In most cases, NOT follows an AND. (Example: Looking for *journalism AND NOT newspapers* would call up those documents that mention journalism but not newspapers.) This operator is an EXCLUDING command, as in "excluding this word."

Note that when users of AltaVista, Excite and Infoseek want to make certain that a word does not appear in the document, they place a minus sign directly in front of the word. (Example: Using the search term *+journalism −newspapers* would generate a report of Web pages that mention journalism but not newspapers.)

NEAR—The NEAR operator indicates that documents must contain the specified words near one another in order to be deemed relevant. (Example: Looking for *Washington NEAR Post* would call up documents that mentioned the two words relatively close together.) Exactly how close the words must appear to one another varies greatly from one search engine to another. In WebCrawler, NEAR means within two words. In OpenText, it means within 80 characters.

Boolean operators can be strung together to create more complex search requests. Parentheses are often used to specify which operations go together. Thus, you could create the search phrase *(journalism AND jobs) AND (reporter OR producer) AND NOT newspaper*. This phrase allows you to search the Web for pages devoted to journalism jobs for reporters or producers without looking at pages that mention newspaper jobs.

Each search engine handles Booleans differently. AltaVista, Excite and Infoseek automatically string keywords together with OR, using plus signs for AND and minus signs for NOT. HotBot automatically strings keywords together with AND and uses the Boolean operators OR and NOT to fine-tune the query. AltaVista's advanced search engine makes use of all the Boolean operators as well as some of its own extras, such as allowing users to specify documents created during a range of dates.

AltaVista, called the favorite among serious researchers on the Web, has a number of additional options for changing the scope of a search.[8] For one thing, you can use a wildcard character (*) to search for plurals and variations of a word. (Example: Searching for *journ** would return documents mentioning journalism, journalists, journals and so on.) AltaVista also lets you search for information on an entire phrase. You must place the phrase inside quotation marks for AltaVista to read it as such. (Example: Searching for "if your mother tells you she loves you" in AltaVista can help you track down the famous quote about the need for verification in journalism: "If your mother tells you she loves you, check it out.")

A variety of additional specialized operators makes AltaVista particularly powerful for searching the Web. The more useful operators for journalists are *domain:domainname*, which allows you to find pages within a specific domain (Example: Searching for +*domain:gov* would return only those pages on government servers); *host:hostname*, which allows you to find pages on a specific host computer (Example: Searching for +*host:census.gov* would return only those pages on the U.S. Census Bureau's host computer); and *title:text*, which allows you to find pages that contain a specified keyword in their title (Example: Searching for *title:statistics* would return pages with the word "statistics" in the title). This last operator is a good way to look for pages devoted largely to the topic that you are interested in.

Keyword search engines like AltaVista and Google offer access to a much wider array of Web pages than directories do. Search engines are especially valuable when:

- You want to obtain information about a very specific topic. You will not find much about "picornaviruses" classified in the Yahoo! directory. However, a quick scan of the Web with a search engine will call up hundreds of pages that mention the subject.

- You want information about a specific phrase. If you want to track down who said "All I know is what I read in the papers," you can go to AltaVista and enter the phrase in quotes. Several pages listing the quote will be displayed, some with the speaker listed.

- You want to narrow down a general topic. The Boolean capabilities of search engines make them well suited for narrowing down a general topic. Instead of sifting through hundreds of pages for information on wildlife endangered by logging outside the United States, you can seek out pages that mention "environment," "wildlife" and "logging" but not "United States."

Metasearch Engines

With the variety of search engines available on the World Wide Web, choosing the right engine for a specific task can be challenging. Metasearch engines were created to alleviate that problem. Rather than maintain its own database of Web pages, a **metasearch engine** takes requests from users, sends those requests out to one or more other search engines and organizes the responses into a single, readable report. In some cases, the metasearch engine simply sums the scores given to a document by each of the various search engines queried. One of the earliest metasearch engines, Metacrawler <http://www. metacrawler.com> works this way. Others, such as Inference Find <(http:// www.ifind.com>, group each Web page into a category that the site generates based on a variety of criteria, including host, location and subject.

One of the better metasearch engines available on the Web today is HuskySearch <http://huskysearch.cs.washington.edu/>, created by Erik Selberg and Oren Etzioni, the authors of Metacrawler. HuskySearch offers users the ability to conduct a fast search (five-second maximum), a regular search (30-second maximum) or a quality search (three-minute maximum). Results from 10 different search engines are displayed in order of relevance; however, the user can select to display them grouped by host site or by clusters of sites pertaining to a specific topic or topics.

Specialized Search Engines

Web directories, search engines and metasearch engines provide an excellent way to conduct a general search of the Web. But for the best results on a specific topic, you may want to use a specialized search engine. **Specialized search engines** gather information for their databases by crawling the Web, much like larger engines do; however, specialized engines crawl only a limited number of sites either within a specific region or that deal with a specific topic. In most cases, specialized search engines function in much the same manner as more general search engines. Specialized search engines of interest to journalists include:

AnyWho <http://www.anywho.com/>, a directory that helps you locate a person or business anywhere in the United States

Education World <http://www.education-world.com>, a database of more than 110,000 education-related sites

Environmental Organization Web Directory <http://www.webdirectory. com/>, which bills itself as the "Earth's biggest environment search engine"

Exes <http://www.exes.com/>, which offers travel-related information

Forum One <http://www.forumone.com/>, which provides Web-based discussions

Medical World Search <http://www.mwsearch.com/>, which searches medical information

NewsBot <http://www.newsbot.com>, the news search engine at HotBot

NewsIndex <http://www.newsindex.com>, the original news search engine

NewsTracker <http://nt.excite.com/>, Excite's news search engine

TOTAVIA   <http://search.totavia.com>,   which is an aviation search engine

MORE INFORMATION FROM THE WEB

Directories and search engines catalog the titles, descriptions and contents of Web pages, but there is more information available on the Web than what is contained on Web pages. Suppose you want to locate someone's e-mail address. If that person has a Web page, you can use a search engine to find the page and the e-mail address. But what if he or she does not have a Web page? In that event, you can use a searchable database. A **searchable database** is a collection of related data that can be searched according to one or more criteria. Web search engines are searchable databases of Web pages. Other searchable databases might contain collections of electronic discussion groups, toll-free numbers or even e-mail addresses.

Web search engines cannot locate information contained in searchable databases because the information does not reside on Web pages. Instead, the database programs create Web pages dynamically based on data that users provide on a **form,** a series of boxes and buttons that allows the user to enter letters, numbers and other information. The searchable database works like this:

1. A user accesses the home page of the specialized database. (Example: The user connects to Yahoo! People Search at <http://people. yahoo.com>; Figure 6.2).

2. The user uses the form provided to enter a series of numbers, letters or words to search for. (Example: The user enters "Rush" and "Limbaugh" in the first and last name boxes under Email Search.)

3. The home page sends commands to the database requesting a list of all matches. The user sees the browser reconnecting to the home page.

4. The program searches for the matches and creates a Web page displaying results on the user's browser. (Example: The Yahoo! People Finder creates a page listing roughly a dozen addresses for Rush Limbaugh, including bigfatidiot@rush.org and madcow24@yahoo.com as well as Limbaugh's correct address, rush@eibnet.com.)

Because the searchable database creates results pages on the fly, users generally cannot successfully bookmark these pages. If you want to see a results page again, you can either save it as a file on your hard drive (clicking on File in the menu bar and selecting Save As) or reenter data on the form page.

Hundreds of searchable databases exist on the Web that are potentially of use to journalists. Here are some of the most commonly used:

Census data—The U.S. Census Bureau's home page <http://www. census.gov/> contains a variety of access tools that allow users to

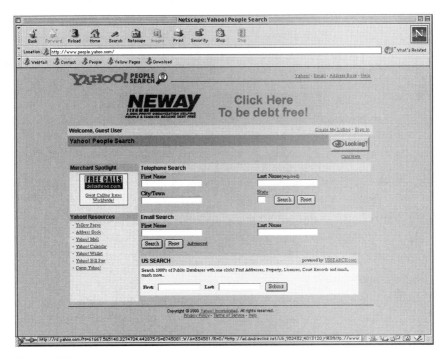

Figure 6.2

The Yahoo! People Search database contains e-mail addresses, telephone numbers and street addresses. Users enter letters, numbers, words and other data using a series of boxes and buttons known as a form. The database then uses the data provided to search for matches.

search the bureau's files for census data pertaining to states, counties, metropolitan statistical areas and cities as well as the nation as a whole.

Aviation data—The Federal Aviation Administration offers access to its online databases of accident and incident reports <http://nasdac. faa.gov/internet/fw_search.htm>. In addition, the commercial site Landings <http://www.landings.com> lists dozens of online aviation databases, many of which are used by journalists covering air disasters.

Businesses—Information on publicly traded corporations can be accessed at the Securities Exchange Commission's EDGAR database <http:// www.sec.gov/edgarhp.htm>. Users can search and view nearly every document these corporations file with the SEC.

Campaign finance—The Campaign Finance Center hosted by Investigative Reporters and Editors <http://www.campaignfinance.org/> offers a wide array of state campaign finance information. The site also contains links to providers of federal election contributions data, including a popular Federal Elections Commission data repository at American University <http://www.soc.american.edu/campfin/>.

Congressional legislation—The Library of Congress gives users the opportunity to search the text of bills, committee reports and other documents through its Thomas Web site <http://thomas.loc.gov/home/thomas2.html>. Articles from the *Congressional Record* can be searched as well.

Experts—ProfNet <http://www.profnet.com>, a collaborative effort of public relations professionals from universities and other research facilities, offers searchable databases of more than 2,000 experts on topics ranging from American politics to zoology. ProfNet is especially useful in locating sources of information on obscure or highly specialized topics.

Internet mailing lists—Liszt <http://www.liszt.com/> is a searchable database of more than 90,000 Internet mailing lists. Liszt also acts as a directory of lists, allowing users to browse by subject.

Nonprofit organizations—Users can locate data about what nonprofit organizations report to the IRS with the Internet Nonprofit Center <http://www.nonprofits.org/library/gov.html>.

Reference materials—My Virtual Reference Desk <http://www.refdesk.com/> lets users browse dictionaries, encyclopedia, a thesaurus and other reference materials. There is even an online calculator and unit converter.

Usenet newsgroups—Users can search through newsgroup postings by using the database at DejaNews <http://www.dejanews.com>.

ZIP codes—Users can get a ZIP code from a place or vice versa with the U.S. Gazetteer site at the Census Bureau <http://www.census.gov/cgi-bin/gazetteer>. Users can also get a ZIP+4 for a specific address using the U.S Postal Service's lookup page <http://www.usps.gov/ncsc/lookups/lookup_zip+4.html>.

Perhaps the best all-around site for exploring specialty search engines and searchable databases is the metasearch engine iSleuth <http://www.isleuth.com/>, which features more than 3,000 specialized search tools on topics ranging from acronyms to zoos. The site also features easy access to a variety of state and regional search engines that allow users to find information from Web sites in specific geographic regions.

SUMMARY

Development of the World Wide Web has moved at an incredible pace. In less than a decade the Web has changed from a little-known research tool to a vital piece of the global information marketplace. Advertisements on billboards, in newspapers and on the television continue to tout business Web pages. Many government agencies, most notably the U.S. Census Bureau, have made vast amounts of public data available on the Web. Some political candidates now worry as much about their Web pages as they do about their other forms of campaigning. All of this development bodes well for the journalist who wants to track down a lot of information in a hurry.

As the amount of information available on the Web changes, so does the way that individuals access that information. Developers have been working to perfect electronic commerce on the Web that would enable more companies to conduct business online. Video and audio applications have become increasingly commonplace. In addition, more and more sites have begun using **Java applets,** small applications that are downloaded from the server and run on a user's computer. The programs, which are written in the Java programming language, can perform a wide array of functions, from helping users search the Web to allowing them to follow a baseball game.[9] The next generation of applications, called **aglets,** are small programs that actually transfer themselves around the Web to actively search for data, deliver messages or communicate with other computers. Several businesses have begun to use aglets to transfer data internally, but transfers between business and individuals are not far off. In the future, combinations of searchable databases, applets, aglets and some future technology could transform the job of reporters, who might even send program robots of their own out to help with an investigation.

NOTES

1. Available online at <http://ajr.newslink.org/ajrcalla.html>.
2. Personal communication, November 12, 1998.
3. Although this chapter refers specifically to Yahoo!, most of the information contained here pertains to all Web directories.
4. According to a company press release dated October 7, 1998.
5. Yahoo!, <http://search.yahoo.com/bin/search?p=pennsylvania+press+women>.
6. Albeit slowly, according to some critics.
7. Available online at <http://www.cnet.com/Content/Reviews/Compare/Search2/ss05.html>.
8. See Search Engine Watch, <http://searchenginewatch.com/facts/major.html>.
9. HuskySearch <http://huskysearch.cs.washington.edu/> offers users the opportunity to download a Java applet that will help them view search results in several different ways. ESPN's SportsZone <http://espn.sportszone.com/> allows users to click on a button that displays a baseball diamond in which users can follow each pitch of their favorite major league game.

7

Getting Data off the Internet
FILE TRANSFER PROTOCOL

Chapter 4 talked about how files can be transferred using electronic mail. That procedure works well for transmitting a file from one user to another, but if you want to make the file available to many different people, e-mail is not the way to go. For one thing, attachments generally require that a human being go through the process of creating the e-mail message and sending the file. Few servers allow users to request files via electronic mail. Those servers that do allow e-mail access to their files generally give such transfers a very low priority, meaning that the user often must wait for several hours or even days before the server sends the file. Moreover, the encoding process makes files about one-third larger than normal, creating a corresponding increase in the time and resources needed to receive the file.

Today, most servers with files to offer make those files available via **file transfer protocol (FTP),** a set of rules governing the transfer of files between two computers using TCP/IP. Like most other types of programs, FTP requires both a server and client in order to operate properly. The FTP server runs constantly, allowing users to log on to the computer, browse through the collection of available files and take a copy of any file to which they have access. The term **download** refers to the process of copying a file from the server to the client computer. Some servers also allow users to **upload,** to copy a file from the client computer to the server. This chapter explains how to take full advantage of the file transfer protocol to move files on the Internet.

FILE TRANSFER PROTOCOL AND ITS USES

The Internet holds a rich assortment of data for journalists, provided they know how to obtain it. File transfer protocol software allows users to reach out across the Net and pull back copies of everything from Census Bureau spreadsheets to word processing documents containing speeches from officials at the Federal Communications Commission. Journalists can also download copies of the latest computer software. For example, chapter 4 made reference to a POP e-mail client known as Eudora Lite. With FTP you can go out on the Internet, locate the program and copy it to your computer free of charge. The same is true of hundreds of thousands of other programs ranging from simulated board games to add-ons that enable a new printer to work with an old word processor.

Not all programs accessible via FTP come free of charge. Some request donations, while others require that users pay a price for the privilege of using the software. Over time, certain designations have arisen to describe the variety of software available over the Internet:

- **Freeware:** Software distributed free of charge. Users can obtain a copy via the Internet and use it as long as they desire.

- **Donationware:** Freeware whose authors ask that users make a donation either to the authors themselves or to a designated charity.

- **Shareware:** Software distributed free of charge, but with the idea that users who decide to keep the program will pay a specific fee to register it. Users registering the software frequently receive technical support and other benefits.

- **Nagware:** Shareware that displays an annoying screen urging users to register the software. The screen often requires that users hit extra keys or simply wait a few seconds in order to get the program to run properly.

- **Dieware:** Shareware designed to stop working after a specific number of days or uses.

USING THE FILE TRANSFER PROTOCOL

Like telnet, FTP allows a client to link with a remote host computer via the Internet. However, FTP does not permit users to make use of any other programs on the host server. The link exists solely for the purpose of transferring files between the two computers. For example, if a reporter wants to obtain a file from a government computer, he or she can log on to the server

---

Where's My File?

Like most programs, FTP can be used either from the Unix prompt on a shell account or from a PC client linked to the Internet via a LAN or SLIP/PPP connection. Remember, if you telnet into a host computer in order to run FTP, then any files you transfer will be moved to and from your shell account. If you want to move files to your local PC, you need to run a separate FTP client on that machine.

---

from a personal computer. The FTP client would then allow the reporter to transfer files between the server and the PC.

Although the ability to log on to a registered account can come in handy, it is much more common for journalists to employ **anonymous FTP,** a system that allows users to transfer publicly accessible files from a host computer to their local machine. A user logs on to the server with the user name "anonymous" or occasionally "ftp." The user then supplies his or her e-mail address as a password. Once the user completes the anonymous log-on process, he or she connects to the server's main FTP directory. An anonymous FTP connection usually allows the user to download any files contained in the server's public (*/pub*) directory, although users sometimes have access to other directories as well.

A wide variety of files can be found on the Internet, including screen savers, games, accessories and a variety of programs that allow users to do everything from create a graphics file to remove the effects of inflation on changes in real estate taxes. However, the most common FTP objective of journalists is data. Government sites such as the one operated by the U.S. Census Bureau offer hundreds if not thousands of files containing electronic government records. Journalists can access these files free of charge and move them to a local computer for later analysis. Thus, a journalist interested in determining the effect that race played in a recent election might go to the Census Bureau's FTP site, obtain a file containing the racial breakdown of his or her city and determine whether voting districts dominated by one particular race voted differently from those of another.

Programs are also popular among journalists, particularly those programs that allow users to access information on the Internet. For example, a number of shareware FTP clients can be found on the Internet, including CuteFTP, FTP Voyager and Internet Neighborhood. This chapter illustrates FTP using the freeware version of WS-FTP, which can be downloaded and used without charge by students, faculty and staff at academic institutions. When the program launches, a Session Properties pop-up window appears. Figure 7.1 shows the pop-up window and illustrates the variety of information required to initiate a connection with a typical FTP host.

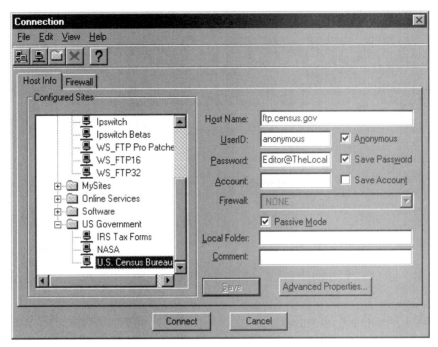

Figure 7.1

The Session Properties pop-up window in WS-FTP allows users to create a separate profile for each FTP server.

Profile Name: Some programs, including WS-FTP, allow the user to save the setup required for connecting to a specific host. This option requires that the user provide a unique name to identify the setup on his or her computer. For example, a user might choose to save the information for connecting to the U.S. Census Bureau under the name "Census."

Host Name/Address: A user must tell the FTP client where to find the host. FTP can connect with a host whether the user provides its DNS name (e.g., <ftp.census.gov>) or its IP address (e.g., <148.129.129.31>).

Host Type: Some programs permit the user to specify a specific host type; however, this option is usually reserved for more advanced users. Even if the program gives the user the option of specifying a host, it is generally best to leave the "Automatic Detect" default in place.

User ID: The FTP host will require the user to provide a user ID in order to access the system. When connecting to an anonymous FTP server, the user ID is usually "anonymous." A user connecting to a server on

Anonymous Log-on

Some clients, including WS-FTP, allow users to simply check a box called "Anonymous" (see figure 7.1). If the user checks the box, the client supplies the user ID and the password.

which he or she has an account should provide the proper user name in order to access that account. Most Windows-based FTP clients allow the user to specify the user name in advance, then automate the connection process.

Password: The FTP server will also require a password. Anonymous FTP servers will accept the user's e-mail address as a password. Some servers verify that the e-mail address is valid, others do not. A user connecting to a specific account will need to provide a valid password for that account. Like the user name process, the password process may or may not be automated.

Once a user has logged onto an FTP server, he or she may use the client to navigate through the server as though a physical connection existed between the two machines. Windows-based clients let the user change directories and move files by simply double-clicking with the left mouse button (Figure 7.2).

Winsock clients such as WS-FTP frequently look like File Manager, Windows Explorer and other familiar programs that are commonly used to manipulate files on a personal computer. The right side of the screen holds the file structure of the host computer, while the left side of the screen shows the file structure for the client computer. A user can generally view, edit, rename or delete files as well as change or create directories on the computer. Copying a file from a remote host to the local computer is a simple matter of double-clicking on the desired file or clicking once on the file and once on an arrow pointing from the host screen to the client screen. Each FTP client has an array of additional options, such as WS-FTP's ability to change file names to all lowercase when uploading them to a host—a useful feature for case-sensitive Unix operating systems.

FILE TRANSFER PROTOCOL
AND THE WORLD WIDE WEB

The World Wide Web has gone a long way toward making FTP seamless. Files are offered as hyperlinks on Web pages. If you want to transfer a file to your computer, just click on the link. The browser asks you where you want to store the file, much the same way that Winsock clients do. Once you

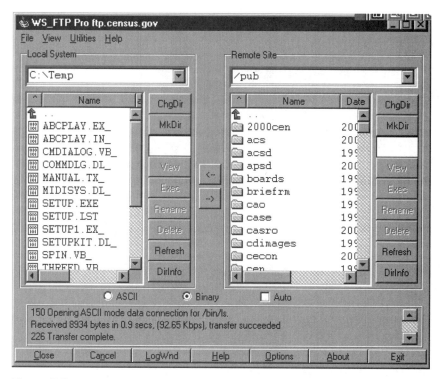

Figure 7.2

WS-FTP screen showing a connection to the U.S. Census Bureau's FTP server. The left side of the screen shows the directory structure on the client computer. The right side of the screen shows the directory structure on the server.

provide a location, the transferal begins. It's that easy. Most of your FTP work will probably be done on the Web, but knowing how FTP works and what happens behind the scenes will help you understand the process on the Web that much better.

FILE COMPRESSION AND DECOMPRESSION

By now you have probably already noticed the most frequently raised complaint about the Internet—it can be pretty darned slow. Users are always looking for ways to speed up their online transactions. Perhaps the most common and useful method of speeding things up is the use of file compression. **File compression** refers to the use of a computer program to temporarily shrink one or more files. A compressed file takes up much less space—sometimes as much as 90 percent to 95 percent less. As a result, it also requires less time to be transmitted over the Internet.

Text-Based FTP

Occasionally users will be forced to use text-based FTP commands. The following commands should get you through the process in a pinch.

- *open*: FTP command to open a connection to a host (e.g., *open ftp.census.gov*).
- *ls*: Unix command to list the directories and files within the current directory.
- *dir*: Unix command to list the directories and files within the current directory. The *dir* command provides more information than the *ls* command does.
- *cd*: Unix command to change the current directory one level down to a specified subdirectory. For example, *cd pub* would change the current directory to *pub*.
- *cdup*: Unix command to change the current directory one level up to a parent directory.
- *get*: FTP command to download a file from the server to the client machine (e.g., *get aareadme.wp*).
- *quit*: FTP command to quit the program.

Almost any kind of computer file can be compressed, from individual text files to the multiple files it takes to run a program such as Netscape Navigator. So why aren't files compressed all the time? It's simple. Compressed files cannot be used in their compressed form. They must be decompressed first. Consider a delivery person riding along on a bike tossing newspapers onto neighborhood porches. The newspapers can be delivered flat, but folding each newspaper a few times makes it easier to toss. The information is still there, but the reader must unfold the paper before he or she can read it. In a sense, that is what happens when a file is compressed. The compression is used only to make the delivery process more efficient.

Although hundreds of file compression methods exist on the Internet, by far the most common among journalists is the ZIP format, a standard in the PC industry. A **ZIP file** is a compressed archive, that is, a file that contains one or more other files in compressed format. ZIP files have a variety of uses, although their primary function is to reduce storage space and online transfer time. ARJ, ARC, Z, TAR, TAZ and GZ files also serve as compression archives. The acronyms refer to the file extensions used to identify each file type, depending on the compression tool used to create them. Compressed archives can also have the extension EXE, which indicates a **self-extracting file,** an executable program that decompresses and extracts files from the attached archive.

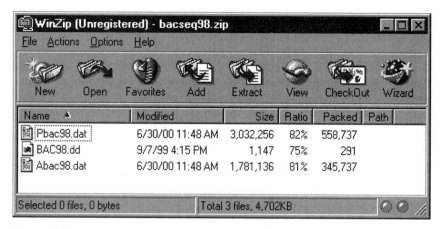

Figure 7.3

WinZip allows you to handle compressed archives. This example shows an archive (bacseq98.zip) containing a plain text document (BAC98.dd) and two data files (Pbac98.dat and Abac98.dat). WinZip compressed the files from their original size f 4,702 K down to 904,765 bytes—a roughly 81 percent reduction in the space needed to hold the files and in the time needed to transfer them from the NHTSA site to your computer.

The most popular program for handling compressed files on the Internet is **WinZip,**[1] a Windows-based program that allows users to compress files and add them to an archive as well as decompress files and extract them from an archive. For example, the National Highway Traffic Safety Administration (NHTSA) maintains a database of fatal accidents in the United States. That data—the Fatality Analysis Reporting System (FARS) database—can be downloaded to your computer using FTP. Figure 7.3 shows a downloadable compressed file containing some of the FARS data.

USING WINZIP

Although reporters may often want to create compressed archives, they are much more likely to use WinZip to decompress and extract files from an archive. Compressed ZIP archives can be found all over the Internet. Reporters may encounter other types of compressed files as well, particularly Z and GZ files; however, WinZip can decompress and extract these types as well. If all these initials and file extensions appear confusing, do not worry. Concentrate instead on the process: (1) someone uses WinZip or another program to create a compressed archive; (2) the compressed archive is attached to an e-mail message or placed on an Internet server; (3) a user obtains the archive either via e-mail or by requesting the file from the server; (4) the user

Why WinZip?

This chapter focuses on WinZip because it is the most prevalent compression program in use on the Internet. However, the concepts discussed apply to other compression programs, such as the DOS-based PKZIP or the Unix-based Zip utility.

decompresses the archive. Once the archive has been obtained and decompressed, the files are ready to use.

In the example of the FARS data (see Figure 7.3), a reporter can download the archive via the Web or FTP. The file is stored in a specified directory on the reporter's hard drive, usually a directory labeled TEMP because it is meant to hold files only temporarily. The reporter starts the WinZip program, chooses to open the archive file and locates it on the hard drive. Once the file has been located, its contents can be viewed. Any or all of the three files can then be extracted. WinZip automatically decompresses files during the extraction process. Extracted files can be placed on any drive the user has access to. Once the files have been successfully extracted and checked for errors, the original ZIP file can be deleted from the temporary directory. The same procedure can be used for Z, GZ and other compressed archives; you can also use WinZip to open these archives and extract the files for future use.

Self-extracting files, that is, compressed archives with the extension EXE, present less of a problem than do ZIP files because the user does not need to possess any special programs in order to extract the files. Self-extracting files contain all necessary instructions for the computer to handle the extraction process. Extracted files are placed in the same directory as the self-extracting file. The user can then move the files around as needed.

SUMMARY

File transfer protocol is not used much by journalists as a stand-alone program anymore. But the protocol itself moves many of the files downloaded via the World Wide Web today. Most of these files are compressed before transfer, which allows them to be moved over the Internet much more quickly. Before these files can be used, they must be decompressed. The dominant program for compressing and decompressing files in Windows is WinZip. If you have an Internet connection, an FTP client or Web browser, and WinZip, you have all the tools necessary to access a wide array of government data over the Internet.

NOTES

1. WinZip is shareware, which means that you must purchase the software if you intend to use it beyond the allowed 21-day evaluation period. Copies of WinZip can be downloaded as self-extracting files from <ftp.winzip.com> or from the company's Web site at <http://www.winzip.com>.

8

Examining a Budget

INTRODUCTION TO SPREADSHEETS

In this chapter you will learn:

- The physical layout of a spread-sheet including columns, rows, and cells

- Formulas for calculating simple difference and percent change

- Cell referencing and the value of relative cell references

- A few simple steps and rules for analyzing a budget

Journalists have a long history of shunning even the most basic mathematics. It is not difficult to find many who admit that their decision to major in journalism was bolstered by the desire to avoid classes such as algebra, statistics and accounting. As a result, too many find themselves unprepared when they discover that one of their first assignments requires them to analyze a government budget and determine where the story lies. The proposed budget increases expenditures by $345,000. Is that a lot? How does it compare to previous years? Which department will receive the largest increase? Will any departments be spending less? In the not-too-distant past, reporters relied on calculators, adding machines or simply a pencil and paper to answer these and other questions. Most survived well enough, provided they had some time. After all, totaling row after row of numbers can be a rather tedious process. Those who didn't have the time often didn't have the story.

Spreadsheet programs such as Excel, Quattro Pro and Lotus 1-2-3 help journalists solve these problems. They permit users to perform calculations rapidly while minimizing the chance for error. A column of numbers that might take hours to tally with a calculator can easily be analyzed in just a few minutes with a spreadsheet program. A person performing the calculations by hand needs to enter each number into the calculator, tell the calculator what to do and write down the answer. That same person, using a spreadsheet, can

What Is a Spreadsheet?

The term *spreadsheet* is somewhat elusive. A spreadsheet is usually understood to mean a two-dimensional file comprised of columns and rows that is used to facilitate mathematical and other operations. However, the term can also refer to the program used to manage these files (i.e., a spreadsheet program, or spreadsheet). In an effort to alleviate the problem, some manufacturers use the term *spreadsheet* for the program and *worksheet* for the file created by the program. This text, following common practice in the field, uses the term *spreadsheet* to refer to either the file or the program used to create it.

total a column of even several thousand numbers with the click of a button. The next few chapters discuss how.

INTRODUCTION TO SPREADSHEETS

A **spreadsheet** is a two-dimensional file, consisting of columns and rows, that is used to facilitate mathematical and other operations. **Columns** run horizontally across a spreadsheet. They are designated by letters—A through Z, then AA, AB, AC and so on. Most spreadsheet programs allow at least 256 columns. The 256th column would be designated "IV." **Rows** run vertically down a spreadsheet. They are designated by Arabic numbers (i.e., 1, 2, 3, etc.). Most spreadsheets can handle at least 8,192 rows. The term **cell** refers to the intersection of a column and a row. The program identifies each cell by its **cell address,** the letter of the intersecting column followed by the number of the intersecting row. Thus, cell addresses can range from A1 through IV8192.

Look at Figure 8.1 to see how a spreadsheet resembles an accountant's ledger. Consider the log in your own checkbook. How is it set up? In all likelihood, the log is divided into columns and rows. The columns might be devoted to items such as Check Number, Date, Description, Payment, Deposit and Balance. Column headings are generally placed in a line at the top of the spreadsheet. This line is called the **header row,** a row within a spreadsheet—generally Row 1—that contains column descriptions. Each row represents an individual entry, such as a check or a deposit. If you were to keep track of your checking account on a spreadsheet, you would still have to enter most of the data regarding each specific check. But you could set up the spreadsheet to do all the math for you.

Creating a spreadsheet that handles the basic mathematics you might use in balancing a checkbook is really quite a simple process. In fact, many journalists regularly employ spreadsheets to keep track of their expense accounts.

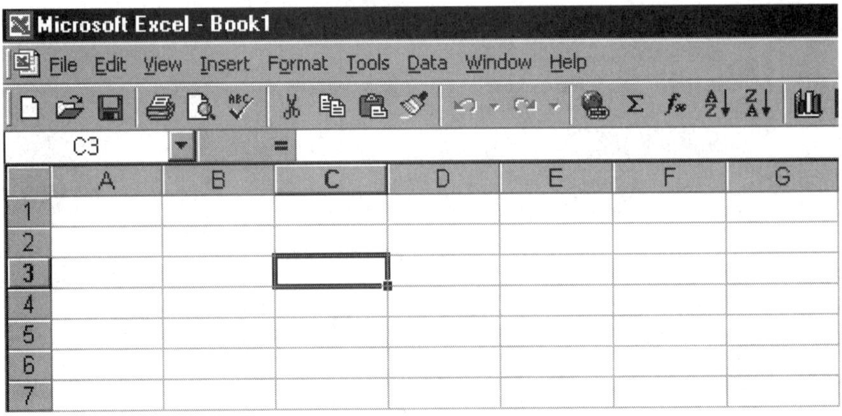

Figure 8.1

A typical spreadsheet showing columns and rows. Cell C3, the intersection of Column C and Row 3, is highlighted.

Consider what happens when you make an entry in your expense log. First, you receive an account with a beginning balance—say $1,000. When you make your first expenditure, you enter the date, a description of expenditure and the amount (e.g., $250.00) under the Expenditure column. Then you subtract the amount of the check from the previous balance in order to obtain the current balance (e.g., $750.00). The math for that task is easy: $1,000 − $250 = $750. Moreover, the logic is straightforward: Current Balance = Previous Balance − Expenditure. If you follow the mathematics and logic involved in that common transaction, you are well on your way to comprehending how a spreadsheet works.

Understand first that spreadsheets handle math in much the same way that adding machines once did. If you wanted to perform the previous calculation on an adding machine, you could hit the plus key, followed by the numbers 1-0-0-0, then the minus key, followed by 2-5-0.[1] Written out longhand, it would look like this: +1000−250. You could type that same sequence into a spreadsheet cell, hit the Enter key and the number 750 would appear as your answer. Modern spreadsheets even make the key sequence a bit easier for humans to read and understand. Users have the option of signaling the start of an equation with an equal sign instead of a plus or minus. Thus, the previous transaction could be accomplished by typing: =1000−250.

Performing calculations like the one just listed is useful, but a cheap calculator can handle the same problem just as easily and often much more conveniently. The value of a spreadsheet lies not in its ability to handle straightforward arithmetic, but rather in its capacity for performing numerous calculations nearly simultaneously. It does this by relying on the logic of an

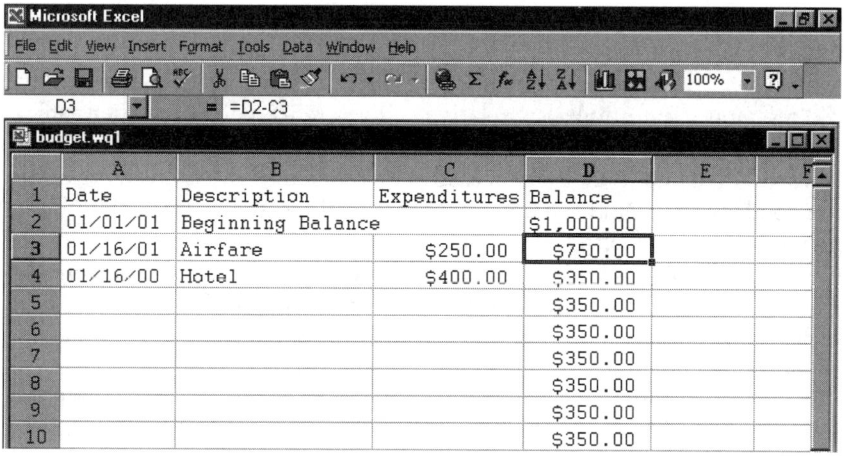

	A	B	C	D	E	F
1	Date	Description	Expenditures	Balance		
2	01/01/01	Beginning Balance		$1,000.00		
3	01/16/01	Airfare	$250.00	$750.00		
4	01/16/00	Hotel	$400.00	$350.00		
5				$350.00		
6				$350.00		
7				$350.00		
8				$350.00		
9				$350.00		
10				$350.00		

Figure 8.2

A spreadsheet expense log with Cell D3 highlighted. Note that the contents of the highlighted cell appear in the white formula bar at the top of the sheet.

operation rather than the mathematics. Consider again the expense account example. The mathematics of the operation was basic: =1000−250. That solved the problem, but only because the previous balance was $1,000 and the check was written out for $250. No matter how many times we run that equation, we will get an answer of $750. If we want to determine the current balance after writing a check for $400, we have to return to the logic of the operation:

Current Balance = Previous Balance − Expenditure

Spreadsheets allow us to use logic rather than just math to solve problems.

Most mathematical operations within a spreadsheet are accomplished not with mathematical equations, but with logical formulas. A spreadsheet **formula** is an equation that describes a calculation and defines the numbers, text or other formulas to be used in that calculation. In other words, a formula tells the computer how to perform a calculation and where to find the data to plug into that equation. But instead of just using the actual numbers to perform calculations, a formula can employ cell references. The term **cell reference** refers to the cell address of the number, text or formula to be used within a formula. Figure 8.2 illustrates how a spreadsheet deals with the expense account example we have been using. Notice that the numeric calculation =1000−250 has been replaced with the spreadsheet formula =D2−C3. The formula in Cell D3 (*Current* Balance) tells the program to take the number in Cell D2 (*Previous* Balance) and subtract from it the number in Cell C3 (Payment). The resulting answer is placed in the cell with the formula, in this case Cell D3. All those cell addresses can sound pretty confusing, but if you pay attention to the logic of the transaction, you will see that it is all rather straightforward.

Unless otherwise instructed, spreadsheet programs make use of relative cell references in formulas. A **relative cell reference** points to other data in relation to the cell in which the reference is located. For example, the formula =D2−C3 located in Cell D3 actually communicates the following steps to the computer: (1) Add the contents of the cell located in this column, one row up (currently Cell D2); (2) Subtract the contents of the cell located in this row, one column to the left (currently Cell C3). Thus, the cell references are all relative to the current location of the formula. This feature means little when the formula is first entered. However, relative cell addressing becomes very useful when the formula is copied from one cell to another.

Figure 8.2 illustrates the value of copying a formula containing relative cell addresses. When the formula in Cell D3 is copied to Cell D4, all the references within the formula change to reflect the new location. Thus, =D2−C3 becomes =D3−C4. When copied to Cell D5, the formula becomes =D4−C5 and so on. In every case, the program is adding the contents of the cell directly above and subtracting the contents of the cell directly to the left. Input the number "400" in Cell C4 and the balance automatically alters to $350. Moreover, the change is reflected in every subsequent cell. Thus, relative cell addresses make it possible to write a formula once at the top of a spreadsheet, then copy the formula down as many as 8,192 rows or across as many as 256 columns. The thousands of individual calculations that would have taken perhaps hours to perform can now be accomplished in under a minute.

EXAMINING A GOVERNMENT BUDGET

Once you have a handle on relative cell references, you can begin to see some of the applications they can have in working with common journalistic subjects such as government budgets. A typical government budget—like those passed by city councils, school boards and other organizations—is a two-sided coin. On the one side are the **expenditures,** what an organization expects to spend during the budget period. Typical expenditures in a school budget might include categories such as teacher salaries, athletics and maintenance. A city budget might allot expenditures for the police and fire departments, the department of public works and the like. On the other side of the coin are the **revenues,** what an organization expects to collect during the budget period. Revenues generally come from property and wage taxes, but they might also be derived from other expected sources such as state or federal funding, parking fines or a variety of service fees. Ideally, all budgets are balanced. In a **balanced budget,** expenditures exactly equal revenues. In fact, one of the first things that a journalist usually looks at when considering what

ENPENDITURE CLASSIFICATION	CURRENT	PROPOSED
TOWN BOARD	$ 111,615.00	$ 99,184.00
TOWN JUSTICES	$ 408,643.00	$ 438,965.00
SUPERVISOR	$ 141,468.00	$ 148,400.00
COMPTROLLER	$ 756,621.00	$ 808,312.00
TAX OFFICE	$ 164,802.00	$ 173,874.00
PURCHASING	$ 245,059.00	$ 251,612.00
ASSESSOR	$ 446,042.00	$ 469,520.00
TOWN CLERK	$ 256,769.00	$ 277,054.00
TOWN ATTORNEY	$ 558,029.00	$ 578,887.00
EMPLOYEE RELATIONS	$ 326,293.00	$ 325,832.00
BUILDINGS (SHARED SERVICES)	$ 876,274.00	$ 880,999.00
FLEET MAINTENANCE	$ 910,792.00	$ 984,704.00
MUTUAL FIRE RADIO	$ 111,040.00	$ 142,448.00
EMERGENCY MEDICAL SERVICE	$1,761,074.00	$1,956,990.00
POLICE DEPARTMENT	$8,014,080.00	$8,532,981.00

Figure 8.3

A typical town budget summary is broken into rows and columns. Each row holds a separate budget item. The columns hold a description of the budget item, the previous year's budget and the proposed budget.

to write about a proposed or newly adopted budget is whether the budget is balanced.

Spreadsheets were designed to tackle problems such as budgets. Like ledgers, checkbooks and expense logs, budgets are broken into rows and columns (Figure 8.3). Each row contains a specific expenditure or revenue source. Revenues and expenditures are grouped separately, usually with all expenditures first and all revenues last. In some cases, the revenues and expenditures appear on the same sheet. In others, they appear on separate sheets. Generally, the first column contains a description of the source of revenue or the recipient of an expenditure. The second column contains the revenues and expenditures for one year. The third and subsequent columns generally contain the revenues and expenditures for other years. Most budgets reserve the column farthest to the right for **projected revenues and expenditures,** the proposed budget for the coming year. If you are covering a budget meeting, the proposed budget is what the organization will usually vote to approve or reject.

At one time, governmental budgets were all worked out by hand and stored on paper. Now, nearly every governmental organization uses a spreadsheet or similar program to keep track of its budget. When the time comes to vote on the budget, the person in charge of that budget (usually the city manager, comptroller or business manager) prints a copy for reporters and the public. Members of the public usually receive a summary of the budget that lists only the main categories within revenues and expenditures (e.g., "Police Dept." or "Wage Taxes"). Reporters often receive a more detailed

---

Check Your Figures

If you obtain a budget (either electronic or paper) from a government agency prior to the budget meeting, be certain to recheck your figures against those presented at the meeting. Budgets can change minutes before a meeting, often for legitimate reasons but sometimes for other purposes as well. In either case, it is important to be certain that you report the correct figures.

---

breakdown of the various categories. For example, the Police Department category might be broken into salaries, uniform allowances, benefits, community education and so on.

Budgets are public records. As a reporter, or a citizen, you have the right to go to your local school board and request a copy of the district's budget. Government agencies will usually provide a written copy of the budget. However, most state and federal laws require that the agency also make its records available in electronic form on request, provided that no additional work is required. In other words, if your local school board manager maintains the district's records on a spreadsheet, you have the right to request that he or she provide you with a copy of that file. Because the law generally prevents governmental organizations from charging more than the basic cost of providing the file, you can usually obtain basic records such as budgets for a minimal fee—often the cost of a few computer diskettes. You can even ask that the district provide you with the file in a specific format, provided they have the capability to do so. Most database and spreadsheet programs permit the user to save files in a variety of formats. Thus, if your local district is using Quattro Pro to handle its budget, you can request that they provide the file in Lotus 1-2-3 format.

Later chapters discuss the finer points of file formats and obtaining electronic records from government agencies. For now it is enough to understand that you can request and usually obtain a government organization's records in electronic format. This feature can be of enormous benefit because you do not have to rekey the data by hand or scan it into your computer. All you need to do is pop the diskette in your floppy drive and open the file in your program. Not only does this feature save the time and effort involved in moving data from paper to computer, it also minimizes the chance that an error will be introduced into the data itself.

ANALYZING A BUDGET WITH A
SPREADSHEET PROGRAM

Spreadsheets frequently serve as the initial analysis tool for journalists interested in learning computer-assisted reporting. The term *analysis* can seem a

---

Making It Pretty

Most spreadsheets have a number of features that allow you to automatically format a cell or a group of cells within your spreadsheet. Often, these features can be found on the button bar or menu bar. Some of the most common formats are:

Character or Numeric		**Numeric Only**	
Bold	**1000**	Comma	1,000
Italics	*1000*	Currency	$1,000.00*
Underline	<u>1000</u>	Percentage	100000%

*Numeric fields generally allow you to adjust the number of decimal points.

---

bit daunting at first. Most journalists learned how to perform mathematical analysis during their high school years. Too many also learned to dislike it. But the word *analysis* itself simply means to examine something that is, by its very nature, complex. Math often helps with the analysis, but it does not drive the analysis. Rather, the ability to think critically is what stimulates the examination. In computer-assisted reporting, the term **interviewing the data** is often used to describe the critical thinking process involved in pulling a story out of a spreadsheet or database. Interviewing data for a story is actually quite similar to interviewing a person:

1. Journalists preparing for an interview need to know something about who, or in this case what, they are interviewing. Think of the traditional 5Ws and the H. *Who* compiled the data? *What* kind of data does the file contain? *When* was it compiled? *Where* did the data come from? *Why* does the government maintain this record? *How* is it stored? These questions can usually be answered by people familiar with the data.

2. Journalists should compose a list of questions before an interview. Some of the questions should be need-to-know questions, while others can fall more into the category of want-to-know.

3. Journalists conducting an interview should usually begin with the easiest questions first, working through progressively more difficult questions during the course of the interview.

If you keep these three steps in mind, you will have a much easier time analyzing computerized public records.

In this chapter I use a typical city budget to illustrate the concept of spreadsheet analysis. The example is a departmental summary derived from the actual budget of Colonie, N.Y., a town of approximately 73,000. Unlike most municipalities, Colonie goes out of its way to make its financial operations available to the public by placing its budget on the Internet in

TOWN BOARD	Current	Proposed
Councilpersons	$ 75,310	$ 93,984
Deputy town supervisor	$ 30,705	$ 0
Office equipment	$ 1,850	$ 1,850
Contractual expenses	$ 3,750	$ 3,350
DEPT. TOTAL	$111,615	$ 99,184

Figure 8.4

A portion of the detailed Colonie town budget showing how cuts in the town board budget were achieved.

spreadsheet format.[2] The town's comptroller makes the budget available either as a Web page or in Excel format so that you can download it and open the file in your spreadsheet program.

You have already seen a portion of the budget summary in Figure 8.3. A **budget summary** provides a department-by-department breakdown of proposed revenues and expenditures. In the full budget, each department's allotted expenditures are laid out in detail. A **detailed budget** breaks revenues and expenditures down on a line-by-line basis. Take, for example, the town board portion of this budget. The department summary shows a proposed decrease in the board's budget, from $111,615 to $99,184. The detailed budget (Figure 8.4) illustrates where that money comes from. The town has proposed removing the deputy town supervisor's allotment. What conclusion do you draw from this change? Actually, you should not draw any conclusions just yet. Consider some of the possibilities. The deputy might have been fired or furloughed. The deputy might have resigned. He or she might have decided to work for free. Or perhaps the deputy is still on the job but the town board has decided to distribute the allotment among one or more other budget categories. The data does not provide an answer to *why* the deputy's allotment has been slashed from the budget, it only indicates that the money has been removed. *Why* is a question better asked of the comptroller or some other official.

Although the detailed budget provides valuable insight into how a governmental organization spends its money, it can take quite a bit of time to analyze. For example, the detailed Colonie town budget fills 1,970 spreadsheet rows for expenditures alone. By contrast, the departmental summary of expenditures covers just 40 rows. If you are unable to obtain a detailed copy of the proposed budget in advance of a meeting, you can use a preliminary analysis of the budget summary for an article on deadline. If you have more time, you can use the detailed budget, though it is still valuable to examine or create a budget summary as well. The following steps provide a beginner's guide to analyzing a government budget in a spreadsheet.

Step 1: *If a budget summary has not been provided, either obtain one or create your own from the detailed budget.*

	A	B	C	D
1	CLASSIFICATION	CURRENT	PROPOSED	$ DIFFERENCE
40	Total Expenditures	$27,946,299	$26,407,734	=C40-B40
41				

Figure 8.5

Cell D40 shows the formula to calculate the actual dollar difference between a proposed total (Cell C40) and the current total (Cell B40). The formula can then be copied and pasted into cells D2 through D39 to determine the budgetary differences for each department. Note that when you hit the Enter key or move out of Cell D40, the formula calculates the actual dollar difference.

Some governmental agencies do not provide a budget summary. If your city council or school board does not provide a budget summary, ask for one. If they cannot provide one, create your own summary from the detailed budget.

Step 2: *Calculate the total proposed budget.*

It is usually good practice to calculate your own budget totals, even if the governmental organization provides its own. If your total does not match the total provided, you can then determine whether you lack all the figures or whether you or the government erred in calculating the proper total. I will discuss how to calculate totals in the next chapter. For now, let us simply assume that the figures are correct and defer a discussion of totals and other aggregate functions until the following chapter.

Calculating the Difference between Two Cells

Step 3: *Calculate the actual dollar difference between the proposed and previous budget totals.*

First, consider the task before you—to determine the difference between two numbers. In this case the numbers consist of the current budget and a proposed (future) budget. The difference is the change from one year to the next. In determining change, you want to subtract the older number from the newer (or future) number. This step ensures that you have a positive number to show an increase from one year to the next or a negative number to show a decrease. Recall that calculating the difference between two numbers in a spreadsheet can be accomplished with a formula containing mathematical operators (like + or −) and relative cell references. Figure 8.5 shows how such a formula can be written.

Copying a Cell Formula

Step 4: *Calculate the actual dollar difference between the proposed and previous budgets for each department.*

Looking at Negatives

Spreadsheets have several different ways to indicate that a number is negative. Often you can choose which method you prefer from among the following options:

Option	Example
Straight negative	$-12,431$
Negative in parentheses	(12,431)
Negative in red	$-12,431$

You already have the formula for calculating the difference between two numbers. To calculate the difference for each department, you simply need to copy the formula throughout the column. Most programs allow users to copy the formula, highlight an entire row and paste. In other words:

1. Highlight the cell that contains the formula that you want to copy.
2. Select the Edit pull-down menu and click on Copy.
3. Highlight the column into which you want to copy the formula. You can do this step by clicking on the top cell into which you want to copy the formula, holding down the mouse button and dragging the cursor down to the last cell into which you want the formula to go. Once the entire area is highlighted, just release the mouse button. Highlighting an area takes some practice, but it is relatively easy once you get the hang of it.
4. Select the Edit pull-down menu and click on Paste.

You can also use the mouse to simply grab the lower right corner of a cell and drag it downward, copying its contents throughout the column. Again, this maneuver requires a bit of practice to do well. You must grab the exact corner of the cell. If not, you may inadvertently move the cell rather than copy its contents. (If you do so, just click on the Edit pull-down menu and select Undo. Experienced users find that using the mouse for this task is a bit easier than the copy and paste routine. As a result, they often write their original formula in the topmost cell of a column (e.g., Cell D2). Remember that using relative cell references means that the formula will change relative to where it is placed. Thus, if the formula in Cell D40 (=C40−B40) were copied into Cell D39, it would change automatically to reflect its new position (=C39−B39).

Calculating Percent Change

Actual dollar differences are useful, but they can be deceiving. For example, in the budget we are using, the largest actual dollar increase ($518,901) was earmarked for the police department. However, 13 departments received a

Converting Decimals

Elementary school math reminder: Remember that all percentages are decimal numbers. The decimal point must be moved two places to the right in order to read the number as a percentage. Thus, .10 is 10 percent, .525 is 52.5 percent, and so on.

greater percentage increase—the largest, a 78.6 percent budgetary increase for community development. Think of it this way. If you were a entry-level reporter or producer, would you rather have a $10,000 pay increase or a 10 percent increase? What if you were the CEO of a newspaper chain or a network anchor? Obviously, the entry-level person would prefer the $10,000 while the higher-up, who is likely to be earning well over $100,000, would prefer the 10 percent. Thus, you must determine the percent change as well as the actual dollar difference.

Step 5: *Calculate the percent change between the proposed and current budget totals.*

Large percentage increases tell you at least as much as actual dollar differences do. But even a huge percentage increase will not necessarily give you your lead. For example, the 78.6 percent increase in the community development allotment cited in our example increased that department's funding by only $2,200. That figure will probably not be the lead-in to your story. However, it does raise a flag indicating that you should ask why the community development budget needs almost twice as much funding as it did the previous year. It may even launch you into an interesting follow-up. And don't forget to look for large decreases as well as increases. The town board budget decreased by 11.1 percent. Why? Recall that the position of the deputy town supervisor had been eliminated from the budget. That story is worth doing.

The formula for calculating percent change can be confusing at first glance. First, consider what percent change tells you. The word *percent* can be taken to mean "for each hundred." When you calculate the percent change between the current budget and a proposed budget, you are determining how many more or fewer dollars will be spent in the proposed budget for every $100 spent in the current budget.

To make that calculation you need only two figures: *the current budget* and the actual dollar *difference* between the current budget and the proposed budget. The percent change is determined by taking the difference and dividing it by the current budget. That calculation could be expressed as:

Percent Change = Difference / Current Budget

It is always a good idea to check your equation to make certain that it works the way you expect it to. You can check it by substituting numbers that you

	A	B	C	D	E
1	CLASSIFICATION	CURRENT	PROPOSED	$ DIFF	% CHG
40	Total Expenditures	$26,407,734	$27,946,229	$1,538,495	=D40/B40
41					

Figure 8.6

Cell E40 shows the formula to calculate the percent difference between a proposed total (Cell C40) and the current total (Cell B40). The formula makes use of the difference contained in Cell D40. Note that when you hit the Enter key or move out of Cell D40, the formula calculates the percent difference, which is .0583. You need to format the cell or column as a percentage with one decimal place to get 5.8 percent.

can easily figure in your head. For example, we all know that 20 is 20 percent of 100. We can substitute the number 20 for Difference and 100 for Current Budget, then do the math. The number 20 divided by 100 yields .20. Remember that percentages are decimals. In order to convert the decimal to a percentage, you simply move the decimal point two places to the right (i.e., multiply it by 100). Thus, .20 is equal to 20 percent.

Once you know the logic behind calculating a percent change, it is a relatively simple matter to write a spreadsheet formula to perform the calculation. Figure 8.6 shows that formula in a spreadsheet. Note that the percent change in this case is .0583, or 5.83 percent. Remember that in order to see the figure as 5.83 percent, you will need to format the cell or column as a percentage. Some spreadsheets allow you to read numbers out to 30 decimal places. Naturally, this feature goes beyond the needs of most journalists. When possible, have the spreadsheet round to no more than one decimal. This task is even easier than it sounds, because all you need to do is specify the number of decimal places. The computer does the rounding for you. Thus, 5.83 percent would be rounded to 5.8 percent. One decimal place is usually enough to illustrate the point to your audience without providing extraneous detail.

Step 6: *Calculate the percentage difference between the proposed and current budget for each department.*

Once again, relative cell references make your work much simpler. If you have correctly entered the formula to calculate the percent change between the current and proposed budget total, you can simply copy that formula to the rest of the column in order to calculate the percent change on a department-by-department basis.

Sorting Data in a Spreadsheet

Step 7: *Sort the departments by actual dollar difference and percent change to determine which will receive the greatest increases or decreases.*

	A	B
1	CLASSIFICATION	CURRENT
2	TOWN BOARD	$111,615
3	TOWN JUSTICES	$408,643
4	SUPERVISOR	$141,468
5	COMPTROLLER	$756,621
6	TAX OFFICE	$164,802

	A	B
1	CLASSIFICATION	CURRENT
2	ANIMAL CONTROL	$111,615
3	ASSESSOR	$408,643
4	BUILDING DEPART	$141,468
5	BUILDINGS	$756,621
6	CIVIL DEFENSE	$164,802

Figure 8.7

The table on the left shows the original table with Column A incorrectly highlighted for a sort. The table on the right illustrates the error that can occur when only a portion of the data is sorted. Note that the CURRENT column remains the same, even though the CLASSIFICATION column has been sorted alphabetically. When performing a sort, the user must be certain to highlight *all* the data to be sorted.

Once you have the actual dollar difference and percent change for each department, you can sort the data in your spreadsheet to determine which departments had the largest increases or decreases. **Sorting** is the term used for ordering items within a spreadsheet, either alphabetically or numerically, in ascending or descending order. Sorting brings out the extremes in the budget, that is, those departments that will receive the largest budgetary increases or decreases. There are essentially two parts to the sort process in a spreadsheet:

1. Highlight the area to be sorted.

There are two caveats about highlighting the data you want to sort. First and most important, spreadsheets will sort only the data that you highlight. If you highlight only a column containing descriptions, the program will sort that *column* only. The remaining columns stay as they are. For example, if you highlighted only the CLASSIFICATION column in the example we have been using, the descriptions would be sorted alphabetically, but the other columns would remain as they are. As Figure 8.7 illustrates, the result would be incorrect data.

The second consideration in highlighting the data to be sorted involves the header row. In the earlier spreadsheet programs, highlighting the header row would mean that the column descriptions would be sorted with the data. For example, if the cell containing the word "CLASSIFICATION" had been highlighted in figure 8.7, it would have been sorted with the data and would appear below "CIVIL DEFENSE." Most programs now allow you to specify whether a header row has been included in the sort area.

2. Sort the data.

Most spreadsheet programs allow you to sort from the menu bar. For example, in Excel you can choose Data and then select Sort. A sort window

Figure 8.8

The Sort pop-up window allows users to sort by any column. If the Header Row radio button has been checked, the header will appear in the Sort By box. If "No header row" is selected, then column letters will appear (e.g., Column A).

will pop up (see Figure 8.8). This sort window is similar in nearly every spreadsheet program. It allows you to choose what column or columns you wish to sort by, whether you would prefer ascending or descending order, and whether you have included a header row in the highlighted area.

One more caution when sorting data: once you sort a spreadsheet it is permanently changed. In most spreadsheets you can remove the sort by selecting Edit from the menu bar and clicking on Undo or by holding down the Control key and pressing Z. However, unlike word processing programs, which allow you to undo several changes, spreadsheet programs permit you to undo only your last input. If you perform a sort and then hit the space bar, you cannot undo the sort. Your only alternatives are to sort the data again or to close the file without saving and revert to your previously saved copy.

IN-DEPTH ANALYSIS OF A BUDGET

Once you complete your analysis of the summary budget and note where the largest increases and decreases occur, you can begin your in-depth analysis of the budget using the detailed version of the budget.

Step 1: *If you don't have a detailed, line-by-line copy of the budget, get one.*

	A	B	C	D	E
1	CLASSIFICATION	CURRENT	PROPOSED	$ DIFF	% CHG
388	Equipment				
389	Office Equip & Furn	$6,500	$6,500	$0	0%
390	Motor Vehicle/Lease	$47,000	$151,000	$104,000	221%
391	Other Equipment	$32,000	$32,000	$0	0%
392					
393	Subtotal	$85,500	$189,000	$104,000	122%

Figure 8.9

The detailed budget provides a line-by-line description of each department's budget. This portion of the Emergency Medical Service budget shows money allotted to the department for equipment. The percent change can flag areas for examination.

The detailed budget provides insight to understanding changes between the current and the proposed budgets. Earlier in this chapter we looked at the town board budget, which had a proposed decrease in funding. An examination of the detailed budget (which was illustrated in figure 8.4) showed that the town council had raised the allotment for councilpersons 25 percent and eliminated funding for a deputy town supervisor. In order to analyze the detailed budget, you must first prepare it in much the same way you did the summary budget.

Step 2: *Calculate the total proposed budget and subtotals for each department.*

Once you calculate the overall total and subtotals for each department, you can then compare these totals to the summary budget totals to make certain that the figures match. Again, any error might be yours, the budgetary agent's or a deliberate attempt at deception.

Steps 3 through 6: *Repeat Steps 3 through 6 from the summary budget examination, this time on the detailed budget.*

Calculate actual dollar and percent changes for the total budget and for each line item. The percent change is particularly important because it allows you to quickly scan down a column in order to uncover large differences between the current and proposed budgets.

Step 7: *If possible, sort the detailed budget by percent change.*

Sorting the detailed budget may be more difficult than sorting the summary budget. Figure 8.9 shows part of the line-by-line budget that matches the summary we have been discussing—in this case, money allotted to the Emergency Medical Service department for equipment. Think about how you might sort the detailed budget. If you considered sorting it as you did the summary budget, you would have a problem. Notice that line items do not

	A		B	C	D	E
1	**CLASSIFICATION**	**DPT**	**CURRENT**	**PROPOSED**	**$ DIFF**	**% CHG**
388	Equipment	EMS2				
389	Office Equip & Furn	EMS2	$6,500	$6,500	$0	0%
390	Motor Vehicle/Lease	EMS2	$47,000	$151,000	$104,000	221%
391	Other Equipment	EMS2	$32,000	$32,000	$0	0%
392						
393	Subtotal	EMS2	$85,500	$189,000	$104,000	122%

Figure 8.10

Adding your own code to a budget can be helpful, especially when it comes to sorting. However, it is important to remember to give each department and subgroup a unique code so that the data does not become muddled.

contain a reference to what department they belong to. If you sorted by percent change, the line item Motor Vehicle/Lease might appear near the top, but you would have no way of determining which department would receive the funding.

Some budget agencies handle this problem by providing a unique code for each department. If not, you can solve the problem yourself by adding a column to the spreadsheet. The new column can hold a reference to each line item's controlling department (see Figure 8.10). For example, you might add an EMS next to all the Emergency Medical Service equipment items and a TB next to town board. Later, when you sorted the items, you would know which department each item belonged to. However, there is one problem with that scheme. EMS equipment items could not be differentiated from EMS capital outlay or other items. You can solve this problem in much the same way as the first. Simply add a number to the department code that indicates the order in which each subgroup appears. For example, equipment could be coded EMS2 and capital outlay could be coded EMS3.

If you plan to add your own codes to a spreadsheet, you should remember two points:

- Make certain that each department and subgroup has its own unique code. If Emergency Medical Services gets EMS, then Electrical Maintenance Services will require a different code. Having two identical codes will confuse the data.
- Keep track of your own coding either on a piece of paper or within a spreadsheet or word processor. No matter how obvious a coding scheme may seem when you create it, you will probably end up wondering what some codes stand for, especially for subgroups within departments.

This kind of problem solving is typical of most CAR projects. Using a spreadsheet to analyze numbers for a story relies more on a journalist's ability to think critically about the numbers than it relies on that journalist's ability to handle math.

ADDITIONAL CONSIDERATIONS IN EXAMINING A BUDGET

Up to this point we have concerned ourselves primarily with the computer-assisted reporting aspect of analyzing a budget. However, there are other things to consider as well. The following rules, while not necessarily comprehensive, serve as a primer for understanding government budgets.

Make No Assumptions

Too often inexperienced journalists assume that something out of the ordinary indicates government corruption. That is usually not the case. There are numerous explanations for any apparent non sequitur. The discrepancy might be the result of normal accounting practices with which you are not familiar, such as new methods of capital depreciation. It might be due to an error on your part, either in mathematics or in logic. The government agency may have simply made a mistake. Computer-assisted reporting does not necessarily provide an answer, but it does provide some questions that should be posed to the budgetary agency.

Look at the Budget over Time

Most governmental agencies provide the current budget and the proposed budget. It is often up to the journalist to request budgets from previous years as well. A good in-depth analysis should utilize at least the previous three years' budgets. Five years is preferable. Looking at budgets over a few years, you can usually obtain a clearer view of trends in governmental spending. And don't forget to index for inflation. Many inflation calculators available on the Internet provide a quick way to calculate the rate of inflation between years.[3] Indexing for inflation can be quite informative. For example, inflation rose 14.9 percent between 1992 and 1997. That means that an item budgeted at $10,000 in 1992 should have been budgeted at $11,492 in 1997 to account for inflation. It is even more important to index during periods of relatively high inflation. Inflation rose 40.5 percent between 1972 and 1977. Thus, an item budgeted at $10,000 in 1972 should have been budgeted at $14,056 in 1977. Inflation alone accounts for the increase.

Compare the Budget to the Budget Narrative

Many budgets are accompanied by a narrative that lays out the organization's mission statement and its goals in developing the budget. Compare this narrative to the budget figures, particularly new funding. Do the figures match the narrative? The narrative might indicate that the budgeting agency wants to address the crime problem, but the proposed budget might not show any additional funding for the police department. How, then, does the agency plan to increase its crime-fighting effort?

Compare Last Year's Budget with What Was Actually Spent

If the budget agency fails to provide one, obtain a line-by-line assessment of what was spent during the previous year. Just because money has been budgeted for something does not necessarily mean that it was spent for that thing. Items that consistently come in under budget could mean that the department is particularly well run, or it could mean that the budgeting agency is trying to look good by budgeting money for one thing only to turn around later and spend the cash on something else. Looking at actual expenses can help you to understand the budget in other ways as well. Is there a budgetary reserve—an amount set aside for unforeseen contingencies? If so, is the reserve carried over from one year to the next or do "unforeseen" problems constantly soak it up? Does the budget include a category or categories for "miscellaneous"? There is nothing intrinsically wrong with a miscellaneous category, but it should comprise only a very small portion of the budget. After all, miscellaneous items are those too small to justify their own line in the budget.

Are there any line items where $0 was spent? That could be interesting. John Kelly of the *Shelbyville News* examined city expenses over a period of years and discovered that even the officials who created the budget sometimes failed to understand where the city's money was going. "We found the county council budgeting money for years in a row for a telephone line that did not exist," Kelly explained. "Minor amount, but huge example of how the county's financial stewards weren't asking enough questions and keeping track of how money was spent. No corruption, just laziness."[4]

SUMMARY

This chapter introduces the idea of a spreadsheet and discusses the most common use of spreadsheets in journalism—analyzing a budget. Computer-assisted reporting involves more than just using a computer. It also requires journalists to make use of basic mathematics (e.g., simple difference and percent change) as well as advanced reporting skills (e.g., knowing what questions to ask, understanding the budget process). As you learn spreadsheet concepts such as relative cell referencing and the use of formulas, do not lose sight of your goal in obtaining these skills—to analyze data for the purpose of producing a story for a medium of mass communication.

NOTES

1. Some adding machines require you to hit a total key as well.

2. You can locate the budget online at <http://ns1.crisny.org/communities/colonie/government/comptroller.colonie.html>.

3. One of the easiest inflation calculators to use is S. Morgan Friedman's at <http://www.westegg.com/inflation/>. You can also download George Landau's Cost of Living calculator at <http://www.NewsEngin.com/neFreeTools.nsf/CPIcalc>. Don't use these tools to calculate the inflation for each number. Just input the number "1000" and calculate the difference between two years. If $1,000 in 1992 is worth $1,149.17 in 1997, the rate of inflation between those two years is 14.917 percent. Create a new column that indexes for inflation, write the appropriate formula and your work is done.

4. John Kelly, "Re: Help: Analyzing a Budget." Message posted to the Computer-Assisted Reporting & Research list, April 5, 1998.

9

News and Numbers

HANDLING SIMPLE SPREADSHEET FILES

In this chapter you will learn:

■ How to simplify common mathematical tasks with a spreadsheet

■ Techniques for doing quick calculations on a range of numbers

■ More tips for making formulas you can copy anywhere

■ How to analyze population data

Budgets may be the most common numeric records that a journalist deals with, but they are not the only ones. Here is a list of records that were used to teach journalists how to use spreadsheets at a recent conference of the National Institute for Computer-Assisted Reporting. Notice the surprising variety of data:

■ AIDS deaths listed by state
■ Major league baseball player salaries
■ Child labor numbers listed by county
■ Crime breakdowns in major U.S. cities

■ Arrests for drug sales and possession
■ Fatal car accidents by manufacturer
■ Senate campaign contributions
■ Uninsured car drivers listed by state
■ County population projections
■ Elementary school data

Clearly, a spreadsheet can be used to analyze more than just budgets. Remember that the program was designed to handle all types of files containing numeric data. As long as files are small enough—no more than 256 columns by 64,000 rows—most spreadsheets can handle them.

This chapter continues the discussion of basic spreadsheet skills by using data regarding doctoral degrees awarded in the United States. The data, compiled by the U.S. Department of Education, provides a breakdown of doctoral degrees by race and by gender. Journalists sometimes receive criticism for focusing too much attention on race and gender issues, particularly in computer-assisted reporting. One reason for this focus is simply that the nation continues to struggle with these issues. Another is that the data is easily available. Government records frequently include race and gender breakdowns. When government agencies provide data concerning political party affiliation, income, IQ, test scores or other relevant attributes, journalists might explore these connections as well. However, it is worth noting that the form of the data as much as its content often leads journalists to a particular story angle or limits the ability to investigate certain areas.

INTRODUCTION TO SPREADSHEET FUNCTIONS

The last chapter discussed how to calculate and copy basic formulas in a spreadsheet using relative cell references. If you want to add the contents of Cells B4 and C4 and place the results in Cell D4, you would go to D4 and type in the formula "=B4+C4." You could then copy the results down an entire column to repeat the calculation for the entire spreadsheet. Formulas work well when you need to calculate figures based on just a few numbers. However, they can become cumbersome for large groups of numbers. For example, consider the task of calculating a total of all the expenditures in a large city budget. To do so using a formula you would need to go to the bottom cell in a column, say Cell B2500, and type in a lengthy list of cells to add (e.g., "=B2+B3+B4+B5+B6" and so on to B2499). This method is easier and probably more accurate than doing the addition on a calculator, but it is still quite time-consuming.

Spreadsheets alleviate the need for inputting long formulas by replacing them with **functions,** predefined formulas that perform calculations in a spreadsheet based on information provided by the user. If you wanted to use a function to handle the problem posed in the previous paragraph you could simply go to Cell B2500, enter the appropriate function and hit the Enter key. The computer adds together all values in the column and returns the total. Many common mathematical tasks involving large groups of numbers have equivalent functions in a spreadsheet, including:

average, which returns the arithmetic mean of a group of numbers

median, which returns the middle value of an odd set of numbers or the arithmetic mean of the two middle values in an even set of numbers

mode, which returns the most commonly recurring value in a set of numbers *sum*, which returns the total value of a set of numbers added together

max, which returns the largest value in a set of numbers

min, which returns the smallest value in a set of numbers

count, which returns a count of how many numbers exist in a set

The *average* and *sum* functions are by far the two most commonly used by journalists.

Spreadsheet function names cannot stand alone within a spreadsheet. If you were to enter the word *sum* in a cell, the program would simply display that word within the cell. You need to let the program know that you are entering a function. You do this by using the at sign (@) in front of the function name.* The @ signals that what follows is a spreadsheet function rather than a label or other data. The user also needs to provide an **argument,** the values that the function uses to perform a calculation. The argument is generally contained in parentheses following the function name. Thus, the format of a typical spreadsheet function is

@function-name(argument)

As is the case with formulas, a function argument can include actual numbers or cell references. If you were to input the function "@sum(2,3,5)," you would get the answer 10 (the sum of 2+3+5). You can also choose to sum specific cells within a spreadsheet. Typing "@sum(a2,b4,c6)" would add together the values in the three specified cells. You may also specify a cell range as your function argument. The term **range** refers to a block of cells within a spreadsheet. Ranges are commonly defined by the leftmost or right-most cell in the top row of the block and its opposite in the bottom row. These cells are separated in the range argument either by a colon (in Excel) or two periods (in Lotus 1-2-3). Figure 9.1 illustrates how a typical sum function would be written to total a column within a spreadsheet. Like formulas, functions can be copied with the relative cell references changing to reflect their new location. Thus, if you were to copy the formula in figure 9.1 to Cell C7, the cell references would change to provide totals for the new columns (i.e., C2:C6).

There are two basic ways to specify a range within a spreadsheet. You can simply type in the range by hand, or you can highlight the range within the spreadsheet using your mouse or cursor keys. To highlight a range, (1) type the at sign; (2) type the function name; (3) type the open parenthesis; (4) highlight the range with your mouse or cursor keys (Note that if you use your cursor keys to highlight the range, you will need to hold down the shift key in order to specify the range.); (5) hit the Enter key to perform the actual calculation.

---

*Note that some spreadsheet programs, such as Excel, will also allow use of the equal sign (=) to signal a function.

	A	B	C	D
1	Race	92–93	93–94	94–95
2	Native American	106	134	130
3	Asian	1582	2025	2690
4	Black	1352	1393	1667
5	Hispanic	827	903	984
6	White	26700	27156	27826
7		@sum(B2:B6)		

Figure 9.1

This spreadsheet file shows a racial breakdown of doctoral degrees granted in the United States (not including nonresident aliens). Cell B7 illustrates how to create an Excel *sum* function to total the values in Column B. In Lotus 1-2-3, the formula would use two periods to specify the range: @sum(B2..B6).

EXAMINING DEMOGRAPHIC DATA

The spreadsheet in Figure 9.1 contains data regarding doctoral degrees awarded in the United States. The data is **demographic,** meaning that it communicates vital or social statistics related to a group. Race, gender, age, education and income are all examples of demographic data. Look at the data and consider how you might examine it for a news story. The previous chapter dealt with determining actual change and percent change between two figures. Certainly you can do the same with this data. But what years should be compared? Comparing the 93–94 data with the 94–95 data would show the change in degrees awarded during the most recent year and would generate a negative headline (e.g., "Figures show 3 percent decline in Native Americans receiving doctoral degrees"). On the other hand, comparing the 92–93 data with the 94–95 data would show the change over three years and would generate a more positive headline (e.g., "Figures show 23 percent jump in Native Americans receiving doctoral degrees"). Either comparison is accurate. Your task will often be to determine which does a better job of presenting the "truth."

In general, the more years you examine, the more accurate you will be in describing your data. The number of degrees awarded to Native Americans rose 26.4 percent from the 92–93 time period to the 93–94 time period. It then fell 3 percent between 93–94 and 94–95. Those two figures are hardly conclusive enough to indicate a trend. If you include the 91–92 figures, which indicate that 118 degrees were awarded that year, you find a decrease of 10.2 percent between 91–92 and 92–93. To recap:

> 91–92/92–93   10.2 percent decrease
> 92–93/93–94   26.4 percent increase
> 93–94/94–95   3 percent decrease

Looking at the figures over a few years, you can see that there has hardly been a trend during the 1990s. A certain amount of fluctuation over time can be expected, so the analysis has not turned up anything too exciting at this point.

CALCULATING PERCENT OF TOTAL

A better way to analyze these numbers might be to determine how many degrees have been earned by members of each race as a percentage of all the degrees awarded. This approach provides you with a way to make better sense of the numbers for your audience. For example, you know that Native Americans constituted roughly 0.8 percent of the U.S. population in 1990. All things being equal, you might reasonably assume that they would receive 0.8 percent of the doctoral degrees awarded in this country. By consulting Web sites operated by the U.S. Census Bureau and the U.S. Department of Education, you have the data necessary to explore whether this assumption holds true.

The logical formula for determining percent of total is rather straightforward:

Percent of total = Portion / Total

Again, it is often useful to substitute known figures into a formula to make certain that you have transcribed it properly. You know, for example, that 40 is 40 percent of 100. If you substitute those numbers into your equation, you get 40 / 100 = .40 or 40 percent. Now that you know that your logic works and that your mathematical formula handles the calculations properly, you can enter the formula into the spreadsheet using cell references (Figure 9.2).

Up to this point, everything you have done to calculate percent of total relates directly to what you learned in the previous chapter. However, there is a problem. If you attempt to copy the formula down the column, you will get an error message. In Lotus 1-2-3, the message will appear as "ERR," while in Excel it will say "#DIV/0." The problem has to do with relative cell referencing. Recall that a relative cell reference points to other data in relation to the cell in which the reference is located. When a formula is copied from one cell to another, the formula changes to reflect its new location. Although this feature is usually beneficial in that it saves the user from having to retype a formula multiple times, it can occasionally pose a problem. For example, in figure 9.2 you can see that copying the formula from Cell C2 to Cell C3 would change it from =B2/B7 to =B3/B8. Whereas B7 had referenced the address of the cell containing the total of all degrees awarded, B8 references a cell that is empty. Thus, you receive an error message.

When you want to write a formula that will be copied from one location to another, but you want the formula to reference a particular cell, you need

	A	B	C	D
1	Race	94–95		
2	Native American	130	=B2/B7	
3	Asian	2690		
4	Black	1667		
5	Hispanic	984		
6	White TOTAL	27826		
7		33297		

Figure 9.2

Calculating a percent of total involves dividing the portion by the total. In this case, you divide the number of degrees awarded to Native Americans (Cell B2) by the total number of degrees (Cell B7). The resulting figure, .0039, indicates that the group received roughly 0.4 percent of all the doctoral degrees awarded.

to use an **absolute reference**—a reference that does not change when the formula is copied from one location to another. An absolute reference is signaled by a dollar sign ($). There are three ways to make a reference absolute:

Absolute column: the column will remain the same no matter where the reference is copied. (Example: $A4. Copied to Column B it would read $A4. Copied to Row 5 it would read $A5.)

Absolute row: the row will remain the same no matter where the reference is copied. (Example: A$4. Copied to Column B it would read B$4. Copied to Row 5 it would read A$4.)

Absolute cell: the column and row will remain the same no matter where the reference is copied. (Example: $A$4. Copied to Column B it would read $A$4. Copied to Row 5 it would read $A$4.)

In general, it is best to use absolute cell references; however, there are occasions when you might want to employ absolute column or row references in order to allow the formula to change slightly when copied throughout a row or column. Figure 9.3 illustrates how an absolute reference would look in our example.

COMPARING DEMOGRAPHIC FIGURES

When examining details related to the U.S. population, journalists and social scientists typically use data from the U.S. Census Bureau to make comparisons. The Census Bureau's Web site <http://www.census.gov> offers a wide variety of material, from recent county-by-county figures to population projections for the nation up until the year 2050. Using the data access tools on the site, it is possible to obtain U.S. population figures in a variety of different

	A	B	C	D
1	Race	**94–95**		
2	Native American	130	=B2/$B$7	
3	Asian	2690		
4	Black	1667		
5	Hispanic	984		
6	White TOTAL	27826		
7		33297		

Figure 9.3

Using an absolute cell reference permits the user to copy a formula anywhere within a spreadsheet while retaining the reference to a specific cell. For example, copying the formula in Cell C2 to Cell C3 would maintain the reference to the total figure in Cell B7, but use the number in Cell B3 as the dividend (i.e., =B3/$B$7).

categories, including race and ethnic origin. These statistics allow you to make comparisons between what you see in a given population, in this case the population of individuals receiving doctoral degrees, and what you might expect to see based on the overall population in the United States. Figure 9.4 shows this comparison based on 1990 census figures and 1993 degree data, the most recent statistics available from the Department of Education.

Notice that Figure 9.4 provides two sets of comparisons, a point difference and a percent difference. The distinction is important, but it can be quite confusing when comparing two percentages. The term **point difference** refers to the number of points separating two percentages. There is a −0.4 point difference between the percentage of Native Americans in the population and the percentage of doctoral degrees earned by Native Americans. Because the two figures are measured in percentages, the tendency is to conclude that there is a 0.4 percent difference between representation in the U.S. population and the population of those earning doctoral degrees. This conclusion is incorrect. A **percent difference** refers to the point difference expressed as a percentage of the expected value. Thus, the 0.4 point difference is actually a 50 percent difference.

It helps to think about the two values not as percentages but as a certain number of percentage points, much like the budget figures in the previous chapter were a certain number of dollars. Looking at U.S. census figures, you see that Native Americans constitute 0.8 percent of the U.S. population (0.8 percentage points). All things being equal, you would expect that Native Americans would also constitute 0.8 percent of those earning doctoral degrees. That figure is your expected value. But Native Americans earned only 0.4 percent of the doctoral degrees (0.4 percentage points). That is a difference of −0.4 points. You expected to find 0.8 percent, so you divide −0.4 by 0.8 and get the value −0.5. You can therefore conclude that Native Americans are underrepresented by 50 percent in the population of those receiving doctoral degrees.

	A	B	C	D	E
1	Race	'90 Pop.	94–95 Degrees	Pt. Diff.	% Diff.
2	Native American	0.8%	0.4%	-0.4	-50.0%
3	Asian	2.8%	8.1%	+5.8	+252.2%
4	Black	11.8%	3.0%	-8.8	-74.6%
5	Hispanic	8.8%	5.0%	-3.8	-43.2%
6	White	75.8%	83.6%	+7.8	+10.3%
7					

Figure 9.4

This chart compares a racial breakdown of doctoral degrees awarded in the 94–95 time period to figures from the 1990 U.S. census. Two comparisons are made: a point difference and a percentage difference. Note that the degree figures do not total 100 percent because the percentages were rounded to one decimal place. Rounding to the nearest place can introduce a minute amount of error (in this case 0.1). Such errors should always be explained to your audience.

Making comparisons among various sets of demographic data can be enlightening, but only if done properly. For example, you might start to draw some conclusions when you compare the racial breakdown of doctoral degrees awarded to the U.S. population. Certainly they indicate some problems. But where do the problems lie? Doctoral programs do not draw students from the general population. They usually draw from the population of students who complete a master's degree program. The U.S. Department of Education provides these figures as well. Figure 9.5 shows a racial comparison of doctoral degrees awarded with previously awarded master's degrees. You will note that the two school years are not back to back. A student does not usually earn a master's degree one year and a doctoral degree the next. It takes time. The actual amount of time varies, but many people who complete their doctoral degrees do so in three to five years. The 1991–92 master's figures represent an arbitrary but acceptable baseline for comparison.

A comparison with U.S census figures had shown that blacks, Hispanics and Native Americans were dramatically underrepresented among doctoral degree recipients. That fact does not change. But looking at figure 9.5, you can see that the underrepresentation of Hispanics and Native Americans might be attributed to the fact that these groups are also underrepresented in the population of master's degree recipients.[1] However, blacks continue to be underrepresented, even when accounting for the percentage of individuals who received a master's degree.

There are several things to keep in mind when making a comparison between two populations:

Be certain that the comparison is valid. Comparing doctoral degree recipients to the general population can illustrate deficiencies with regard to the equal representation of all races and ethnicities, but such deficiences may be beyond the control of those who run the doctoral

	A	B	C	D	E
1	Race	91–92 Masters	94–95 Doc.	Pt. Diff.	% Diff.
2	Native American	0.4%	0.4%	0.0	0%
3	Asian	4.1%	8.1%	+4.0	+97.6%
4	Black	5.8%	3.0%	-2.8	-48.3%
5	Hispanic	3.0%	5.0%	+2.0	+66.7%
6	White	86.6%	83.6%	-3.0	-3.4%
7					

Figure 9.5

Comparing doctoral graduates with the population of master's degree recipients accounts for many of the previously seen differences, particularly among Native Americans and Hispanics. However, there remains a noticeable difference between the percentage of master's recipients who are black and the percent of those who receive doctoral degrees.

programs. Likewise, racial representation in a profession should be compared to the population of individuals who have the minimum qualifications for that job (e.g., a college, postgraduate or trade school degree).

Percentages should be used to compare unequal populations. Comparing the 1.87 million Native Americans counted in the 1990 U.S. census with the 130 individuals who received a doctoral degree in the 94–95 school year does not tell you much. Saying that Native Americans constituted 0.8 percent of the population but only 0.4 percent of the doctoral class provides a more solid basis of comparison.

When comparing percentages, point differences need to be distinguished from percent differences. Think of percentages as number of points. If a figure rises from 25 percent to 50 percent, it has increased 25 points, or 100 percent.

USING PER CAPITA FIGURES

Understanding very large or very small numbers can be difficult. As a journalist, it is your task to help make the complex easier to comprehend. One way to simplify numbers is to calculate a **per capita figure,** a figure that represents the number of people or items for each unit of a population. Journalists use per capita rates to help their audience comprehend percentages that are very small or very large—usually less than 1 or greater than 1 million.

For example, the U.S. national debt currently runs at approximately $5.6 trillion. That number is so large that many people have a problem understanding it. To make it easier, you could calculate the U.S. national debt per person (per capita)—showing your audience that each U.S. citizen would have to donate nearly $21,000 in order to wipe out the debt. Calculating per capita figures for large numbers is an uncomplicated process. All you need to do is take the number and divide it by the population that you are using for comparison. In the national debt example, you simply take the national debt and divide by the U.S. population to determine the amount of debt per person.

Per capita calculations work well with small figures as well. Journalists usually use percentages to describe a portion of a whole. Remember that "per*cent*" is nothing more than the number of one thing that you have for every 100 of another. If you were to observe that 52 percent of the U.S. population is female, you are really saying that for every 100 residents of the United States, 52 are female. However, it becomes more difficult to describe portions below 1 percent of a given population. For these smaller figures, it is advisable to just change the unit of measurement from 100 to 1,000 or more. In fact, that is exactly what the World Village Project <http://www.worldvillage.org/> does in an attempt to dramatize various conditions in the world community. Rather than stating that 0.1 percent of the world population owns a computer, the project says that "if our world were a village consisting of 1,000 people, only one person would own a computer."

CALCULATING PER CAPITA FIGURES FOR SMALL NUMBERS

To calculate a per capita figure, you need to have only three values: (1) the entity to be measured; (2) the population against which it is to be measured; and (3) the unit that you would like to use as the per capita rate. Divide the entity to be measured by the population to determine a percent (per 100) figure and multiply that number by the per capita unit that you would select (e.g., per 1,000). Represented as a logical equation, this calculation would look like the following:

Per 1,000 Rate = (# of Units / Population) * 1000

To get the rate per 10,000 or 50,000, you could easily substitute the appropriate figure in the place of 1,000.

In an effort to clarify the calculation of per capita figures, let's examine rates of tuberculosis in the United States broken down by race. Figure 9.6 shows the 1990 U.S. census figures alongside 1997 data related to cases of tuberculosis. The percentage of the population is so small as to carry little meaning for the audience. Rather than use it, you can convert that percentage to a per capita rate—in this case the rate of tuberculosis per 50,000 members of a given race. Why 50,000? Actually, there are two reasons. First and most important, you want to pick a number that is large enough to make the smallest number greater than 1 so that it becomes easier to understand. In this instance, you would have to multiply the smallest percentage by a

	A	B	C	D	E
1	Race	1990 Pop.	TB Cases	%	
2	Native American	1,866,807	264	0.014 %	
3	Asian	6,994,302	3,883	0.055 %	
4	Black	29,284,596	6,610	0.023 %	
5	Hispanic	21,900,089	4,228	0.019 %	
6	White **Total**	188,424,773	4,872	0.003 %	
7		248,709,873	19,851	0.008 %	

Figure 9.6

A breakdown of the 1990 U.S. population data alongside 1997 figures of tuberculosis cases. Notice how little information the percentage figures communicate to the audience.

little more than 38,000 in order to get a figure above 1. So why jump to 50,000? It simply aids comprehension to use round numbers. That said, the choice of 50,000 remains a somewhat arbitrary one. You could just as easily calculate the rate per 100,000 or even 1 million residents and still have a usable and easily understood figure.

Using the logic of your calculation, you need to divide the number of tuberculosis cases for each race by the total population of that race. You then multiply that figure by 50,000. Converting the logic to a spreadsheet formula, you get

$$=(b2/c2)*50000$$

Because you have already calculated the percentage, you could also simply multiply that percentage by 50,000 (e.g., $=d2*50000$). Figure 9.7 shows both formulas. The results hold a bit more interest. Rather than saying that 0.008 percent of the U.S population has tuberculosis, you can say that the disease affects 4 of every 50,000 U.S. residents. You can also show that the infection rate varies considerably among the races, from a low of roughly one case per 50,000 whites to a high of approximately 27 cases per 50,000 Asians in the United States.

If the numbers seem a bit too clean, they are. The rates are actually 1.29 per 50,000 whites and 27.40 per 50,000 Asians. Some journalists prefer to leave per capita rates in whole figures. Although 1.29 cases per 50,000 may be a more precise figure, it creates an illogical picture in the mind. Does the ".29" mean that a person has a slight infection? However, as an option, you may want to consider simply increasing the per capita unit, thus citing an infection rate of roughly 13 per 500,000 whites and 274 per 500,000 Asians. Both options are accurate, though one is less precise than the other. The decision on whether to use whole numbers or decimals should be made by you and possibly others in the newsroom; however, you should make an effort to make the more precise figures available to your audience, either on your

	A	B	C	D	E
1	Race	1990 Pop.	TB Cases	%	Per 50 K
2	Native American	1,866,807	264	0.014 %	=(b2/c2)*50000
3	Asian	6,994,302	3,883	0.055 %	=d3*50000
4	Black	29,284,596	6,610	0.023 %	
5	Hispanic	21,900,089	4,228	0.019 %	
6	White **Total**	188,424,773	4,872	0.003 %	
7		248,709,873	19,851	0.008 %	

Figure 9.7

You can calculate the number of cases of tuberculosis per 50,000 members of each population by dividing the number of cases by the population and multiplying the resulting percentage by 50,000. Column E shows two different formulas to calculate this figure.

company Web site or through an accompanying **nerd box,** a sidebar that explains the methodology of your study, including all the technical details as well as any assumptions that you may have made.

USING RATIOS

Related to percentages and per capita rates is the idea of ratios. A **ratio** is a comparison that states the number of units of one thing for each unit of another. For example, you might discuss the ratio of people to television sets in a nation. In the United States, there are roughly five television sets for every four people, a ratio of 5 to 4. On the other end of the spectrum are countries like Afghanistan, which has approximately one set for every 237 residents (a ratio of 237 to 1).

A ratio is essentially a fraction. For example, using figures from the U.S. Census Bureau, you might look at the number of children living with single moms (mothers with sole custody of a child) compared to those living with single dads in the United States. Census figures show that among the roughly 15.2 million U.S. children living with one parent, 12.7 million live with their mother. The remaining 2.5 million live with their father. These figures give you a ratio of 12.7 million to 2.5 million, hardly an easy figure to comprehend. Because the number is a fraction, you could use basic math to easily reduce the ratio by dividing each number by 1 million, leaving a ratio of 12.7 to 2.5. But that figure is still fairly difficult to swallow.

Instead of bombarding the audience with complex numbers, most journalists work to make ratios as easy to understand as possible. The simplest way is to just divide the larger number by the smaller number. The larger number becomes the "ratio of" and the smaller number becomes the "ratio to." Dividing 12.7 million by 2.5 million, you get 5.08—a ratio of roughly 5 to 1. For every child living with his or her single father, approximately five live with their single mothers. Simple division makes complex ratios smaller and easy to understand.

Like per capita numbers, ratios are sometimes so small that they actually become more difficult to understand. For example, the ratio of children with neither parent home all day to those with at least one parent at home is 1.77 to 1. You could just use the figure of 1.77 to 1. As another option, you could use a less accurate but easier to understand ratio of nearly 2 to 1. To make the ratio a bit more precise, you could multiply each number by 4 and report a ratio of approximately 7 to 4 (actually 7.06 to 4). Again, you and others in your newsroom will decide how to deal with this problem.

Ratios are useful for comparing two related figures. In the earlier example, you compared children living with single parents by the gender of those parents. Although it is possible to derive a ratio for any two numbers, care must be exercised. You could, for example, compare the ratio of children living with single mothers to children living in poverty; however, since not every child living with a single mother is living in poverty, the comparison has no value. There is no logical connection between the two. Other ratios, such as the number of children living with single mothers in the labor force to single mothers not in the labor force would have more validity. Just remember that any comparison you make must meet the test of common sense.

USING CENSUS DATA

This chapter relies heavily on data available from the U.S. Census Bureau. Technically speaking, a **census** is a count of an entire population, usually including some numeric descriptions and characteristics of that population. The important point to remember is that the entire population is included in the analysis. The term **population** refers generically to any defined group of people or things. Populations can be as widely varied as people living in Chile, journalists or even marbles in a jar. If you count the number of marbles in a jar, you have taken a census of those marbles.

Federal law mandates that the government conduct a census of the population every 10 years. Citizens are required by law to cooperate with the census. Why the big deal? There are at least two good reasons. First, the government uses data gathered from the census to apportion seats in the U.S. House of Representatives. As state populations grow or decline, those states gain or lose seats in the 435-member House. Just as important, the government uses census figures to help determine how to spend billions of dollars in federal and state funds each year.[2] The information is used to help plan schools and hospitals as well as to help government officials determine which areas of the nation need additional funding for roads and public transportation.

Although you might assume that all data available from the Census Bureau is gathered by taking a census, a head count of the U.S. population, that is not always the case. In fact, when the bureau conducts its decennial (every

10 years) census, it collects data in two different ways. First, it administers a short form. The **short form,** sometimes called the 100 percent questionnaire, contains a limited number of basic questions about race, gender, housing and so on that are administered to every person and household in the United States. The short form actually goes to only five of every six housing units. The remaining one in six units receive what is known as, not surprisingly, a long form. The **long form,** sometimes called the sample questionnaire, contains all the questions of the short form as well as 58 items about social and economic factors such as income, occupation and schooling. The Census Bureau estimates that it takes respondents approximately 14 minutes to complete the short form. Respondents require just over three times as much time, on average, to complete the long form.

The basic data from the short form constitutes a census of the U.S. population. Because the data represents a census, you might think that it is free from error. That is not necessarily the case. Any census is subject to **measurement error,** mistakes resulting from the way the study subjects are counted or measured. Because of problems, either in the questionnaire or in the way it is administered, subjects may be counted twice or they may not be counted at all. In fact, the Census Bureau has been criticized for problems that led to the underrepresentation of minorities in the 1990 census. Unfortunately, there is no reliable way to determine the extent to which measurement error distorts the results of a census. As a result, journalists usually use the census figures as they appear, while acknowledging the general types of problems that might be present in the data.

Contrary to short form census figures, data on the long form is drawn from a sample. A **sample** is a fragment selected from a population. Ideally, a sample should match the population from which it was drawn. In other words, if you drew a sample of 100 people living in the United States in 1990, you might expect that 49 would be male and 51 would be female. Moreover, you would expect that one of those people would be a Native American or Alaskan Native, three would be Asian or Pacific Islander, 9 would be Hispanic (of any race), 12 would be black and most of the remaining 75 would be white. As you might imagine, the odds of a given sample matching the population exactly are pretty slim. Although samples rarely come that close to matching the population from which they were drawn, some are better than others.

For most purposes, the value of a sample lies in how well it represents the population or, as researchers say, how well it can be "generalized" to the population. Like a census, a sample can have some degree of measurement error. It can also suffer from **sampling error,** differences between the sample and the population that are due to simple chance. Journalists usually account for sampling error by noting the results of the sample (e.g., 11 Hispanics out of a sample of 100) and then listing a range within which the actual figure for the population will fall. For example, you might say that 11 percent of your sample population is Hispanic. Depending on a number of considerations—such as the size of the sample—you might mathematically determine that the actual proportion of Hispanics in the population is 11 percent, plus or minus 1.1 percentage points, which puts the population somewhere between 9.9 and 12.1 percent.

While it may seem that samples are less accurate than censuses, the Census Bureau itself acknowledges that sampling may be more effective at measuring some segments of society than a census is:

> Because the errors associated with sampling error can be more easily measured than other types of error, they get more attention. But error from other sources are present throughout the census process and can reduce the quality of results more than sampling error. In fact, sampling is the primary tool we have for controlling and reducing the negative consequences of error from other sources.[3]

In other words, the ability to control for sampling error mathematically re-duces the systematic problems caused by other sources of error, including measurement error.

So, what does this explanation mean? The Census Bureau makes its short and long form decennial data available to the public as summary tape files, or STFs. Summary Tape File 1 contains data collected from the short form. Because this data represents a 100 percent census count, journalists can use the exact data for comparisons. In fact, Philip Meyer suggests that journalists use this data to check the validity of the many polls they receive.[4] By contrast, Summary Tape File 3 contains data collected from the long form. Because this census represents data collected from a sample, it exhibits sampling error. Before using this data, journalists should become familiar with the bureau's discussion of error in Appendix C of the documentation for the STF3 file.[5]

SUMMARY

This chapter introduced the concept of spreadsheet functions, which dramat-ically reduce the amount of typing that a journalist must do when analyzing a budget. Functions can perform hundreds of calculations in a fraction of the time that would be required otherwise. Some basic mathematical concepts were also reviewed, including the use of per capita figures, ratios, and simple percentages. Knowledge of these simple techniques is an absolute must for the journalist interested in using computer-assisted reporting tools to analyze government data.

NOTES

1. It should be noted that some doctoral programs accept students with bachelor's degrees. The students may or may not earn a master's degree during the course of their doctoral studies.

Census 2000

The 1990 census was more than twice as expensive per housing unit as the 1970 census (in 1990 dollars). Despite the increased expenditures, the Census Bureau still drew criticism for its systematic measurement errors. Largely because of these problems, the National Research Council formed a panel to study how the census is conducted. In 1994, the panel concluded that "a fundamentally redesigned census that relies more heavily on sampling and statistical estimates would be more accurate and cost-effective than past efforts that have relied on trying to physically count every person in the nation."[6] The question of how to conduct the census remained a hotly debated issue into 1999, with Democrats championing statistical sampling while Republicans argued that a head count remained the only option available under the Constitution, which calls for an "actual enumeration" of the population.[7] In the end, the head count won out.

2. According to the Census Bureau, "In 1990, about $125 billion was distributed to state, local and tribal governments and about half of this money was distributed using formulas involving census population data." See <http://www.census.gov/dmd/www/advisory.htm>.

3. From "Questions and Answers about Census 2000," available online from the U.S. Census Bureau at <http://www.census.gov/dmd/www/advisory.htm>.

4. Philip Meyer, *The New Precision Journalism* (Bloomington: Indiana University Press, 1991), 214.

5. Available online at <http://www.census.gov/td/stf3/append_c.html>.

6. Cheryl Greenhouse, "Statistical Sampling, Estimation Techniques Would Yield More Accurate, Less Costly Census." Press release from the National Research Council, November 18, 1994. Available online at <http://www2.nas.edu/whatsnew/23ea.html>.

7. Toni Horst, "The Census Sampling Issue," *The Dismal Scientist*, September 8, 1998. Available online at <http://www.dismal.com/thoughts/census_sample.stm>.

10

Accessing Official Data the Easy Way

BRINGING DATA INTO A SPREADSHEET

In this chapter you will learn:

- How to obtain spreadsheet data files

- Various file formats and how to distinguish them

- How to bring data into a spreadsheet

- What parsing is and how to do it

In the mid-1980s, a reporter at a small weekly newspaper in Pennsylvania found himself assigned to cover the local city council's annual budget meeting. Having reported such meetings for a daily newspaper in the past, he knew enough to get a copy of the budget ahead of time. He also knew that he had a long night ahead of him, punching numbers into a calculator and double-checking both the city's figures and his own math. But this time he decided to try using a new computer program he had recently learned. Rather than do the calculations by hand, he entered the numbers into a spreadsheet and, lo and behold, he cut his "math time" by more than half. Having never heard of computer-assisted reporting, he patted himself on the back for his ingenuity and continued using spreadsheets to cover all kinds of number stories throughout his career at the paper.

Had I been looking at the big picture instead of congratulating myself, I might have figured out that I could have saved even more time and greatly reduced the chance of making a mistake with the data. How? By realizing that I could have simply asked the city manager for a copy of the budget in a spreadsheet file rather than on paper. Spreadsheets were not invented for journalists. They were developed to help businesses and other agencies keep track of their cash flow. Many local, state and federal workers have been using spreadsheets since the programs were introduced in the 1970s. Federal Freedom of Information Act laws give journalists the right to obtain most of the files created by those spreadsheet programs. Many states have followed suit. This chapter is devoted to giving you the technical knowledge needed to access and use those files.

LOCATING AND OBTAINING SPREADSHEET DATA

When KBIA-TV reporter Kalleen Capps tried to obtain information about dog and cat licenses from local government officials in Columbia, Mo., she was told that the data was stored in a "proprietary format." The data could only be read with a special program, the officials told her, and they could not give the program to her because that would be a violation of copyright laws. Not to be dissuaded, she asked for more details on the program. After a few questions, it became apparent to her that the "special program" was a piece of off-the-shelf software that the station had on most of its computers. More-over, the program could read and save data in any of more than two dozen different formats that could be read by virtually any spreadsheet program available. The officials were not trying to deceive her. They simply did not know the capabilities of their own program. Luckily, she did. And, as a result, she got the story.

The following sections describe just some of the ways spreadsheet files can be obtained.

Create the Data Yourself

Journalists can create data themselves. For example, many journalists use spreadsheets to keep track of their expenses while on the road. They enter the data by hand and then use the program to handle all the math.

Enter the Data from Paper

Some government agencies still use ledger books instead of spreadsheet programs to keep track of their finances. In such cases, the journalist can simply obtain a copy of the ledger and input the numbers directly into the spreadsheet.

Scan the Data into a File

Some government data is available in typewritten or book form. Although such data can usually be obtained in some computer format, it is sometimes easier or more expedient to simply scan the data into a file. To scan data, a journalist uses a **scanner,** a piece of computer hardware, looking much like a copier, that takes a picture of something and transforms it into a computer file. The journalist can then make use of **optical character recognition (OCR) software,** programs that enable the user to transform a picture of text into a word processing document.

Get the Files on Some Storage Medium

Government data often can be obtained by simply requesting it in its original storage medium. For example, you can request that your local city manager give you a copy of the budget on a 3.5-inch floppy disk. Other storage media include CD-ROMs, nine-track tapes and data cartridges. Small files can fit onto a floppy disk, while larger files may have to be obtained on other media. Just remember to be certain that you can read files on the medium you have requested.

Download the Files from the Internet

Many data files can be obtained directly from the Internet. There are two basic ways to download files. First, you can use a browser to access them on the Web. Second, you can use a file transfer protocol program to download the files directly from an FTP site. In many cases, the data is already available on the Internet. Other times you may make a specific request that a government agency make a certain data file available to you via the Internet.

WORKING WITH VARIOUS FILE FORMATS

Where you obtain the data is not as important as the format in which it arrives. Regardless of the source, most files that you obtain will be in one of four formats: data format, generic text format, Web table format or PDF format.

Data Format Files

Data format refers to those files that were created for use by common spreadsheet, database or other data programs. Most spreadsheet and database programs can open a wide variety of data formats. This feature is known as **importing,** bringing a file of a different format into the program you are using. In addition to bringing in files of another format, most programs can also handle **exporting,** transforming their own files into formats easily read by other programs. For example, Excel (a spreadsheet program) can easily import files created by Quattro Pro (a spreadsheet program from a different manufacturer). Foxpro (a database program) can save its files in Excel format so that the program can open them directly. If a government agency used either a spreadsheet or a database program to create its files, that agency should be able to easily save those files in a format that can be read by your software.

To open a file that was saved in a different data format,

1. *Locate the file.*   Click on File in the menu bar, select Open from the pull-down menu and locate the file on your drive.
2. *Choose the file type.*   At the bottom of the pull-down window you will see a selection that allows you to choose Files of type (Fig-

Figure 10.1

The Open pop-up window allows users to open files of different types. Here, the Quattro Pro file type is selected, displaying one file available to be opened.

ure 10.1). Click on the downward arrow and you will be able to scroll through the various file types.

3. *Open the file.*   Click on Open.

As I have noted, there are occasions when government officials honestly do not know how to transform files from one format to another. You may have to explain the process to them if you want the data. It is quite simple. To save a file in a different format,

1. *Start the save process.*   Click on File in the menu bar and select Save As from the pull-down menu.

2. *Choose the type of file you want to create.*   At the bottom of the pull-down window you will see a selection that allows you to choose Save as type. Click on the downward arrow and you will be able to scroll through the various file types.

3. *Save the file.*   Click on Save.

Generic Text Files

Importing and exporting data format files is a relatively simple process. But it is not always possible to obtain a file in a data format. Indeed, most government data is stored in a generic text format. It's easy to see why. **Generic text** files lack the formatting codes that some programs put in. As a result, they generally take up less space. Perhaps more important, generic text files can be read by virtually any commercially available program. If the goal is to make a certain bit of data available to as many people as possible, generic text format is the way to go.

By far the most common generic text format is the **American Standard Code for Information Interchange (ASCII),** a basic set of characters used and understood by nearly every computer in the world. ASCII files can be read and created by virtually any program, from a free word processing program to an advanced statistical software package. They also account for the bulk of the files transferred over the Internet. Why then is it more difficult for spreadsheets to read ASCII files? Remember that a spreadsheet program organizes data into columns and rows. Database programs do essentially the same thing, organizing data into fields and records. But other programs don't use this organization method. As a result, in order to read plain text files, spreadsheet programs need to perform **parsing,** a process of placing text into appropriate columns.

To make the task of parsing easier, computer programmers have come up with a variety of ways to format ASCII data so that programs can determine what data goes in which columns. The two most common of these formats are delimited and fixed-column format (Figure 10.2). **Delimited text files** make use of a specific symbol to separate the data into columns. The symbol used is usually a comma. Such files are often referred to as being in "comma-separated values," or CSV, format. However, other characters or even tabs can be used as delimiters. Delimited text files often use quotation marks to further mark fields containing characters (letters, symbols and just about anything else except numbers). This feature is especially important if some of the columns have commas already in them. By contrast, **fixed-column format** files, sometimes called **fixed-width format** files, physically line the data up into columns, with each column representing a single character. For example, the fixed format file in figure 11.2 uses Columns 1 through 20 for the name, Columns 21 through 40 for the address, Columns 41 through 55 for the city, 56 and 57 for the state and 58 through 62 for the ZIP code.

The Parsing Process   All you do when you parse a file is divide the text into columns. The basic process is roughly the same whether the file is in delimited or fixed format. The difference lies in how the program decides where the columns begin and end. Lotus 1-2-3 uses the Parse command to parcel data into columns. In Excel, parsing is handled by the Text to Columns command found under the Data pull-down menu. In both programs, the process is essentially the same:

1.   Use File and Open to access the text file that you would like to parse.

```
Regular text file
Leigh Roberts 49 Cleveland Ave. Scranton PA 18510
Jonathan Zalinski 178 Church St. Baton Rouge LA 70810

Delimited (comma-separated values) format
"Leigh Roberts","49 Cleveland
Ave.","Scranton","PA",18510
"Jonathan Zalinski","178 Church St.","Baton
Rouge","LA",70810

Fixed-column format
Leigh Roberts        49 Cleveland Ave.     Scranton
```

Figure 10.2

This figure illustrates how the most common ASCII text file formats store and display data.

2. Choose whether the file is delimited or fixed-column format. The program will display the file, so you can determine the format at this point if you haven't already done so.
3. Tell the program how to decide where the column breaks should go. With a delimited file, you simply tell the program what the delimiter is (comma, semicolon, etc.) and whether quotation marks or some other symbols are used to delineate text. With a fixed-column file, you need to insert the column breaks by clicking on the appropriate locations with your mouse.
4. The program will show you how the data will look before actually parsing it. It may also allow you to choose different data formats for each column.

Common Parsing Problems Any number of minor errors can pop up when you parse a bit of text. Here is a list of the most common problems:

An extra line of text. When you parse a specific piece of data, some spreadsheets will occasionally duplicate the last line of your selection. If you notice that the last line of text appears to be duplicated, you can simply delete it.

A date appears. Sometimes the spreadsheet program will mistake a numeric range as a date during the parsing process. For example, the age range "05-09" appears in your spreadsheet as "9-May." To fix the problem, change the Cell Format to Text and reenter the range by hand. You can often perform this task quickly by typing a single quote before the text, as in "'05-09." The program interprets what follows as text.

Leading zeroes are dropped. When spreadsheets see a column of numbers, they usually determine that the column's data type is numeric. Sometimes, that assumption is incorrect. Suppose you are importing a column of ZIP codes. Numeric calculations are not performed on ZIP codes, but the program doesn't know that. It assumes they are numeric data. As a result, it eliminates any leading zeros in that column. For example, it transforms the ZIP code "00704" into "704." Any fields in which you do not intend to perform mathematical functions should be parsed as text fields to avoid this problem.

Column overflow. When importing a fixed-column format file, it is not unusual for users to guess column breaks by looking at the first few rows of data. However, there may be some unusually long entries much farther down in the spreadsheet. If you place a column break in the wrong place, you might see a data entry like

1887271   1.

The "1" on the right side of the entry was supposed to be parsed in the other column. There are two ways to solve this problem. First, you can simply fix it manually by deleting the "1" from the end of one column and placing it at the beginning of another. That solution works if there are only a few errors. As an alternative, you can try to find the largest bit of overflow and then reparse the data accordingly. Thus, if you found a column like

1725843   761,

you could simply parse the data again and move the offending column break three spaces to the left.

Web Files

One of the richest and most accessible sources of data for a journalist is the World Wide Web. Many of the ways to locate information on the Web were discussed in chapters 6 and 7. However, it is also useful to review how we can use the data that we access. First, realize that it is possible to download actual spreadsheet files from the Web. Most spreadsheets on the Internet and Web appear in Lotus 1-2-3 format. For example, FedStats <http://www.fedstats. gov/> features numerous Lotus files, identifiable by their three-digit file extensions, that is .wks, .wk1, .wk2 and so on. To use these files, all you have to do is download them to your computer. Just click on the file you want and you are invited to select a destination for it on your computer. Once you've downloaded a Lotus file, you can simply import it into whatever spreadsheet program you are using. The same is true of Excel files such as those currently offered by the U.S. Census Bureau. Smaller database files, usually with the extension .dbf, can be downloaded and imported into a spreadsheet program the same way. FedStats and other sites also offer data in CSV and other

ASCII formats. These files can be downloaded, imported and parsed as discussed earlier in this chapter.

It is also possible to obtain data that appears directly on a Web page. To do so, simply highlight the figures on your screen, copy the data, paste it into your spreadsheet and then parse it as you would a generic text file. For example, suppose you are looking at some mortality figures on the site operated by the Centers for Disease Control and Prevention <http://wonder. cdc.gov/injury.shtml> and you want to pull the numbers into a spreadsheet for analysis.

1. *Call up the figures with your Web browser.* From the Injury Mortality page, you can select United States and All-Injury. When you click on Submit, the U.S. death figures will appear on your screen.

2. *Highlight the figures on your screen.* Using your mouse, click at the end of the data that you want to access. Hold the mouse button down and drag your cursor to the top of the dataset, including the column headers but not the other information at the top of the screen. In this case, you will see a row that says "85+." Click on the right side of the Female Rate in that row. Draw your cursor up to the left side of the row that begins with "Group." Be sure to go all the way to the edge of your screen in order to include the spaces on the left side. (Note: Dragging from the bottom up allows you to highlight the entire dataset, including blank spaces, more easily.)

3. *Copy the data to temporary memory.* Hold down the Control key and press C to copy the data.

4. *Paste the data.* Go to your spreadsheet program. Click once in Cell A1 of a blank spreadsheet. Hold down the Control key and press V to paste the data. The data is moved from temporary memory into your spreadsheet.

5. *Parse the data.* Go ahead and parse the data as discussed earlier in this chapter. Select fixed-column format for data type. The program will probably put the column guides in for you. If so, you may adjust them as needed. If not, you may put them in yourself.

Copying data from a typical Web page into a spreadsheet works well because the data remains in roughly the same pattern of columns and rows. Moving data from a Web table is not quite as simple. Although you can copy data from a table, the row and column layout is lost when you paste it into your spreadsheet. However, there is an easy way to overcome this problem. Simply save the file you are viewing and open it directly in your spreadsheet program. The following procedure works in most modern spreadsheet programs:

1. *Call up the page in your Web browser.*

2. *Save the file.*   Click on File in your Web browser and select Save As. Once you do so, a pop-up box will appear asking you to choose a location for the file.

3. *Choose a location on your local drive for the file.*   You may save it anywhere that you deem appropriate. Often a temporary ("temp") directory is the best location because you will be importing the file into a spreadsheet.

4. *Start your spreadsheet program.*

5. *Locate the file's directory.*   Click on File and select Open. Locate the directory in which you saved the file.

6. *Choose the appropriate file type.*   In the Files of Type box near the bottom, select HTML Documents.

7. *Open the file.*   Click on Open and the file should appear in your spreadsheet. The look may be a bit confusing, but the file can be edited and used like any other spreadsheet. You can even remove the formatting if you like. (For example, in Excel you can highlight the table, click on Format in the menu bar, select Autoformat and pick the Table Format "None" option.)

PDF Files

The lack of formatting in generic text files presents some problems when users try to publish certain types of documents over the Web. However, another option exists. **Portable Document Format, or PDF,** is a universal file format intended to allow users to distribute, over the Internet and Web, documents that retain their original format. Files are converted from their original format to PDF with a program called Acrobat, available for purchase from Adobe Systems. The company distributes a client program, called Acrobat Reader, that can be downloaded free of charge from its Web site.[1] Acrobat Reader allows users to view and print PDF files. Unfortunately, it does not allow users to easily import PDF files into a spreadsheet or database.

There are several options for getting data from a PDF file into a spreadsheet. The easiest, and most expensive, solution is to purchase the full Acrobat program from Adobe. You can also purchase programs from other manufacturers that convert PDF files to more readable formats.[2] What many journalists do instead is work around the problem. Some of these workarounds can be highly technical.[3] Here I present a process that is tedious but technically simple. It involves copying data from the PDF file, much as you would from a Web site. However, unlike data copied from a Web site (or data obtained by opening a HTML file in a spreadsheet), data copied from a PDF file loses its row and column table structure. No matter how many spaces separate data in a PDF file, only one space appears when it is copied from the screen. The result is that it becomes very difficult for the program to determine where to place the column breaks. Some additional formatting is needed before you can use it in a spreadsheet.

The following process works well for bringing *numeric* data into a spreadsheet file. To copy the data to your spreadsheet, make sure you download a copy of Acrobat Reader from Adobe, then perform the following steps:

1. *Save your PDF file to disk.* Acrobat Reader does not allow you to copy a PDF file that has been activated through a Web browser.

2. *Start Acrobat Reader.*

3. *Open the PDF file.* Click on File in your menu bar and select Open.

4. *Set the program to Select Text.* There are a variety of ways to do this. You can click on the small abc icon in the tool bar; click on Tools in the menu bar and choose Select Text; or just press Ctrl+Shift+4 on the keyboard.

5. *Highlight the data you want to copy.*

6. *Copy the data from the PDF file.* Hold down the Control key and press C.

7. *Paste the data into the spreadsheet.* Go to Cell A1 in your spreadsheet, hold down the Control key and press V.

The data is now in the spreadsheet, but you will notice that it appears jumbled together. Here comes the tricky part. In order to help the program recognize where to put the column breaks, you will have to reformat the data by hand. This task is not difficult, but it is a bit tedious.

Before walking through the steps, first consider what you need to do. Figure 10.3 shows a bit of data related to hate crimes that was obtained from a PDF file made available online by the FBI. Note that the data appear to be jumbled together. The easiest way to make the program recognize columns would be to tell it that the file is delimited by spaces, that is, to simply replace all the spaces with delimiters. However, that approach presents a problem. The descriptions at the beginning of this data can be one word ("Anti-White"), two words ("Sexual Orientation") or even three words ("Anti-Other Religious Group"). Using spaces as delimiters would put each word in a different column and would create a flawed table. With a small table like this one, it might be possible to make corrections by hand, but imagine doing manual corrections for thousands of rows and hundreds of columns. Luckily, there is another solution. You can insert a delimiter that will let the computer do most of the work for you.

Instead of replacing all spaces with delimiters, you want to place delimiters between columns of numbers. The solution is to have the program search out numbers that are preceded by spaces and replace those spaces with delimiters. Consider the following process:

1. *Highlight Column A.* Click once on the A atop the first column.

```
Incidents Offenses Victims Offenders
Total 8,049 9,861 10,255 8,474
Single-Bias Incidents
Race: 4,710 5,898 6,084 5,444
Anti-White 993 1,267 1,293 1,520
Anti-Black 3,120 3,838 3,951 3,301
Anti-American Indian/Alaskan Native 36 44 46 45
Anti-Asian/Pacific Islander 347 437 466 351
Anti-Multi-Racial Group 214 312 328 227
Religion: 1,385 1,483 1,586 792
Anti-Jewish 1,087 1,159 1,247 598
Anti-Catholic 31 32 32 16
Anti-Protestant 53 59 61 19
Anti-Islamic 28 31 32 22
Anti-Other Religious Group 159 173 184 120
Anti-Multi-Religious Group 24 26 27 11
Anti-Atheism/Agnosticism/etc. 3 3 3 6
Sexual Orientation: 1,102 1,375 1,401 1,315
Anti-Male Homosexual 760 912 927 1,032
Anti-Female Homosexual 188 229 236 158
Anti-Homosexual 133 210 214 103
Anti-Heterosexual 12 14 14 14
Anti-Bisexual 9 10 10 8
Ethnicity/National Origin: 836 1,083 1,132 906
Anti-Hispanic 491 636 649 614
Anti-Other Ethnicity/National Origin 345 447 483 292
Disability: 12 12 12 14
Anti-Physical 9 9 9 11
Anti-Mental 3 3 3 3
```

Figure 10.3

Raw data copied from a PDF file on hate crime in the United States.

2. *Start the Find and Replace procedure.*   Click on Edit in the menu bar and select Replace.

3. *Replace the spaces preceding numbers with a delimiter.*   Remember, you only want to replace those numbers with spaces in front of them. Under Find What type " 0" (note the space before the number). Under Replace With type ";0" (I recommend a semicolon rather than a comma to ensure that 2,100 is read as 2100, not 2 and 100). Repeat this procedure for numbers 1 through 9. When you finish, your document should look like that in Figure 10.4.

4. *Parse the file.*   You can now parse the file as a generic text file delimited by semicolons. The column headers ("Incidents," "Offenses," "Victims" and "Offenders") will have to be placed by hand, but no further editing should be necessary.

```
Incidents Offenses Victims Offenders
Total;8,049;9,861;10,255;8,474
Single-Bias Incidents
Race:;4,710;5,898;6,084;5,444
Anti-White;993;1,267;1,293;1,520
Anti-Black;3,120;3,838;3,951;3,301
Anti-American Indian/Alaskan Native;36;44;46;45
Anti-Asian/Pacific Islander;347;437;466;351
Anti-Multi-Racial Group;214;312;328;227
Religion:;1,385;1,483;1,586;792
Anti-Jewish;1,087;1,159;1,247;598
Anti-Catholic;31;32;32;16
Anti-Protestant;53;59;61;19
Anti-Islamic;28;31;32;22
Anti-Other Religious Group;159;173;184;120
Anti-Multi-Religious Group;24;26;27;11
Anti-Atheism/Agnosticism/etc.;3;3;3;6
Sexual Orientation:;1,102;1,375;1,401;1,315
Anti-Male Homosexual;760;912;927;1,032
Anti-Female Homosexual;188;229;236;158
Anti-Homosexual;133;210;214;103
Anti-Heterosexual;12;14;14;14
Anti-Bisexual;9;10;10;8
Ethnicity/National Origin:;836;1,083;1,132;906
Anti-Hispanic;491;636;649;614
Anti-Other Ethnicity/National Origin;345;447;483;292
Disability:;12;12;12;14
Anti-Physical;9;9;9;11
Anti-Mental;3;3;3;3
```

Figure 10.4

After you have used Find and Replace, all the numbers in the data are preceded by semicolons instead of spaces. These semicolons can now serve as delimiters and show the program where to place column breaks.

SUMMARY

Some data simply cannot be easily handled. The NICAR-L mailing list has hosted numerous parsing discussions that deal with particularly troublesome problems and that offer highly technical solutions utilizing programming code in PERL, Visual Basic, FoxPro, SAS or C++. If you choose to specialize in computer-assisted reporting, you may be drawn into these computer science discussions yourself at some point. Meanwhile, it is enough to realize that most journalists help each other when they encounter problems. Some even volunteer to write the code for you, e-mail you a copy at no charge and then coach you in how to use it.

Luckily, most government data that journalists want to obtain can be imported or easily downloaded and parsed. Remember that journalists tend to get spreadsheet data in one of five ways: they create it themselves from scratch; they enter it by hand from a paper source; they scan it from a paper source; they obtain it on some kind of storage medium; or they download it over the Internet or the World Wide Web.

Although the source of the data is certainly important in judging its reliability, it has no bearing on how journalists use it in a spreadsheet. What matters is its format. Data format files can be opened or imported directly into a spreadsheet. Generic text files, whether in delimited or fixed-column format, must be parsed into columns before they can be used, even data copied from Web pages. Web pages containing tables can be opened directly into a spreadsheet. PDF files are more troublesome and require either a special program or some tedious effort to prepare them for use.

NOTES

1. The program can be accessed at <http://www.adobe.com/prodindex/acrobat/readstep.html>.
2. Aerial from Ambia <www.ambia.com> is one such option.
3. One way of working around the PDF problem involves using PostScript printer drivers to capture the document in a generic text file. Another is to place the data on a Web site and use online forms that convert PDF files to text.

11

Databases and Journalism

AN INTRODUCTION

For most of America, it has never been a safer time to drive. Traffic fatalities have dropped dramatically over the past three decades. Unless you happen to be in Philadelphia. There traffic deaths have risen 50 percent in the last 10 years, making the 1990s possibly the worst traffic decade in that city's history. When Bob Warner and the team at the *Philadelphia Daily News* decided to investigate this problem, they did so by examining nearly 5 million records of traffic accidents and tickets provided by state, federal and local agencies. That analysis resulted in a series of articles that looked at everything from pointing out dangerous roads and intersections to exploring possible solutions for the problems they had identified.

In this chapter you will learn:

- What a database is

- Differences between spread-sheets and databases

- What databases let you do

- How to ask questions of a database

The *Daily News* series relied heavily on good reporting, reporting that included in-depth analysis of several computerized databases. In the most basic sense, a **database** is a group of related data organized so that it can be accessed easily and quickly. Perhaps the most common database that you use is the phone book. It is a collection of data that is organized alphabetically, last name first, so that you can get information from it quickly. Computer databases work much the same way. However, whereas a phone book allows you to use names to look up phone numbers, that same database on computer would allow you to use a phone number to find someone's name, to look for the name of a person who lives at a given address or even to list the phone numbers of everyone who lives on a certain street. You could even go further and count the number of people with listed numbers in the entire database or on a given street. In short, a computerized database offers more flexibility.

But databases give journalists more than just flexibility. They enable them to report stories more quickly and easily than would otherwise be possible. Take, for example, the story of Bob Anderson, former environmental reporter with *The Advocate* in Baton Rouge, La. In 1996, Bob had reported on mercury in the flesh of fish caught in various Louisiana waters. His article pointed out which bodies of water contained fish with high levels of mercury and which had fish that were safer to eat. One year later, after taking a one-day seminar in computer-assisted reporting, he did the same story again. As he explains:

> The reporting part of the two stories was much the same. It involved talking to toxicologists about what levels were dangerous for the general public, what levels were dangerous for specific parts of the population, like children and pregnant women, and what levels were low enough that the toxicologists would let their own children consume the fish. Where the computer made a major difference was in the hours spent totaling and analyzing the data.[1]

The project entailed gathering about five years' worth of data on more than 100 bodies of water in the state. The fish were of different sizes and varieties. It was extremely painstaking work to do by hand. Each time a new stream came in during the first year, Bob had to manually change the alphabetical listing of sites and refigure the numbers. Doing the same story a year later, all those tasks were handled with a few keystrokes. Moreover, Bob was now able to quickly rank the sites by the average concentrations in different types of fish, analyze the relationship of species to mercury level and compare the importance of size. All because he used a computer database.

WHAT IS A DATABASE?

The term *database* is an elusive one. While it's true that the phone book is a kind of database, that's not usually what you picture when you hear the term. Instead, people tend to think of databases as being computerized. But that's not particularly helpful either. After all, a spreadsheet file is a kind of database too. Rather than try to come up with a de facto definition of a database, I have put together a working definition. For our purposes, a database is:

A group of related data. There must be some unifying feature to a database. It is a collection of things or people (e.g., traffic accidents, restaurant inspections, AIDS patients, etc.).

Organized into one or more tables. The data is organized into one or more tables laid out in a format that looks much like the columns and rows of a spreadsheet.

Stored for use by a computer. The data is kept in a file that is stored electronically, magnetically, optically or in some other form readable by computer.

Intended to be analyzed by database software. As you will see, some data is suited to analysis by a spreadsheet while other data is better examined with a database manager.

There are two basic types of databases: relational and nonrelational. A **nonrelational database,** sometimes called a **flat-file database,** is a single, stand-alone table of data. For example, a single file containing the names and addresses of your contacts would be a flat-file database. By contrast, a **relational database** is a collection of two or more tables that are intended to be used in conjunction with each other. Relational databases allow comparisons between two or more tables in the database. For example, a state might maintain one table with driver's license data and another with data about traffic stops. Rather than writing all the information about a driver in the traffic stops table, the state lists only the driver's license number. A database management program could then reference that number in the license table to pull out all the information needed. This procedure conserves time spent transcribing the data as well as space on the computer. Relational databases will be discussed in greater detail in chapter 14.

HOW DO SPREADSHEETS AND DATABASES COMPARE?

Most databases look a lot like spreadsheets, at least on the screen. They are generally organized into columns and rows. In a database, each row represents a **record,** a collection of individual data items pertaining to one entry in the database. For example, a driver's license database would contain one record for every license issued. A record is made up of fields, roughly equivalent to columns in a spreadsheet. A **field** is an area of a database record where a specific bit of data is stored. Each record in a driver's license database would contain a number of fields, which would in turn hold individual data items. Field 1 might contain the driver's first name, Field 2 would hold the middle name and so on.

A flat-file database and a spreadsheet data file are usually interchangeable from a technical standpoint. Any file that you use in a spreadsheet can be imported into a database. Likewise, many flat-file database files can be imported into a spreadsheet. Spreadsheet and database programs can each store data format files. What matters is not so much the structure of the file as what you intend to do with it. You can use a spreadsheet to perform database functions. But in some cases that task would be like using a screwdriver to pound in a nail. You can also use a database to perform most spreadsheet functions. But again, that task might be like using a hammer to drive a screw. What you want to do is use the right tool for the job. Although both spreadsheet and database programs can sort and search data, there are significant differences between the two programs.

In general, a spreadsheet is best used for:

Math. If the file you want to examine has a lot of numbers that need to be added, multiplied, subtracted or divided, a spreadsheet is probably the best choice. Spreadsheets work well for budgets, payrolls and other number projects. Calculations are the primary function of a spreadsheet program.

Small files. Excel can handle up to 65,536 rows or records and up to 256 columns or fields. Other spreadsheet programs can handle files of roughly the same size. If a file is larger than this, you shouldn't try to use a spreadsheet to analyze it.

By contrast, a database program is best suited for:

Nonnumeric data. A spreadsheet can be used to examine nonnumeric data, but that analysis is superficial or very difficult. Database programs are better suited for this purpose.

Large files. Although database programs vary, most can easily handle a hundred thousand rows or more. Many can handle files that contain millions of rows of data.[2]

Multiple users. A spreadsheet is altered during the process of analysis. Databases remain in their original form. Therefore, a database is better when you want a large number of people in the newsroom to have access to the data.

Grouping data. A spreadsheet program can add an entire column together, but it becomes difficult to group data together. For example, if you have a table of campaign donors, a spreadsheet can give you the total for all donors. But it is easier for a database to break that information down by city or county.

WHAT IS IN A DATABASE?

A database can consist of hundreds of fields. Keeping track of even a few fields can sometimes be confusing. That's why the people who create databases also create record layouts to go with them. A **record layout** is a listing of the names of all fields contained in a database, along with some information about those fields. The type of information can vary greatly. If a field name is confusing or ambiguous (e.g., "Tdate"), a record layout should provide a description of what the name means (e.g., "Transfer date" or "Transaction date"). Record layouts will also usually say how long a field is and whether the contents are in character or numeric format. Some even provide starting points for each field. For example, if a record is 100 characters long, the record layout may specify that the ID field begins at space 1 and runs for 11 spaces. The LastName field begins at space 12 and runs for 20 spaces and so on. Figure 11.1 shows what a typical record layout looks like.

Field	Fieldname	Type	Width	Description
01	ESCYEAR	C	4	ESCHEAT YEAR
02	OWNERLNAME	C	25	OWNER LAST NAME
03	OWNERFNAME	C	15	OWNER FIRST NAME
04	OWNERMINIT	C	1	OWNER MIDDLE INITIAL
05	TRUSTLNAME	C	25	CO-OWNER LAST NAME

Figure 11.1

This is a portion of the record layout for the Unclaimed Property System in Connecticut. Notice that it provides the field number, field name, data type (character or numeric), field width and a description of the field.

Some record layouts also serve as data dictionaries. A **data dictionary** is a reference that allows you to decode what's in a database. Although many databases consist of comprehensible references, such as M for male and F for female, not all databases are so easy to understand. You might encounter a field called Race and find that it contains numbers from 1 to 9. In order to understand what those numbers mean, you need a data dictionary that lists all the codes and what they stand for. For example, a data dictionary might list the Race field and codes as follows: 1=African American 2=Asian American 3=Native American (and so on). For databases with few codes, the data dictionary is sometimes combined on one sheet with the record layout. In other cases, the data dictionary can span dozens or even hundreds of pages.

WHAT DO DATABASES LET YOU DO?

Basically, a database lets you search the data. Want to see what kinds of repairs a specific plane had before it crashed? Just search for the plane's tail number and registration numbers in the Federal Aviation Administration's database of Service Difficulty Reports.[3] That is how Ford Fessenden and the staff at *Newsday* began looking into the crash of TWA Flight 800. The team was able to call up a list of every problem that the aircraft had encountered during its lifetime as well as problems encountered by similar aircraft. The series of stories that followed, which examined the causes of the crash as well as the human toll it took, eventually earned *Newsday* the 1997 Pulitzer Prize for Spot News Reporting.[4]

When you search a database, you can be very specific in both what you search for and how it is displayed. Your search can be broken down into three specific tasks:

Sorting. A database allows you to sort data in either ascending or descending order, alphabetically or numerically.

Field Names

Every database record is made up of one or more fields. Each field has a unique field name. Different database programs place different limitations on what you can use for field names and how long they can be. Some programs require that field names be only one word or up to 10 letters or numbers. Others, such as Microsoft Access, allow you to use spaces and up to 64 characters.

As a rule, it is better to keep field names short, easy to remember and no more than one word long.

Filtering. A database allows you to limit your examination to only one part of the data. For example, instead of looking at a record of gun dealers throughout the United States, you could limit your inspection to the state of North Carolina or the city of Greenville or even Greenville Boulevard.

Grouping. A database allows you to group data together in a variety of ways. Using a database of arson fires, you could list every city in the database together with the number of arsons in each city (arsons grouped by city). Or you could list the total amount of arson damage in each state (a sum of damage grouped by state).

You could also combine two or more of these tasks. For example, you might tell the database to display a list of the arson fires in each city (grouping) in descending order by number of fires (sorting) but only for cities in New Jersey (filtering).

Imagine that you had a list of all the people convicted for driving under the influence of alcohol in your community. The database consists of one record for each conviction. Each record contains several fields—let's say FirstName, LastName, City, State, Age, Gender, Race, BloodAlcohol, ArrestDate, Sentence. A real database would obviously contain more data than just these fields, but we'll keep our example simple. Now imagine that you wanted to look for patterns in the data.

You could start by sorting the data. Sorting by LastName would generate an alphabetical list (not really of much use). Sorting by Gender would give you a list of the females first, followed by males. Again, that sort is not particularly useful, though some patterns might emerge. Sorting by Blood-Alcohol would be more interesting. Does a pattern seem to emerge at the low or high end of the sort? Do you find more males at one end or the other? Do you find more whites on one end or the other? Sorting by ArrestDate might be interesting as well. Do there seem to be patterns based in the arrest dates (e.g., more arrests near major holidays or near the end or beginning of a month)? These patterns might emerge out of a simple sort.

You could start grouping the data as well. Arrests could be grouped by City to examine whether police seem to be targeting out-of-towners. BloodAlcohol could be grouped by Gender to find out if the men arrested had a higher or lower average blood alcohol content than the women did. Perhaps patterns would emerge from a combination of grouping and sorting. You could group by ArrestDate and then sort the results to determine which date or dates had the most arrests. Filtering might bring out additional patterns. You could look at the arrests of local residents only. Are more blacks arrested than whites? How does that finding compare to the local population ratio? As you can see, the three basic pattern-searching techniques for a database can be used in a wide variety of ways. These techniques will be discussed at greater length in the chapters that follow.

HOW DO DATABASES WORK?

Chapter 8 discussed the concept of interviewing the data. The same idea holds true for examining a database, perhaps even more so. When you work with a spreadsheet, you make changes to the spreadsheet itself. If you save the spreadsheet, those changes become permanent. Perform a sort and the sort remains. Calculate a column total and that total is now a permanent part of the spreadsheet. These changes are fine, because spreadsheets are designed to perform calculations on the fly and reflect changes immediately.

Things are different with a database. Instead of making changes to the database itself, you create a **query,** a formal request for information from a database. The database management program then uses that query to create a temporary table reflecting what you asked for. This procedure is known as querying a database. For example, suppose you have a database about legal immigrants to the United States. You want to examine the records of those immigrants who came into the country from Ireland in June. To do so you create a query that basically tells the database management program, "Show me a table containing an alphabetical list of the people who immigrated to the United States from Ireland in June." The computer then creates a temporary table that displays the information you requested. You can save that new table, or you can run a new query and erase the old one. No matter which you do, the immigrants database remains in its original form.

The most basic type of query, and by far the most commonly used in computer-assisted reporting, is the select query. A **select query** allows the user to choose which data from a table should be displayed and the manner in which it should be displayed. With all the jargon in computer-assisted reporting, it's easy to get confused. But think about that definition for a moment. All you are doing when you are querying a database is telling the computer what you want to see and how you want to see it. That's all there is to it.

The QEQ Approach

Preparing a query for a database—what is often referred to as building a query—is easy once you get used to it. But as you're learning, it's better to break the preparation down into three steps: question, expectation and query (QEQ).

Question The first step is to figure out exactly what your question is. That question should be expressed in straightforward human terms (e.g., "How many arson fires did each city report last year?"). This step may sound simple, but too often people have only a vague idea about what they're looking for. Instead of starting with the question, they begin by worrying about what buttons to push on the computer. If you don't have a clear question, you won't get a clear answer.

Expectation Once you have a question in mind, think about what the answer will look like in some kind of table form. If you want to see how many arson fires each city reported last year, your answer will probably look like a table of two columns. The left column would contain the names of the cities and the right column would contain the number of fires each city reported last year.

Ensuring that your expectations are realistic requires some familiarity with what databases are capable of doing. If you want to find out which city had the most arson fires last year, your answer will not be a table that contains only the city's name. But you could ask the computer to create a list of cities and the number of arson fires reported in each and to sort the list so that the city with the most fires appears at the top.

Query Once you have stated the question and you have an expectation of what your answer will look like, you are ready to build the query. The simplest way to build a query is to ask the computer to create a table that matches your expectations.

Imagine that you have a table that contains all the campaign contributions made by political action committees. First, you come up with a question that you want to ask (e.g., "Which PAC gave the most money to Senator Monroe's campaign?"). Next, you envision your answer (e.g., "The answer will be a table of two columns. The left will contain a list of PACs. The right will contain their total contributions to Senator Monroe's campaign, sorted in descending order."). Only then do you build your query (e.g., "Show me a table containing all the PACs and the total of their contributions in descending order, but only for Senator Monroe's campaign.") As you can see, the query flows directly out of your expectations.

Journalists working with databases can encounter problems in any stage of the query process. First, they may not have a specific question in mind when they build the query. Ask them what they are doing and they may talk about "grouping," "filtering" and "sorting" instead of "trying to find out which PAC gave the most money to Senator Monroe." Always focus on the reporting. The computer commands are a means, not an end. The second problem that database journalists face is an inability to properly envision what their answer will look like. Remember that any answer a database gives you will be in table format, consisting of columns and rows. You can't begin to build a good query until you have a clear idea of what the answer will look like in that form. Finally, journalists can make an error in the query itself. They may have a clear idea of what they want and expect, but then ask for something totally different. Computers are not "smart"; they simply handle basic tasks quickly. And they do exactly what you *tell* them to do, even if it would be obvious to any human being that it was not what you *meant* for them to do.

Queries in Action

It's important not to get bogged down in all this talk of searching, grouping, filtering and sorting. Instead, let's look at some real-world stories and how they were reported using databases. For example, look at the lead of this story, the first in James Walsh's three-part series on car theft that appeared in the *Minneapolis Star Tribune:*

> The first time Amy Hewitt reported her car stolen, the new 1993 Dodge Spirit was found abandoned in Powderhorn Park—along with a shotgun in the back seat that had been used in a drive-by shooting.
>
> The next time, the thief dumped it a few blocks from her house in south Minneapolis. The third time? The details are fuzzy now. Then there was that night last fall when Hewitt and her husband had both their cars stolen.[5]

Trying to find the people who had been victimized the most by car thieves would be a daunting task using paper records. With databases, it's easy. Consider how you would approach this task. First, identify your question (e.g., "What individuals had their cars stolen most often?"). Second, consider what your answer would look like. You need to identify individuals and car thefts. Ideally, your answer would be a table of two columns, VictimName and CountOfThefts. Most databases break names into two fields, First and Last. Thus imagine a database with three columns: First, Last and CountOfThefts. At this point you can come up with your query (e.g., "Show me a table containing the First field, the Last field and a Count field. Then sort it in descending order by the Count"). In Minneapolis, Amy Hewitt's name appeared among those at the top.[6]

The data also helped add depth to the series' second story, which dealt with the lack of punishment for car thieves in the Minneapolis/St. Paul area:

> The lack of hard consequences for a widespread, costly crime is the norm.
>
> Take the 33-year-old Minneapolis man with six auto-theft convictions over seven years: Five times he was sent to the county workhouse for a few months, once to prison.

Identifying Individuals

Imagine you went through the process of asking who had their car stolen most and the answer came up "John Smith" or "Mary Brown." Your reportorial skepticism should kick in at this point. The obvious problem is that some names are more common than others. Many different John Smiths may have had their car stolen.

When using a database to group information about individuals, you need to guarantee that you identify the individuals correctly. The best way is to use a unique identifier such as a social security number (federal ID) or driver's license number. In a car theft database, you might try the vehicle identification number.

If no unique identifiers are available, you need to fall back on traditional reporting to bolster your database analysis. You could use the First, Last and Address fields, but there might be two John Smiths at the same address. Or you might miss a Mary Brown because she moved three times in the last year. The computer helps your reporting effort, but it doesn't do all the work for you.

> How about this 37-year-old from Bloomington? Nine convictions in four years—four workhouse stays, one trip to prison.[7]

You can run a query similar to the one discussed earlier in order to identify individuals arrested for stealing cars. Then the task becomes one of simply filtering out only those records pertaining to that individual. For example, imagine that your search turned up the 33-year-old Minneapolis man that Walsh mentioned. The results would display his social security number (e.g., 555-55-5555) or other unique identifier in one column and a count of his convictions in the second. With the social security number, you could then obtain the full records of all his convictions. Your question would be "What were the dispositions of this man's auto-theft convictions?" The answer you want is a table containing all the fields of all the records pertaining to that man. Your query is "Show me a table containing all the records where the social security number is 555-55-5555."

Good data adds depth to a story. It also adds authority. Notice how the data is used in the following passage to bolster anecdotal evidence received from victims and police officers:

> A burgeoning black market for hot cars—and a relatively easy ride if you're caught—have made Minnesota and Minneapolis prime territory for auto thieves. Police tell victims they'll probably never make an arrest, prosecutors admit they seldom push cases to conviction and legislators acknowledge that state laws don't really intend to lock car thieves away.
>
> Even the most hardened car thief will serve no more than 2½ years in prison, a Star Tribune analysis of years of police and court data shows.[8]

The series uses a variety of anecdotes to put a human face on the problem. But it drives the point home with a statistic. Your question is "What is the maximum sentence that was handed down to a car thief?" You have two choices for the answer. You can see a list of convicted car thieves and their sentences, as we discussed earlier. Or you can see just a number representing the maximum sentence handed down. In the latter case, your query would be "Show me a table containing the maximum sentence handed down to a car thief."

A Query Breakdown

Basic database queries, the ones journalists use for the bulk of their computer-assisted reporting work, can be broken down into five parts:*

1. *Show me a table.* Every query begins with what amounts to "Show me a table." You are asking the database management program to show you a table containing your answer.
2. *Containing these fields or aggregates.* Your query specifies which fields you want to see; in effect, it filters the fields. The query specifies the order in which you want to see those fields. You can ask for the FirstName followed by the LastName field or vice versa. You can also specify which aggregates you want to see. **Aggregates** are computer functions used to create groupings of some sort. The most common aggregates are Sum, Average and Count, but you can find a variety of others such as Min, Max and even Standard Deviation. In a query, they are treated much like fields.
3. *From this table.* From this database program where to find the fields that you want.
4. *Limit it to these records.* A query can filter a database so that only certain records appear. You ask for only those records that match certain criteria (e.g., "where the social security number is equal to 555-55-5555" or "having a number of convictions greater than 4").
5. *Sort it this way.* A query can specify how you want your answer table sorted. You can sort in ascending or descending order. You can also sort on more than one field. This last feature is useful when you want to sort by name. You can sort by last name and then by first name.

That's all there is to it. Once you come up with a question and envision your answer, you just ask for a table that provides the answer for you. Here are some examples.

Q: What can be found in the Traffic Safety database?
A: *Show me a table containing all the fields from the TrafficSafety database.*

---

*Parts 1 through 3 are necessary. Parts 4 and 5 are optional.

Q: What are the names of those people listed in the police database of murder victims?

A: *Show me a table that contains the FirstName and LastName fields from the MurderVictims database.*

Q: How many railway accidents were there in each state listed in the Railway database?

A: *Show me a table containing State field and a Count from the Railway database.*

Q: What group received the most grant money according to the National Endowment for the Arts database?

A: *Show me a table containing Group field and a Count from the NEA database. Sort it by the Count in descending order.*

Q: How many loans were reported from New Jersey under the Home Mortgage Disclosure Act?

A: *Show me a table containing a Count from the HMDA database where the State field is equal to "NJ".*

Only when you understand the logic behind queries are you ready to get on the computer and begin creating your own.

SUMMARY

Databases have become among the most valuable information resources available to journalists. Learning how to use them properly requires that you first understand how they work. Databases consist of numerous records, and each record contains one or more fields. To get information from a database you determine what question you want to ask, imagine what the results will look like and then create a query in the database management program. Queries are requests to display data. They don't touch the original database; rather, they tell the database management program to create a temporary table that displays the information as you requested. Most queries begin with what amounts to "Show me a table containing." You can then select which fields or aggregates you want to see and the order in which you want them displayed. You can also indicate how you would like the results sorted, grouped or filtered.

Once you understand the logic behind working with databases, it becomes a question of learning how to put that knowledge to use with the actual computer software. The two chapters that follow discuss the most common ways of building queries in a database management program. The information may seem a bit confusing at first. Just remember that all you are doing is asking questions. Everything else is simply learning *how* to ask those questions.

NOTES

1. Bob Anderson, personal communication, May 1, 1997.

2. Microsoft reports that Access is capable of handling single databases that range up to 1 gigabyte in size, with linked tables stretching that limit to the size of your storage device. However, a number of reporters have discovered problems in dealing with large databases in Microsoft Access. As a result, many recommend using Microsoft FoxPro or some other program for handling larger databases.

3. Service Difficulty Reports, or SDRs, detail the repair or maintenance problems experienced by aircraft in the United States. They are compiled by the Federal Aviation Administration.

4. For details, see the Pulitzer Prize Board's description online at <http://www.pulitzer.org/year/1997/spot-news-reporting/works-2-1/index.html>.

5. James Walsh, "While Officials Do Little, Minneapolis Car Thefts Mount," *Minneapolis Star-Tribune*, April 19, 1998. Available online at <http://www2.startribune.com/cgi-bin/stOnLine/article?thisStory=10033591>.

6. A "Victim's Stories" section in the series noted that about 300 people had their cars stolen more than four times.

7. James Walsh, "Car Thieves Have to Work Pretty Hard to Go to Prison," *Minneapolis Star-Tribune*, April 20, 1998. Available online at <http://www2.startribune.com/cgi-bin/stOnLine/article?thisStory=10033813>.

8. Ibid.

12

Mining Government Records for Information
A STRUCTURED APPROACH

In this chapter you will learn:

- How database management programs deal with databases

- A structured way to ask questions of databases

- How to translate common questions into the language of database programs

- How reporters use these skills to do their job more quickly and easily

North Carolina state law requires that every restaurant be inspected at least four times a year. But Janet Roberts and Chris Davis at the *Morning Star* in Wilmington, N.C., discovered that many local restaurants were falling through the cracks. In fact, nearly one out of every three restaurants in New Hanover County skipped at least one inspection during the year prior to the newspaper's investigation. Sifting through the 1,400-plus inspection records by hand would have been a daunting task. But using a computer to analyze the health department's database, staff members were able to perform a complex analysis that allowed them to pinpoint the skipped inspections while taking into account a variety of special circumstances. The resulting article and sidebars examined not only how frequently restaurants were inspected, but also how they fared. Reporters even analyzed the inspection process to determine what inspectors looked for during their three-hour visits.

Doing a complex analysis like the one performed by the *Morning Star* team requires a structured approach to the data. You need to understand not only what you want to ask, but also how to translate that question into a format that the computer can understand. This chapter explores the underlying language that runs most database programs. Building on what was discussed in the previous chapter, we will walk through the process of creating a basic query that will help you get what you want from a database. Explanations may sound a bit technical at times, but keep in mind that all we are talking about is translating a basic question into a language that the computer can understand.

A STRUCTURED APPROACH

In the previous chapter, we discussed the three steps in preparing a query for a database: question, expectation and query. The first step of the process has nothing to do with the computer. It has everything to do with being a good reporter. After all, that's a large part of what reporters do—come up with questions and uncover answers. Once you have the question, you have to envision what your answer will look like in table form. Again, this step doesn't necessarily involve the computer. Most answers take the form of some kind of list. Want to find out who gave the most to Bush's election campaign? Your answer will be a list of Bush contributors, with the total amount that each person gave, sorted so that the person who gave the most is at the top of the list. Whether you're looking up your answer in a book or on the computer, you should have some expectation of what that answer will look like.

The final task is creating the query. Query building usually takes one of two forms: Query by Example or Structured Query Language. **Query by Example,** often referred to as QBE, involves using your mouse to build a query by selecting from various options on the screen. In general, QBE is a bit easier to use; however, it is also much less powerful. We will discuss QBE more fully in the following chapter. First, we will explore **Structured Query Language (SQL),** the industry-standard query language used by most database management programs. SQL (pronounced either "S-Q-L" or as an acronym, "sequel") is the primary method of building queries in programs such as Microsoft Visual FoxPro, Oracle and many others. Much of the early work in computer-assisted reporting was done by reporters using SQL. In fact, some of the more advanced computer-assisted reporting professionals still prefer SQL, which allows reporters to handle larger databases and perform more complex operations. SQL allows you to translate your human language question into an English-based query that the computer can understand. A typical SQL query might look something like this: *select * from fec99 where city = "New York" order by contrib*. That phrase may seem a bit confusing right now, but it will all become clear within the pages that follow.

Although QBE may be easier, you are going to learn SQL first. Why? Because SQL forces you to take a structured approach to building a query. It requires that you ask for information in a specific way. Perhaps more important, it is *the* database language. Most QBE programs simply take your query and turn it into an SQL statement before submitting it to the program. In a sense, tackling SQL first cuts out the intermediary. Finally, by learning both SQL and QBE, you can choose the best method for whatever task you face.

OVERVIEW OF SQL

It is helpful to remember that SQL is a language. Like any other language, it has a vocabulary and a syntax—rules governing how the words in that vocabulary are used. Luckily for us, the SQL vocabulary is rather limited. In fact, in order to perform most data queries, you need to become familiar with only about two dozen words, symbols or combinations. Of these, the following six stand out as the most important.

select ("show me a table containing"): Nearly every data query begins with what amounts to "Show me a table containing." The SQL equivalent for this phrase is "select."

from ("from"): Because you can select data from any table you have access to, you need to specify where the data you want will come from. The "from" clause is used for that.

where ("but only those records where"): There are occasions when you will want to filter the records before you look at them. For example, you might only want to look at arson fires in Missouri. To filter records, use the "where" clause (e.g., where state = "Missouri").

group by ("aggregate using these fields"): When you want to create totals, generate averages or perform other mathematical functions, the "group by" clause *must* be used to tell the computer what fields you want totals or averages for.

having ("but only those records where"): The "having" clause is a way to filter by aggregates. For example, you can create a table that counts the number of times a person has reported his or her car stolen and then selects only those people who filed four or more reports.

order by ("sorted by"): This clause allows you to sort your table in ascending or descending order, by whatever criteria you choose.

Okay, now take a deep breath. All these symbols, aggregates, clauses and functions may not seem a lot like journalism right now. But as we walk back through each of these "words" and discuss how they are used, you will see how they allow you to do what you really want to do—interview the database.

The *Select* Statement

Most data queries consist of a single *select* statement. The other five major words or phrases are usually referred to as **clauses,** distinct parts of a *select*

Case Sensitivity

As a rule, SQL statements are not case sensitive. The computer will give you an answer whether you write *Select FirstName*, *SELECT FirstName* or *select firstname*. It is usually easiest to simply write your statements in all lowercase letters, but it is your choice.

statement. As you might imagine, *select* statements begin with the word "select." This word is followed by the fields or aggregates that you want to see, in the order you want to see them. Each field or aggregate is separated by a comma. If you want to see a name in proper speaking order, you would write *select first, last*. If you want to see them in reverse order, you would simply write *select last, first*. If you want to include the middle initial, it might be *select first, middle, last*. It's that easy.

There are times when you will want to see every field in a database. Rather than forcing you to type out each field name, SQL provides a shortcut. You can use the asterisk (*) as a wildcard. Generally speaking, a **wildcard** is a character that matches all characters or groups of characters, rather than a single character, when doing a search comparison. So here, the wildcard effectively says "all the fields, no matter what their names are." Figure 12.1 illustrates some of the different options in a *select* statement.

Using the wildcard in a *select* statement is the most common way to browse through a database in SQL and should usually be your first step in analyzing data. Browsing a database in this manner allows you to do several things:

Make sure the field names in the database match your record layout. Sometimes the database you obtain may not match the record layout you have received. It could be that you got the wrong layout. On the other hand, it could also mean that the agency giving you the database decided to remove a few fields before giving you the data. When you obtain a database from a government agency, it's always good practice to also get a copy of the blank paper form that was used to gather data. If you're looking at driver's license records, get a copy of a driver's license application. The fields from the paper form, the record layout and your database should all match. If not, you need to find out why.

Take a look at what the database contains. By looking at the data, you can determine whether it is what you expected. You can also decide if you need a data dictionary to decipher any codes in the database. Also, note the form the data takes. Is it in all lowercase, all capital letters or initial capitals only? This form is important when you want to filter the data.

Look at only one field (FirstName) select firstname	*Example:* *Sam* *Bernard* *Barbara*
Look at two fields (FirstName and LastName) select firstname, lastname	*Example:* *Sam* *Donaldson* *Bernard* *Shaw* *Barbara* *Walters*
Change the order in which fields are viewed select lastname, firstname	*Example:* *Donaldson* *Sam* *Shaw* *Bernard* *Walters* *Barbara*
Look at all the fields in a database select *	

Figure 12.1

Some examples of how you can choose and order fields in a *select* statement.

Search for errors in the data. By examining each field in a handful of records, you can look for potential problems such as misspelled names. Some databases have cities that are spelled more than a dozen different ways (e.g., "St Louis," "St. Louis," "Saint Louis," "St. Louise," "St. Luis" and so on). Studying the errors can give you a handle on how reliable the database is.

Look for patterns. Simply browsing the data is a good first step to analyzing it. Seeing what's there can also stir questions in your mind and prompt you to search for the answers.

The *From* Clause

Once you have listed the fields that you want, you need to specify the table or database they are coming from. You use the *from* clause for this task, and specify the table that contains the fields you want to view. For example, to see the contents of the First field from the table called "tvdatabase" you would write *select first from tvdatabase*.

SQL allows you to write your *select* statement out on one long line if you want to. While the computer has no problem reading this format, humans do. As a result, it is usually better to place each clause on a separate line. Thus,

select first
from tvdatabase

One more thing is worth mentioning here. Different programs handle SQL differently. Most require the use of a semicolon, though they use it in different ways. For example, Microsoft Visual FoxPro, the SQL program most commonly used by journalists, requires that you end each line with a semicolon to tell the program "don't do it yet." So, in FoxPro, the SQL would look like this:

> *select first;*
> *from tvdatabase*

It tells the program "Show me a table containing the first field (not yet) from the tvdatabase table." Oracle and other database programs handle the semicolon differently. In those programs, the semicolon tells the computer "go do it." There, the SQL might read:

> *select first*
> *from tvdatabase;*

This instruction tells the program "Show me a table containing the first field from the tvdatabase table (go do it)." If you're confused by these differences, you're not alone. Veteran CAR journalists take some time getting used to using the semicolon properly when they switch from one program to another. For our purposes, I will assume that most of you will be using a FoxPro-like program rather than an Oracle-like program. As such, each SQL line will end with a semicolon before you hit the Enter key to go to a new line.

The *select* statement tells the computer what fields or aggregates you want to see. The *from* clause identifies the table containing the data. The remaining clauses are what allow you to filter, group and sort the results of your query.

The *Where* Clause

Most filtering in SQL is done with the *where* clause. Basically, *where* tells the computer to limit what it shows you to only those records that match the criteria you specify (i.e., *where ThisField = ThatCriterion*). To illustrate the point, let's take a look at the restaurant inspection database mentioned at the beginning of this chapter.[1] First, you can choose what you want to see and the order in which you want to see it. Let's take a look at the names of the various restaurants and the grade they received during their inspections:

> *select name, grade;*
> *from rest*

This command generates a list of all the restaurant names and the grades. But what if you only wanted to see Aponte's Pizza? That is a job for the *where* clause:

> *select name, grade;*
> *from rest;*
> *where name = "APONTE'S PIZZA"*

Acceptable Symbols in a *Where* Clause

=	"Equal to" or "exactly"
<	"Less than"
<=	"Less than or equal to"
>	"Greater than"
>=	"Greater than or equal to"
<>	"Not equal to"

You will no doubt notice a couple things about the *where* clause. First, the criterion—"APONTE'S PIZZA"—is in all capital letters. While it is true that SQL statements are not case sensitive, search criteria are. In other words, if you searched for "Aponte's Pizza" or "aponte's pizza," you wouldn't get any results. Any good database is designed so that the contents of each field are standardized—all lowercase letters, all capital letters or initial capitals only. The second thing you should notice is that the search criterion is in quotation marks. SQL requires that all criteria in character format be enclosed by quotation marks. Criteria for numeric fields are not enclosed by quotation marks.

The previous example uses the equal sign (=) to specify a search criterion. You can also use less than (<) and greater than (>) separately or in conjunction with one another as in less than or equal to (<=) or not equal to (<>). This strategy works well with any numeric data that you have to deal with. Using the Rest database, you can identify those restaurants that failed to attain a score of at least 8,000 (a B) on a given inspection. To do so, you ask the computer to show you all the names and grades of all restaurants that had a score of less than 8,000:

```
select name, grade;
from rest;
where score < 8000
```

Note that you do not have to specify "score" in the *select* line. All the *select* line does is tell the computer what you want to actually see, in this case, the restaurant name and grade.

"Greater than," "less than" and other operators can be used with character data as well. It works alphabetically—"B" is greater than "A" and so on. This feature is especially useful when you want to filter results that are "not equal" to your criterion. For example, you might want to look at only those restaurants that are not defunct (identified by a "D" in the Status field). To do so:

```
select name, grade;
from rest;
where status <> "D"
```

The program searches through the database and displays only those records that do not have a "D" in the Status field.

When filtering with character fields, you have another option as well. You can search for records that only partially match your criterion. In other words, you can look for records that are *like* your criterion rather than equal to it. To perform this task, you use a wildcard (%) in place of one or more parts of your query.[2] For example, there are multiple Burger King restaurants in the database. They are designated "Burger King 1," "Burger King 2" and so on. To generate a list of only Burger King restaurants, you could use the *like* feature:

> *select name, grade;*
> *from rest;*
> *where name like "BURGER KING%"*

Remember that a wildcard matches all characters in a search. So here, the *select* statement tells the program "Show me a table containing the name and grade fields from the Rest table, but only those records where the name is 'BURGER KING[whatever].'" Using *like*, the wildcard can appear at the end of a criterion ("BURGER KING%"), at the beginning ("%CAFÉ"), in the middle ("KENTUCKY%CHICKEN") or at both ends ("%PIZZA%"). It all depends on what you want to see.

It is possible to specify more than one criterion for a filter. In fact, once you get rolling, you will probably want to use this feature often. For example, you can search for all the Hardee's restaurants that received a grade other than A during at least one inspection. To do so,

> *select name, grade;*
> *from rest;*
> *where name like "HARDEE%" and grade <> "A"*

When you use *and*, a record must match both criteria in order to be displayed. If you want to display records that match either criterion, you can use *or*. For example, to display all the Burger King and Hardee's restaurants in town, you would write:

> *select name, grade;*
> *from rest;*
> *where name like "HARDEE%" or name like "BURGER KING%"*

The *and* and *or* options can be used multiple times to tweak your query as much as you desire.

Aggregates and Other "County Things"

You have just explored how to filter fields and records. The second task that databases allow you to perform is the grouping together of records. **Grouping,** sometimes referred to as **aggregating,** involves performing a variety of

Common Mistakes

Beginning SQLers commonly make the mistake of repeating the term "where" when they are using multiple filters in their *where* clause. The word "where" should not be repeated, although the field name must be repeated if used twice.

Incorrect

- *where city = "Baton Rouge" or where city = "New Orleans"*

Incorrect

- *where city = "Baton Rouge" or "New Orleans"*

Correct

- *where city = "Baton Rouge" or city = "New Orleans"*

mathematical functions on a specific field or fields. For example, you might ask the program to *count* the number of records in the database, to *sum* the amount of money given to a specific candidate or to give the *average* age of drivers in each state. The functions that are used to create these groupings are known as **aggregates.** If this explanation sounds a bit technical to you, you're not alone. Just remember that aggregates generate numbers. Richard Mullins, academic adviser to the National Institute for Computer-Assisted Reporting (NICAR), often emphasizes this fact in his teaching by referring to aggregates as simply "county things"—things that count.

In SQL, aggregates are treated for the most part like fields. They are used primarily in the top line of your *select* statement. An aggregate is usually signified by the name of the aggregate, followed by the field to be aggregated in parentheses. For example, if you wanted to generate an average score on the inspections, you would write: *select average(score) from rest.* Finding the lowest or minimum score in the database can be done the same way: *select min(score) from rest.* To count the number of IDs in the restaurant inspection database, you would write: *select count(id) from rest.* The aggregate *count(id)* counts the number of times that the ID field contains data. If there are 500 records and 10 of them are missing ID numbers, *count(id)* would return the number "490."

Instead of counting the number of times that data occurs in one specific field, you can count the number of times that data occurs in *any* field. For this task, you would use *count(*).* For example, each of the 10 records that are missing IDs contain data in at least one other field. If we use the *select* statement *select count(*) from rest,* we get a result of "500," or the number of records in the database.

You can ask for multiple aggregates in a *select* statement the same way you ask for multiple fields, by simply separating the aggregates with commas.

Effect of the *Group by* Clause

select grade, count(grade) from rest

GRADE	CountOfGRADE
A	1411

select grade, count(grade) from rest;
group by grade

GRADE	CountOfGRADE
A	1215
B	169
C	27

Figure 12.2

The top table was generated by combining an aggregate and a nonaggregate (field) without using *group by*. The lower table includes the *group by* statement. Notice the difference between the two tables. The moral of the story: whenever a field and an aggregate are used together, you must include a *group by* statement to tell the computer how you want to view the resulting table.

If you want to ask for the sum of the contributions in the Federal Election Commission (FEC) database as well as the number of contributions and the average contribution, you could write the following: *select sum(contribution), count(contribution), average(contribution) from fec*. The resulting table would display three columns, with one number in each column.

Combining Aggregates and Fields with *Group By*

The real fun (and power) of aggregates comes when you combine them with fields. There are numerous uses for such combinations. In the restaurant inspection story, for instance, you might want a breakdown of the grades—how many As, Bs, and so on were handed out. For this information, you need to ask for the possible grades and a count of the number of times each grade appears. Your answer would consist of a table of two columns. The left column would contain the possible grades (A, B, C), and the right column would contain the number of those grades given (see figure 12.2, lower table). At this point, you can probably write the first line of your *select* statement: *select grade, count(grade) from rest*. It would seem that this *select* statement would give you the lower table in figure 12.2. But that's not what you would get. Instead, the left column would contain the last grade entered into the database—in this case an A—while the right column would contain the number "1411," representing the total number of grades in the database (Figure 12.2, top table). Why? Because you didn't tell the program that you want to *group* your answers together *by* grade.

The **group by** clause tells the computer to group aggregates together by a specific field. In this case, you would write: *group by grade*. This statement indicates that you want to group your "count" by type of grade.

Group by can be one of the most confusing topics to understand for journalists new to SQL. After all, it seems obvious from the first line of the *select* statement that you are asking for two things: a list of grades given and the number of each type given. But remember that computers are not intelligent, at least not yet. All they do is run the commands that are given to them. And those commands must be very precise. Tell the computer to show you the Grade field and count the Grade field, and that's exactly what it does. If you want the answer split up (i.e., grouped), then you need to specify that as well (Figure 12.2).

When you are combining fields and aggregates in a *select* statement, it is crucial that you remember to include *all* selected fields in the *group by* clause. Let's say you want to look at a count not only of the various grades given out, but also of the scores within each grade. You would need to ask the program to generate a list of every possible grade and score combination along with a count representing the number of times that combination occurred. This query would answer, for example, how many As got a score of 9,000, and it would point out whether any Bs were handed out to restaurants with a score of 9,000. Recall that the asterisk (*) acts as a wildcard, allowing you to get a count even if both the grade and score fields are blank. So to run this query, you need to start with the following *select* statement: *select grade, score, count(*) from rest;*. If you run this query as is, you would get an answer that is obviously wrong. It would show the last item in the Grade field ("A"), the last item in the Score field ("9450") and a count representing the total number of records in the database ("1411"). You need to include a *group by* clause. But suppose you only include the Grade field in the *group by*, leaving out the Score field. Your answer would still be incorrect (Figure 12.3). Remember that computers are not intelligent. If you tell a program to group by Grade, it will not necessarily assume that you want to group by Score as well, even though both fields appear in your *select* statement. You need to specify this information yourself, as in the following:

    select grade, score, count(*) from rest;
    group by grade, score

Only with *all* selected fields included in the *group by* clause do you get the correct result.

The *Having* Clause

With the *where* clause we discussed one way of filtering a database—limiting your search to only those records that match certain criteria in one or more fields. But the *where* clause does not work with aggregates. For example, imagine that instead of concentrating on the number of inspections per res-

A Bad *Group By* clause

select grade, score, count(grade) from rest;
group by grade

GRADE	SCORE	CountOfGRADE
A	9450	1215
B	8400	169
C	7000	27

Figure 12.3

When combining more than one field with an aggregate, you must include *every* field in the *group by* clause. If not, you will get an answer that is incorrect—like the one here. This example has grouped only by grade. So it appears that every A grade received a score of 9450, every B a score of 8400 and every C a score of 7000. A quick glance at the database would show that these numbers are not correct.

taurant you want to look at the number of inspections per address. The *select* statement would read as follows:

> *select address, count(address) from rest;*
> *group by address*

Let's further assume that you want to look at only those addresses that have had more than four inspections. If you tried to pull up this information with a *where* clause (e.g., *where count(address) > 4*), you would get an error message. It is not possible to filter aggregates with a *where* clause. For that, you need to use *having*.

Having is a *where* clause for aggregates. The *where* and *having* clauses both come after the *group by* clause in your *select* statement. So using the previous example, you might write the following *select* statement:

> *select address, count(address) from rest;*
> *group by address;*
> *having count(address) > 4*

This *select* statement would return a table consisting of two columns. The left column would contain a list of addresses, while the right column would contain a list of how many inspections were conducted at each address. The table would be filtered so that only those addresses that had more than four inspections appear.

It should also be noted that the *having* clause can be combined with a *where* clause in your *select* statement. For example, imagine that you want to look only at Market Street addresses that have had more than four inspections. For this task, you would add a *where* clause to specify the street name you are seeking, as follows:

> *select address, count(address) from rest;*
> *group by address;*

having count(address) > 4;
where street like "%Market%"

This statement creates a table similar to the previous one, except that only Market Street addresses appear. It also shows how these simple clauses can be used to create powerful and often complex queries.

The *Order by* Clause

Now that we have discussed searching, filtering and aggregating data with Structured Query Language, we can at last approach the concept of **sorting** data. Data within a database can be sorted two very basic ways: ascending (1..2..3 or A..B..C) or descending (3..2..1 or C..B..A). To sort, you simply tell the program which field or fields you wish to sort by and the direction in which you want them sorted. To do so, use the *order by* clause.

Again using the restaurant inspection database, let's sort the data in ascending order by Grade. The following statement would work for this query:

*select * from rest;*
order by grade

Note that you do not have to specify that the data should be sorted in ascending or alphabetical order. Ascending is the default search order. If you want to reverse it—to sort in descending order—you simply add *desc* behind the field name:

*select * from rest;*
order by grade desc

You can specify multiple sort criteria within an *order by* clause. Suppose you want to sort the data by grade first and then alphabetically by the name of the business. You can do this by specifying Grade first, then Name, as in:

*select * from rest;*
order by grade, name

If you want to sort by grade in descending order and name in ascending order, you can do that too:

*select * from rest;*
order by grade desc, name

SQL offers tremendous flexibility in the way you view the results of your search.

SOME SQL SHORTHAND

As you probably have already noticed, SQL can quickly become complex. It can also become a bit cumbersome to write and rewrite your queries. Fortunately, there are some shorthand techniques that make writing SQL a bit easier. The most helpful, even necessary, of these techniques is the use of numbers to reference fields in your *select* statement. For example, imagine that you have written the following *select* statement:

> select name, address, insp__yy, count(*) from rest;
> group by name, address, insp__yy;
> where insp__yy=95;
> order by name, insp__yy desc

SQL provides a useful shortcut to save you the trouble of having to type field names over and over. Instead of using the name, you can use a number that represents the order in which the field appears in your *select* statement. In the previous example, you could use *1* for *name* (the field that appears first in your statement), *2* for *address*, and *3* for *insp__yy*. These numbers can serve as substitutes for the field names in most instances. So you can rewrite this query as:

> select name, address, insp__yy, count(*) from rest;
> group by 1, 2, 3;
> where insp__yy=95;
> order by 1, 3 desc

Note that I said that numbers could be substituted "in most instances." Numbers do not work with the *where* or *having* clauses. Why? Because the computer has a hard time calculating a statement like *where 3=95* or *having 4 > 5*. But in most other instances, the shorthand solution works well.

SUMMARY

SQL seems a bit daunting at first. However, once you practice writing queries you will find that it becomes quite easy to translate basic questions into SQL so that you can actively interview the database. Remember, all you are doing is asking a question of the database. Formulate your question in English. Envision what the answer would look like in table form. Finally, translate that question into an SQL query. A few tips will help you turn your vision of an answer into reality:

> Ask yourself, "What fields and aggregates will be displayed in the answer?" Then place those fields and aggregates in the *select* line in the order you'd like to see them.
>
> Ask yourself, "What table contains the fields I'm interested in?" That table appears in your *from* clause.
>
> Ask yourself, "Did I use both fields and aggregates?" If the answer is yes, you need to include all the fields (but not the aggregates) in a *group by* clause.
>
> Ask yourself, "Do I want to look at only some of the records?" If the answer is yes, you need to include a *where* clause to specify which records you want to include.

Ask yourself, "Do I want to filter by any of the aggregates?" If the answer is yes, you need to include a *having* clause to specify the criteria that aggregates must meet in order to be included.

Ask yourself, "Do I want to sort the results in any way?" If the answer is yes, you need to include an *order by* clause and specify what field or aggregate should be used to sort the results and whether you want those results in ascending or descending order.

In the beginning, you should walk through each step carefully. But before long, you will be (rightly) concentrating more on creating the original question than on the query.

END NOTES

1. The *Morning Star* makes the database available in several formats at <http://starnews.wilmington.net/temp/restnet.html>.

2. It is worth noting that wildcards may vary from one program to another. While the asterisk (*) is the most common wildcard, many SQL programs use the percent sign (%) exclusively in *like* commands.

CHAPTER

13

Mining Government Records for Information

QUERYING BY EXAMPLE

In the previous chapter, we explored query building. We noted that building queries for a database usually takes one of two forms. **Structured Query Language (SQL),** the industry-standard query language used by most database management programs, is the primary method of building queries in programs such as Microsoft Visual FoxPro, Oracle and many others. SQL enables you to translate your human language question into an English-based query that the computer can understand. SQL is powerful and flexible, but it is also difficult

In this chapter you will learn:

- The advantages and disadvantages of querying by example

- How to design a query in Microsoft Access using examples

- How to translate common questions into QBE queries

- How reporters use these skills to do their job more quickly and easily

to learn and use. In an effort to make things a bit easier, other programs—such as Microsoft's Access and Borland's Paradox—allow users to build queries by providing examples. This **Query by Example,** or **QBE,** method involves using your mouse to build a query by selecting from various options on the screen. Querying by example is easier than SQL because the user does not need to learn a new language in order to build a query. As a result, many reporters choose to forgo some of the power of SQL and stick with the ease-of-use offered by QBE. This chapter largely mirrors the previous one, but with an emphasis on query building with QBE rather than SQL.

OVERVIEW OF QBE

Structured Query Language, the language of most database programs, offers reporters many advantages. It forces reporters to take a structured approach

161

to databases—in a sense, to look at them the way that the computer looks at them. It makes it easier for reporters to perceive a query as a logical sequence of events or tasks. It also gives them the power to directly alter those tasks in very detailed ways. But these benefits come at a cost. SQL is a language, and like any language it requires a lot of practice to master. Few reporters have the time to spend learning the intricacies of SQL. Even those who do may find it cumbersome writing line after line when working under deadline pressure. As a result, many prefer to use the query-by-example method.

Querying by example is just what it sounds like. The program allows you to choose your database, fields and aggregates from a list of possible choices. You can decide how to sort the results and finish your query because it provides you with examples for filtering the data. As you might imagine, QBE is a very user-friendly way to ask questions of a database. This chapter is designed to introduce you to the concept of querying by example. Utilizing the restaurants database discussed in the previous chapter, we will explore how to create a query, how to select fields, how to use aggregates, how to apply filters and how to sort your results. In order to demonstrate the concepts, I will be using Microsoft Access 2000. Although some journalists make use of Access's more advanced features such as Web-Enabled Information Sharing, most use the database management program primarily for interviewing databases. The program does allow users to formulate questions in SQL; however, its user-friendly QBE feature is what makes it arguably the most popular database manager among journalists.

INTRODUCTION TO ACCESS 2000

Access 2000 is a powerful database manager that we will only begin to explore in this chapter. Although this text is not meant to be an Access tutorial, I do need to briefly discuss some of the program's features.

Access is a relational database program. Remember that a relational database is a collection of several tables that are intended to be used in conjunction with one another. Most programs, including dBASE and Microsoft's own FoxPro, store individual tables in separate files. These files commonly end with the three-digit extension .dbf (e.g., rest.dbf), which marks them as database files. FoxPro and dBASE then allow users to create queries that utilize one or more of these files while maintaining them as separate files. By contrast, Access uses its own format for storing files. One table or a set of related tables are stored together in a single database file with the extension .mdb (e.g., rest.mdb). Because the tables are stored together, journalists using QBE techniques can pick and choose fields, aggregates and more. It is an easy yet versatile system.

All you need to create a query in Access is an existing .mdb file. If none exist, you can easily create one from existing .dbf files.[1] Once you have an Access database open, the program offers you two ways to create a query: Query Wizard and Design View. **Wizards** are utilities within a program that

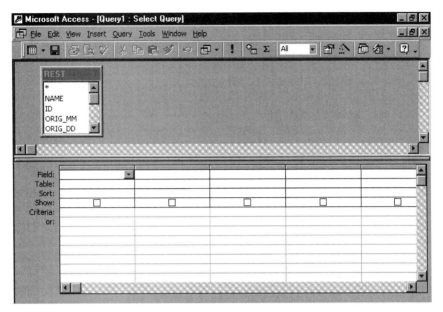

Figure 13.1

The Microsoft Access QBE grid (Design View) allows users to select fields from a list, specify criteria by which to limit the query and decide whether and how to sort the results. The QBE grid shown here contains the *Rest* table used in an investigation of restaurants conducted by the *Morning Star* in Wilmington, N.C.

guide users through potentially difficult tasks in that program. In Access, the Query Wizard takes you through each step in the process of building a query. It is simple to use, but far too limited and time-consuming for day-to-day use. By contrast, Design View is much more versatile. To enter Design View, you must double-click on the "Create a Query in Design View" icon. You will then be asked which tables from the open .mdb file you would like to include in your query.

Once you add the table or tables you are interested in, Access brings up the query **design view,** or **QBE grid,** the area in Access where the user can build queries by example (Figure 13.1). The upper portion of the grid window displays the table or tables that the user selects for use in the query. The lower portion of the screen contains the QBE grid itself. From here, you can begin building your query.

QBE QUERY BUILDING

Whether you are using SQL or QBE, you must go through the three QEQ steps in preparing a query for a database: question, expectation and query.

First, you must come up with a question to ask the database (e.g., "Who gave the most to Bush's election campaign?"). Next, you need to envision what your answer will look like in table format (e.g., "a table of two columns, the left with Bush contributors and the right with the total amount that each person gave, sorted so that the person who gave the most is at the top of the list"). Finally, you build a query that will create a table matching your expected answer. Coming up with a question and an expected answer do not necessarily involve the use of a computer. But how you go about building a query depends on the program that you are using. In Access, the easiest way to build a query is with the QBE grid.

Think of the QBE grid as your query. If you want a field included in your answer, you must specify it in the QBE grid. If you want to use an aggregate, it must appear on the grid. The same applies if you want to use a filter or specify the order in which your results should be sorted. The trick to creating a good query in the QBE grid is matching the grid to your expected answer.

First, let's look at the columns. Each column is designed to hold a specific field from one of the tables within the database. Fields are specified in the top row of the QBE grid. There are two primary ways to add a field to your query. First, you can click on a field in the table and drag it to the Field row. Second, you can double-click on any field in the table and it will automatically appear in the Field row.

Now let's look at the rows:

Field contains the names of the fields that will be used to obtain your answer.

Table contains the name of the table in which the field at the top of the grid column appears.

Sort allows you to sort your results by the field at the top of the grid column. You can specify Ascending, Descending or Not Sorted.

Show allows you to decide whether the field at the top of the grid column will be displayed in your answer. Each column contains a box. If you want the field to be displayed in your answer, leave the box checked. If not, click on the box to indicate that the field should not be displayed.

Criteria allows you to limit the records to be displayed based on the contents of the field at the top of the grid column (similar to the *and* in SQL).

Or allows you to increase the potential number of records to be displayed by specifying additional search criteria (similar to the *or* in SQL).

Total allows you to create an aggregate based on the field at the top of the grid column. This row is not shown initially, but may be activated by the user.

Selecting the Fields You Want

The first step in matching your query to your expected answer is to make sure you include the right fields in the right order. If you want to see names in

Field:	FIRST	LAST	
Table:	REST	REST	
Sort:			
Show:	☑	☑	
Criteria:			
Or:			

Figure 13.2

The QBE grid should be set up to match your expected results. The query here would display a table of two columns. The left column would contain first names in the table, and the right column could contain the last names.

proper speaking order, you would double-click on the First field and then double-click on the Last field. If you want to see names in reverse order, simply double-click on the Last field and then double-click on the First field. The key here is to match your QBE grid to your expected answer (Figure 13.2).

Access also allows you to rearrange the fields once you have selected them. To illustrate the process, let's assume you have selected the name fields in reverse order and you would like to change them to proper speaking order. To reorder the fields:

1. *Highlight the column containing the field you want to move.* Click on the gray area above the Last field. The entire column containing the Last field name should be highlighted.

2. *Grab the column.* Position your cursor in the gray area above the Last field name, click and hold down your left mouse button.

3. *Drag the field to the desired location.* With your left mouse button depressed, move the cursor to the right until the column separator on the right side of the First field is highlighted.

4. *Drop the field.* Release your mouse button. The fields should now be in proper speaking order.

Once you have specified one or more fields, you can run your query. To run a query in Access, click on Query in the menu bar and select Run or simply click on the exclamation point (!) in your toolbar.

Browsing a Database

There are times when you will want to see every field in a database. Rather than forcing you to drag or double-click on every field, Access provides a shortcut. You can use the asterisk as a wildcard. Remember that a **wildcard** is a character that matches all characters or groups of characters, rather than a single character, when doing a search comparison. So here, the wildcard effectively says "all the fields, no matter what their names are." Running a query using the field wildcard is the most common way to browse through a database and should usually be your first step in analyzing data.

To illustrate the point, let's look at the Rest database discussed in the previous chapter. Recall that this database is one that Janet Roberts and Chris Davis of the *Morning Star* in Wilmington, N.C., used in their investigation of local restaurant inspections. Using database management software, they discovered that nearly one out of every three restaurants in New Hanover County skipped at least one inspection during the year prior to the newspaper's investigation.

Here are the steps you follow to browse all fields in the Rest database once you have the database open and the appropriate table selected:

1. *Add the wildcard.*   Double-click on the asterisk (*) located at the top of the field list. "REST.*" appears in the upper left corner of the QBE grid. You will see that the program has automatically placed "REST" in the table row, indicating that the selected fields appear in the Rest table.

2. *Run the query.*   Click on the exclamation point (!) in the toolbar. The contents of the Rest table will be displayed on your screen.

Notice that the QBE grid disappears when you run a query. That is because the program switches automatically from Design View (where the queries are produced) to Datasheet View (where the results are shown). You can also switch between these two views and SQL View (where you can view and alter the program-created SQL) by clicking on View in the menu bar and selecting the appropriate view.[2]

Adding Aggregates and Other "County Things"

In addition to allowing you to simply view records, databases also allow you to group records together. As we noted in the previous chapter, **grouping,** sometimes referred to as **aggregating,** involves performing a variety of mathematical functions on a specific field or fields. For example, you might ask the program to *count* the number of records in the database, to *sum* the amount of money given to a specific candidate or to give the *average* age of drivers in each state. The functions that are used to create these groupings are known as aggregates. If this explanation sounds a bit technical, just remember that aggregates simply generate numbers. Richard Mullins, academic adviser to the National Institute for Computer-Assisted Reporting (NICAR), often emphasizes this fact in his teaching by referring to aggregates as simply "county things"—things that count.

Aggregates are handled a bit differently in QBE than in SQL. In order to add an aggregate, you first need to determine which field that aggregate will be applied to (i.e., which field you want to total, count, average, etc.). Once that field has been added to the QBE grid, you then need to specify how you want to aggregate the data. In Access, you do this by adding a new row, called

Total, to the QBE grid. You can then specify whether you want to group data by that field or use it as an aggregate. For example, let's assume you want to look at the average score of restaurants in the databases. To do so:

1. *Add the field you want to aggregate.* Double-click on the Score field to add it to the QBE grid.

2. *Add the Total row.* Right-click on the QBE grid. A pop-up menu should appear. Select Totals from the menu. The new row should appear with "Group By" in the Score column.

3. *Choose the aggregate you want to use.* Click on the downward arrow to the right of "Group By" in the Score column. A pop-up menu should appear. Select Avg from the menu to generate an average of the Score field.

4. *Run the query.* Click on the exclamation point (!) in the toolbar. The single number that is displayed represents the average score of all restaurants in the database (e.g., "9164.35152374"). If you wanted to get the minimum score instead of an average, you could follow these exact steps but choose Min instead of Avg from the pop-up menu. To count the number of IDs in the database, you would follow these steps but add the ID field instead of the Score field and select Count instead of Avg from the pop-up menu. The aggregate Count counts the number of times that a field contains data. For example, we might do a count of the ID field. If there are 500 records and 10 of them are missing ID numbers, a *count* of ID would return the number "490."

Combining Aggregates and Fields with *Group By*

The real fun (and power) of aggregates comes when you combine them with fields. There are numerous uses for such combinations. In the restaurant inspection story, for instance, you might want a breakdown of the grades—how many As, Bs, and so on were handed out. For this information, you need to ask for the possible grades and a count of the number of times each grade appears. Your answer would look like a table of two columns. The left column would contain the possible grades (A, B, C), and the right column would contain the number of those grades given.[3]

Mixing aggregates and nonaggregates (fields) is dangerous business when you're using SQL, where you must be sure to include all the nonaggregates in a separate *group by* statement or risk getting wildly inaccurate results. Queries that seem obvious to you are often not so obvious to the computer. Consider the example in the previous paragraph. When you ask the computer to show you the grade field and a count of the grade field, it seems obvious that you want the count grouped by grade (i.e., the number of As, Bs, Cs, and so on). But the computer doesn't understand that. You have to tell it to group your count by the Grade field. In fact, you have to group by every nonaggregate

	GRADE	CountOfGRADE
υ	A	1215
	B	169
	C	27

Figure 13.3

This table shows the results of mixing an aggregate (CountOfGRADE) with a non-aggregate (GRADE field) in a query.

that you add to the query. In SQL, you have to remember to perform this step by hand. Query by Example makes it easier by forcing you to designate every field selected as either an aggregate or a nonaggregate.

To illustrate the process, let's build a query to generate a count of the various grades given out. You need to ask the program to generate a list of every possible grade along with a count representing the number of times that grade occurred:

1. *Add the fields.* Double-click on the Grade field to add it to the QBE grid. Then double-click on the Grade field again to add it a second time. Your QBE grid should have "GRADE" in the first and second columns.

2. *Add the Total row.* Right-click on the QBE grid. A pop-up menu should appear. Select Totals from the menu. The new row should appear with "Group By" in all the columns that contain field names.

3. *Choose the aggregate you want to use.* Click on the downward arrow to the right of Group By in the Grade column on the right. A pop-up menu should appear. Select Count from the menu to generate a count of the Grade field. Notice that "Group By" remains in the other column.

4. *Run the query.* Click on the exclamation point (!) in the toolbar. Three rows will appear (Figure 13.3). The left column of each row represents the grade handed out (A, B or C). The right column represents the number of times each grade was handed out.

QBE simplifies the query process by forcing you to communicate your desires to the computer in a way that it "understands." The result, ideally, is a table that matches your expected answer.

Selecting the Records You Want

QBE makes it easy to select the records you want to view—to "filter" the database. In order to create a filter, all you need to do is supply the criteria that records must meet in order to be included. For example, suppose you want to see restaurant names and the inspection grades that they have re-

Acceptable Symbols in a *Where* Clause

=	"Equal to" or "exactly"
<	"Less than"
<=	"Less than or equal to"
>	"Greater than"
>=	"Greater than or equal to"
<>	"Not equal to"

ceived, but only for those records pertaining to Aponte's Pizza. Once you have the database open and the table added, you can follow a few simple steps to build a query in Access's QBE grid:

1. *Add the fields you want to see.* Double-click on the Name field and then the Grade field to add them to the QBE grid.

2. *Add the filter you want to use.* Underneath the Name field in the QBE grid you will see a row for Criteria. Click once in the box to place your cursor there and then type in "Aponte's Pizza."

3. *Run the query.* Click on the exclamation point (!) in the toolbar. All the records with "Aponte's Pizza" in the Name field would be displayed.

Note that unlike SQL, most QBE search criteria are not case sensitive. In other words, if you searched for "APONTE'S PIZZA" or "aponte's pizza," you would still get the correct results.

This example supposes that you are looking for records containing data that exactly matches your search criteria. In other words, it assumes that you are asking to see all the records where *FieldContents=SearchCriterion*. However, there are times when you might want to see all the records containing data that are greater than (>) or less than (<) your criterion. You can limit your search easily by placing the appropriate symbol in front of your criterion. Using the Rest table, you can identify those restaurants that failed to attain a score of at least 8,000 (a B) on a given inspection. Once you have the database open and the table added, follow these steps:

1. *Add the fields you want to see.* Double-click on the Name field and then the Grade field to add them to the QBE grid.

2. *Add the field you want to filter by.* Double-click on the Score field to add it to the QBE grid.

3. *Hide the filter field.* Even though you want to filter by the Score field, you do not have to include it in your results. The Show row contains boxes with checkmarks in them. If a box is checked, it will be shown. Click in the box below the Score field to remove the

checkmark and tell the program that you do not want it to show the Score field.

4. *Add the filter you want to use.*   In this case, you want to see all those records with scores of less than 8,000. Underneath the Score field in the QBE grid you will see a row for Criteria. Click once in the box to place your cursor there and then type in "<8000" (don't put a comma in the number).

5. *Run the query.*   Click on the exclamation point (!) in the toolbar. The names and grades of all records with scores of less than 8,000 will be displayed.

"Greater than," "less than" and other operators can be used with character data as well. The procedure works alphabetically—"B" is greater than "A" and so on. This feature is especially useful when you want to filter results that are "not equal" to your criterion. For example, you might want to look at only those restaurants that are not defunct (identified by a "D" in the Status field).

When filtering with character fields, you have another option as well. You can search for records that only partially match your criterion. In other words, you can look for records that are *like* your criterion rather than equal to it. For this search, you use a wildcard in place of one or more parts of your query. In SQL, the wildcard was a percentage sign (%). In QBE, the wildcard is an asterisk (*). You can use this asterisk in place of all or part of a specific criterion. For example, multiple Burger King restaurants in the database are designated "Burger King 1," "Burger King 2" and so on. To generate a list of only Burger King restaurants, you could use the wildcard feature:

1. *Add the fields you want to see.*   Double-click on the Name field and then the Grade field to add them to the QBE grid.

2. *Add the filter you want to use.*   In the Criteria row of the Name column, type "Burger King*." You don't need to enclose the field in quotation marks; the program will do this for you, writing the criteria out properly (i.e., *like "Burger King*"*).

3. *Run the query.*   Click on the exclamation point (!) in the toolbar. The Name and Grade field of all records that reference any of the Burger Kings in the database will be displayed.

Remember that a wildcard matches all characters in a search. So here, the query tells the program to show all the records where the Name field begins with Burger King, regardless of how it ends. The wildcard can appear at the end of a criterion ("BURGER KING*"), at the beginning ("*CAFÉ"), in the middle ("KENTUCKY*CHICKEN") or at both ends ("*PIZZA*"). It all depends on what you want to see.

It is possible to specify more than one criterion for a filter. In fact, once you get rolling, you will probably want to utilize this feature often. For example, here's how you can search for all the Hardee's restaurants that got a grade other than A during at least one inspection:

1. *Add the fields you want to see.* Double-click on the Name field and then the Grade field to add them to the QBE grid.

2. *Add the filters you want to use.* You want to add criteria in two different columns, Name and Grade. In the Criteria row of the Name column, type "Hardee*." In the Criteria row of the Grade column, type "grade <> A."

3. *Run the query.* Click on the exclamation point (!) in the toolbar. The Name and Grade field of all records that reference any of the Hardee's restaurants that also got a grade other than A will be displayed.

When you place criteria in the Criteria row, a record must match *all* those criteria in order to be displayed. If you place criteria in the Or row, a record can match *any* of the criteria in order to be included. Figure 13.4 shows some of the different ways to filter records in the QBE grid.

As is the case with most of these new concepts, filters may seem a bit confusing at first. Although the use of a single filter (e.g., "Aponte's Pizza") is rather straightforward, multiple filters can be a bit more complicated. But with a little practice, you will see that even multiple filters will soon become easy to use.

Sorting the Results

Now that we have discussed searching, filtering and aggregating data with QBE, we can approach the concept of sorting data. Data within a database can be sorted two very basic ways: ascending (1..2..3 or A..B..C) or descending (3..2..1 or C..B..A). To sort, you simply tell the program which field or fields you wish to sort by and the direction in which you want them sorted. Again using the restaurant inspection database, let's sort the data in ascending order by grade. Here's how:

1. *Add the wildcard.* Double-click on the asterisk (*) located at the top of the field list. "REST*" appears in the upper left corner of the QBE grid. You will see that the program has automatically placed "REST" in the table row, indicating that the selected fields appear in the Rest table.

2. *Add the field you want to sort by.* Double-click on the Grade field.

3. *Hide the sort field.* Even though you want to sort by the Grade field, you do not have to include it in your results. Click in the box located in the Show row below Grade to remove the checkmark and tell the program that you do not want it to show the Grade field.

4. *Select the sort order.* Click on the arrow in the Sort row on the right side of the Grade column. Select Ascending from the choices.

5. *Run the query.* Click on the exclamation point (!) in the toolbar. The contents of the Rest table will be displayed on your screen

Query #1: Display the name and grade of records for Aponte's Pizza

Field:	FIRST	GRADE	
Table:	REST	REST	
Sort:			
Show:	☑	☑	☐
Criteria:	"Aponte's Pizza"		
Or:			

Query #2: Display the name and grade of records for restaurants with a score under 8,000

Field:	FIRST	GRADE	SCORE
Table:	REST	REST	REST
Sort:			
Show:	☑	☑	☐
Criteria:			< 8000
Or:			

Query #3: Display the name and grade of records for all Burger King restaurants

Field:	FIRST	GRADE	
Table:	REST	REST	
Sort:			
Show:	☑	☑	☐
Criteria:	Like "Burger King*"		
Or:			

Query #4: Display the name and grade of records for all Hardee's that didn't get an A

Field:	FIRST	GRADE	
Table:	REST	REST	
Sort:			
Show:	☑	☑	☐
Criteria:	Like "Hardee*"	<> "A"	
Or:			

Query #5: Display the name and grade of records forall Hardee's and Burger Kings

Field:	FIRST	GRADE	
Table:	REST	REST	
Sort:			
Show:	☑	☑	☐
Criteria:	Like "Hardee*"		
Or:	Like "Burger King*"		

Query #6: Display all fields for all restaurants inspected or established in September

Field:	REST*	INSP_MM	ORIG_MM
Table:	REST	REST	REST
Sort:			
Show:	☑	☐	☐
Criteria:			
Or:		9	9

sorted in ascending order by grade. Because Grade is a character field, the data is sorted in alphabetical order, with the As at the top of the results table.

In QBE, sorting is just a matter of telling the computer which fields you want to sort by and whether you want them in ascending or descending order.

You can also choose to sort by more than one field. For example, you can add the Name field to our previous sort in order to sort the results alphabetically by the restaurant name. To do so:

1. *Switch to Design View.* Either click on the View tool on the left side of your toolbar or click on View in the Menu bar and select Design View.

2. *Add the new sort criterion.* Double-click on the Name field to add it to the QBE grid.

3. *Hide the new sort field.* Click in the Show row box below Name to remove the checkmark and tell the program that you do not want it to show the Name field.

4. *Select the sort order.* Click on the arrow in the Sort row on the right side of the Name column. Select Ascending from the choices.

5. *Run the query.* Click on the exclamation point (!) in the toolbar. The sorted contents of the Rest table will be displayed.

Access sorts according to the order in which your sort criteria are selected. Because Grade is the leftmost sort column, the program sorts alphabetically by grade first. Then it sorts each grade alphabetically by name. Thus, all the restaurants with As are displayed alphabetically, followed by an alphabetical listing of the restaurants with Bs, and finally the restaurants with Cs.

SUMMARY

Although QBE is easier to understand than SQL, it can still seem confusing. Just remember the basic steps of query building. You are interviewing the database. Formulate your question in English. Envision what the answer would look like in table form. Finally, translate that question into a QBE query. A few tips will help you turn your vision of an answer into reality:

1. Ask yourself, "What fields will be displayed in the answer?" Then place those fields in the QBE grid in the order you'd like to see them.

◀ **Figure 13.4**

The six query examples here illustrate some of the versatility of Access's QBE grid. You can look at records that match one criterion or multiple criteria. You can also choose to look at records that match all your criteria or at records that match any one of your criteria.

2. Ask yourself, "Will aggregates be displayed in the answer?" If the answer is yes, add the fields that you plan to aggregate and right click to add and adjust the Totals row.

3. Ask yourself, "Do I want to look at only some of the records?" If the answer is yes, you need to include the Criteria row and some examples to specify which records you want to include.

4. Ask yourself, "Do I want to sort the results in any way?" If the answer is yes, you need to specify what fields or aggregates should be used to sort the results and whether you want those results in ascending or descending order.

Answer these questions, and you will find yourself interviewing databases much sooner than you might think.

NOTES

1. To create a .mdb file from existing .dbf files in Access, simply click on File in the menu bar, select New and choose Database from among the various options. You will be asked to give your new .mdb file a name and to save it. Next, click on File in the menu bar again, select Get External Data and choose Import. At the bottom of your screen, change Files of Type to the appropriate .dbf file type (commonly "dBASE IV") and double-click on the table you want to add to your database. You may repeat the Import process to add additional tables to the .mdb file.

2. Access also allows you to switch views from the toolbar.

3. For an example, see figure 12.2 in the previous chapter.

14

Searching for the Expected and the Unexpected
LINKING DATABASES

David Milliron of the *Atlanta Journal-Constitution* had a problem on his hands. The state of Georgia has a law requiring background checks on certified teachers. When teachers apply for certification or recertification, they are required to disclose whether or not they had been convicted of a crime other than minor traffic violations. But Milliron and the staff at the newspaper knew that no one ever checked to make sure that teachers were telling the truth on their applications. Milliron observed,

In this chapter you will learn:

■ What relational databases are and how to use them properly

■ How to match tables that were not intended to be matched

■ Ways to identify or designate key fields

■ Methods for joining databases in SQL and QBE

> We knew that there was a major loophole in the state's background check procedure. The burden of conducting the background checks isn't at the licensure end, but rather up to the local school districts—all 180 of them in Georgia. And the law says that only when you're newly hired at a school district as a certified employee shall a background check be conducted, so we knew there was the potential for a lot of people to have grand-fathered in because as long as they remain in the same system and lie on their re-certification application, they potentially go undetected.[1]

The problem: how could the team determine whether teachers were falling through cracks in the system and, if so, identify those teachers? After all, it wasn't like the journalists could obtain a database of criminal teachers. They were looking for data that the state department of education and local school districts had missed.

But Milliron had an idea where to look. From his experience with other computer-assisted reporting projects, he knew that government agencies were voracious data collectors. He realized that the state must maintain a database of certified teachers and another of criminals. In order to answer his questions, he would need to join the two databases together. Wherever there was a match, he would have a teacher who was also a criminal.

USING RELATIONAL DATABASES

Chapter 11 defines a database as a group of related data organized into one or more tables stored for use by a computer and intended to be analyzed by database management software. A single stand-alone table of data is known as a nonrelational, or flat-file, database. It is designed to be used independently. A computerized address book is a good example of a nonrelational database. By contrast, a relational database is a collection of two or more tables meant to be used in conjunction. They are *related* to each other. Consider the list of traffic offenses maintained by your state's department of motor vehicles. Each time a person receives a traffic ticket, a great deal of information is gathered by the state—first name, last name, address, city, state, zip, violation, location and so on. Many people receive more than one traffic violation.

Keeping all this information in a flat-file database means lots of wasted time, money and storage space. Each time a person receives a traffic ticket, state employees would have to enter every bit of data pertaining to both the offense and the driver. This procedure would in effect duplicate information that the state already has in its driver's license database. Instead of spending a lot of effort in duplicating this information, the state could easily reference it by including just the offender's license number. Later, when the information is needed, users could cross-reference the two tables (Figure 14.1).

MATCHMAKING

Linking two tables within a database involves little more effort than querying a stand-alone table. The real fun comes when you start to explore the possibility of linking two tables that were not originally intended to be used together. This kind of matchmaking lies at the core of many top computer-assisted reporting stories. Matching allows you to do stories that compare accidents against traffic tickets to explore correlations between those who get tickets and those involved in accidents; compare drunk-driving convictions with school bus drivers to look for drunk school bus drivers; compare lists of voters in the last election to Social Security Administration death records in an effort to uncover voter fraud (people who voted after they died); compare lists of campaign contributors to the voting records of public officials to explore connections between who gave money to a candidate and how that candidate voted once in office. As you can see, the possibilities are limited only by your imagination.

Driver's License Table	Offenses Table
LicenseNum	ReportNum
First	*LicenseNum*
Middle	Violation
Last	Section
Street	Thoroughfare
Apartment	Type
City	Intersection
State	Distance
Zip	Direction
Birthdate	Speed
Issued	Accident
Expires	AccidentRepNum
Sex	
Height	
Eyes	
Class	
Endorse	
Restrict	
Donor	

Figure 14.1

This figure lists fields in hypothetical driver's license and traffic offense tables. In a flat-file database, all 30 unduplicated fields would have to be stored in a single table. A relational database allows you to split the fields into two separate tables. When a driver receives a citation, data personnel just need to enter his or her license number. The traffic offense table can then be cross-referenced with the driver's license table to get the remaining information.

Consider the example used to introduce this chapter. David Milliron of the *Atlanta Journal-Constitution* wanted to uncover information about school employees in the state of Georgia who had criminal records. He knew that the state didn't maintain a database of criminal school employees. Instead, he would have to locate a database of criminals and compare it to a database of school employees.

Milliron tracked down the databases that would be required to perform the analysis. First, he wanted a list of everyone who had been convicted of a crime in the state of Georgia. This information actually came from two databases— one containing the names of people who spent time in a state prison or correctional facility (since 1971) and another of people who had been paroled or sentenced to probation (since 1978).[2] He also needed a list of everyone who worked in the Georgia public school system. Again, he obtained the information from two databases—one containing the names of licensed teachers and another containing the names of other public school employees.

After cleaning up the data, Milliron used Microsoft Access to analyze the records. He was amazed by the results: 1.5 percent of all currently employed K–12 school workers had committed crimes serious enough to warrant time in a state prison or correctional facility or to warrant a sentence of parole or probation. These figures formed the lead of the *Journal-Constitution*'s story, written by Doug Cummings:

> Parents who assume all teachers, school bus drivers and other school employees have been checked for a criminal past are wrong.
>
> Despite a 1994 state law requiring fingerprinting and criminal background checks, nearly 3,000 school employees in Georgia have criminal records. That's about 1.5 percent of public school employees.[3]

The *Journal-Constitution* story—and a concurrent special by Richard Belcher and Chris Cantergiani on project cosponsor WSB-TV—could not have been done without some creative matchmaking.

USING KEY FIELDS

When you join two tables, you are looking for matches. In the *Journal-Constitution* case, the team essentially wanted to join a table of school employees to a table of criminals. Whenever a person in the school employees table also appeared in the criminals table, the team had a match. The program stores all these matches in a new temporary table of criminal school employees.

Now at this point you might be asking yourself how a database program can tell whether the person in Table A is the same person in Table B. Typically the program uses a **key field,** a field that uniquely identifies each record in a table, usually so that it can be cross-referenced with another table or tables. In a table of school employee records, each record (an entry referring to a specific employee) might be uniquely identified by that employee's social security number.[4] Likewise, each record in the table of criminals might also be uniquely identified by a social security number. In this case, the social security number field would serve as a key field. To join the two tables together, the program need only look for instances where a social security number in Table A matched a social security number in Table B.

MATCHING WITHOUT A KEY FIELD

Unfortunately for the investigative team in the Georgia case, the state department of education decided to **redact,** or delete, the social security number field before turning over the school employees table. Most Freedom of Information legislation allows government agencies to redact fields in instances where that information might harm any interest protected by exemptions under that legislation. Georgia department of education officials felt that the newspaper's request was such an instance despite the state attorney general's advice to the contrary.

As the computer-assisted reporting expert on the team, Milliron had to figure out a way to match two tables without using social security numbers. He needed a **composite key field,** two or more fields used together to uniquely identify a record in much the same way as a single key field. The initial response might be to simply match names from the two databases. But an individual's name is not necessarily unique. James Johnson the teacher may not be the same James Johnson who was convicted of cruelty to children. Adding individual addresses would limit the number of incorrect matches, but it would also mean missing anyone who had moved or had maintained two or more addresses. Instead, Milliron chose to include the date of birth field. Even so, he recognized that errors could creep in. For example, you might have two people who shared the same birth date and the same name, particularly if it were a common name. Without a key field, the team needed to take special care to avoid false matches. As Milliron describes it,

> Our analysis involved matching names and dates of births, and discarding matches with slight inconsistencies. I created what I call a "demographic" table of each database. The eyeballs did the final absolute cuts.

In this case, the computer simply couldn't be trusted to handle the job. The journalists needed to use their skill as reporters to make the ultimate decision of whether a person in Table A was the same person in Table B.

In ideal circumstances, tables should be matched using a key field such as a social security number. If no key field exists, matches can still be made when a combination of fields can uniquely identify a person. However, extra care must be taken to ensure that no false matches are made—to guarantee that the person you have named as a criminal school employee is in fact both a criminal and a school employee. The computer can't do this job for you. You will have to make these decisions for yourself. Just remember to be conservative in your matching. If you have any doubt that the match is a true one, make a few phone calls. If you can't absolutely verify the accuracy of a match, then you must discard it from your analysis.

JOINING TABLES IN SQL

Joining tables in SQL involves three basic steps: (1) specifying the fields and where they come from; (2) specifying the tables to be joined; and (3) specifying the key fields that will be used. These steps are handled by three different parts of the *select* statement: *select, from* and *where.*

SQL Joining: *Select*

Remember that every SQL query begins with the word "select." The *select* portion of your statement allows you to specify which fields or aggregates you want to see and the order in which you want to see those fields. When using two or more tables you need to be very specific, telling the computer not only what fields you want but also the tables in which they are found. To write this *select* statement, place the table name first, followed by a period and then the field name. Here's an example: *select employees.first, employees.last, employees.years, criminals.offense;*. This statement effectively tells the computer "show me a table" that consists of the First, Last and Years fields from the employees database and the Offense field from the criminals database.

Note that you will need to use both the table name and field name anywhere you would normally reference only the field name in your *select* statement. This procedure is true of all clauses in the *select* statement. For example, instead of writing "order by last," as you would in a nonjoined statement, you would have to write "order by employees.last." Although the program you are using may accept some field names without the table name—principally those that appear in one table only—you are opening the door to error in your data analysis if you don't use both names.

SQL Joining: *From*

The *from* clause tells the program which tables will be used in the join. While this step may appear a bit redundant given that you have already specified the table names, it is necessary. In fact, there are instances in which an experienced journalist will join to a second table even if he or she does not select any fields from that table.[5]

The *from* clause in an SQL join looks much like the *from* clause in a query, except that multiple tables are separated by commas. In this example, *from employees, criminals;*, the first table name is followed by a comma and then the second table name.

SQL Joining: *Where*

The *where* clause forms the heart of joins in SQL. It is here that you tell the computer what key fields you will be using to join the two databases. Remember that a join is nothing more than a search for matches. A new table is created that shows the results wherever the contents of the key field in Table A match the contents of the key field in Table B. Here's an example: *where employees.ssn = criminals.ssn;*. If a social security number in the employees table matches a social security number in the criminals table, you have a match.

Remembering to include a key field match in your *where* clause is crucial. Otherwise, the computer does not know how to look for matches. Without instructions, it will create a **Cartesian product,** sometimes called a **cross product,** which matches every record in Table A with every record in Table B. When Milliron joined the table of criminals with the table of school employees properly, using a composite key field, he discovered 2,931 matches. If he had not included any key field, he would have gotten more than 200 billion matches—the 1,153,759 criminal records multiplied by the 187,071 school employee records. Obviously there would not be 200 billion criminal school employees in the state of Georgia. Whenever the number of matches that you receive is dramatically higher than you expected, you probably have a problem with your key field.

Note that the *where* clause can still be used as a filter even when it is used to join two tables together. You utilize filters the same way you would specify multiple filter criteria using *and*. For example, if you wanted to look only at the records of those employees convicted of perjury, you might write, *where employees.ssn = criminals.ssn and criminals.offense="PERJURY";*. Again, remember that there is no need to repeat the "where" when using multiple criteria (see chapter 12 for examples).

SQL Joining: A Complete Query

Putting all the pieces together, let's look at an entire query as it would appear in a program such as Microsoft Visual FoxPro. Suppose you want to see the first name, last name, years of service and criminal offense of all school employees who were convicted on charges of drug or firearms possession, sorted in alphabetical order by last names. The query might appear as follows:

> *select employees.first, employees.last, employees.years, criminals.offense;*
> *from employees, criminals;*
> *where employees.ssn = criminals.ssn and criminals.ssn like "%POSS%";*
> *order by employees.last*

This query specifies the source of each field, the tables to be joined and the key field used to join them.

SQL Joining: Shorthand

You may have noticed that joining two or more tables together requires a lot of extra typing. Luckily Microsoft FoxPro and many other programs that handle SQL allow you to use a kind of shorthand in joins. This shorthand method enables you to specify abbreviations for tables instead of repeatedly typing table names throughout your *select* statement. Instead, you can use just one or two letters to identify a table. In order to use this technique, you need to specify the shorthand table names immediately after the actual table names in your *from* clause. Here's an example: *from employees e, criminals c*. This *from* clause would allow you to use the letter *e* for employees and *c* for criminals throughout your *select* statement. Thus, the earlier *select* statement would appear as

> *select e.first, e.last, e.years, c.offense;*
> *from employees e, criminals c;*
> *where e.ssn = c.ssn and c.ssn like "%POSS%";*
> *order by e.last*

The longer your *select* statement, the more typing—not to mention time— you save by using abbreviations.

Note that although you do not have to use the first initial of the table, doing so makes it easier to remember which shorthand reference matches which table. When two tables share the same first initial (e.g., "criminals" and "customers") you can choose to either use a different single initial for each (e.g., "c" and "u") or, if you find it easier, use two letters to identify each table (e.g., "cr" and "cu").

JOINING TABLES WITH QBE

At first glance, joining tables seems much easier in a Query by Example environment than it is in SQL. After all, programs like Microsoft Access keep track of everything for you. You don't have to specify which field comes from which table each time you use that field. The program will track the tables you are joining as well, ensuring that each is included in the join. Unfortunately, all these nice features require that the tables you intend to join be contained within the same database. Thus, while working with a preexisting relational database—one that was designed for the purpose of cross-referencing tables—is quite easy in a QBE environment, working with tables that were not designed to be used together can be a bit trickier.

QBE: Tables Designed to Be Joined

First, let's look at databases containing tables that were designed to be used together. Access and other QBE programs make working with such databases a snap. Because these tables were designed to be used together, they were given key fields so that you could search for matches. When these key fields share the same name, as they usually do, Access performs the join for you. All you need to do is specify the tables to be used once, and you can proceed as you would with any other query.

For example, let's imagine you want to use a department of transportation Access database (see figure 14.1) to generate a list of the home cities of drivers and the number of violations per city. To do so, you would have to:

1. *Open the database file.* Click on File in the menu bar and select Open. Locate the .mdb file and double-click on it.

2. *Enter Design View.* Double-click on the "Create a Query in Design View" icon. You will then be asked which tables from the open .mdb file you would like to include in your query.

3. *Select the tables to be queried.* Double-click on each table that you want to add to the query (e.g., "Driver's Licenses" and "Offenses"). Notice that Access will create a line connecting the key fields between the two tables.

4. *Complete the query.*   Double-click on the City field in the Driver's Licenses table and the Violation field in the Offenses database. Include the Total row and select Count under the Violation column.

5. *Run the query.*   Click on the exclamation point (!) in the toolbar. The contents of your join will be displayed on your screen with cities in the left column and a count of offenses in the right column.

Access takes care of all the details for you. As a result, querying a preexisting relational database is no more difficult than querying a stand-alone table.

QBE: Tables Not Designed to Be Joined

In order to create a QBE query in Access that draws data from tables that were not designed to be joined, both of those tables must first be placed into a relational database file. Recall that a relational database is a collection of two or more tables intended to be used together. In Access, relational databases are stored as Microsoft database (.mdb) files. Thus, using Access to join tables that were not designed to be joined involves three steps: (1) creating a new database; (2) importing the tables into that database; and (3) specifying the key field or fields that allow those tables to be joined.

Step 1: *Create the new database*
   Creating a new database in Access is a relatively simple process. For example, let's assume you want to create a new database called Criminal Teachers. To do so:

1. *Create the database.*   Click on File in the menu bar and select New. If the "Database" choice is highlighted, just click OK. A pop-up window should appear.

2. *Name the database.*   Type in the name of the database (e.g., "Criminal Teachers") and click on Create. Note that you do not need to specify the extension .mdb. The program will add that for you.

The database is created and a new pop-up window appears to help you through the next step of database creation.

Step 2: *Import tables into the new database*
   Once the database is created, you need to add tables to it. To do so:

1. *Start the import process.*   Click on File in the menu bar and select Get External Data and then Import Tables. The Import pop-up window should appear.

2. *Find the tables to add.*   Use your mouse to locate the tables on your hard drive. Note that you will have to identify the type of tables you are importing (e.g., .dbf files) by using the Files of Type bar at the bottom. Usually, .dbf files can be imported as "dBase IV" files.

3. *Add the tables.*   Double-click on the file to add the table to your database. A message should appear telling you that the table has been successfully added.

Step 3: *Specify the relationships*

Once the tables are in the database, you still need to tell the program how they are related to one another. In Access, like in most QBE programs, you need to specify this relationship only once. Here's how:

1. *Specify the tables.*   Since one database may consist of many different tables, you will need to specify which databases will be linked to one another. Click on Tools in the menu bar and select Relationships. The Relationships pop-up window should appear along with a list of the tables in the database. Double-click the tables you want to relate.

2. *Specify the key field(s).*   Remember that tables are related (or joined) by key fields. To specify a key field, simply click on the field in the first table and drag it over the second table. Note that you can specify a composite key field by holding down the Control key and clicking on one field at a time. When all the fields are highlighted, drag them on top of the second table. The Edit Relationships pop-up window should appear, and the fields you selected will be in the left column.

3. *Specify the relationships.*   Once the key fields from the first table have been defined, you need to define the key fields in the second table and tell the program which fields are connected to which. The Edit Relationships pop-up window already has the key fields from the first table in it. Use your mouse to select a matching field (from the second table) for each field selected. Click on each row in the right column to select the appropriate matching fields.

4. *Create the join.*   Click on the Create button. The joined fields should now be connected by lines from one table to the other. Don't worry if you make a mistake; you can always repeat the process to reedit the relationships.

Once the relationships are specified, the join is complete. You can then go about querying the joined tables as though they were one flat-file database.

SUMMARY

The ability to link unrelated tables represents a potent weapon in the computer-assisted reporter's arsenal. It gives reporters the opportunity to uncover information that once would have been nearly impossible to find. Take, for example, a voter fraud story done in 1990 by George Landau and Tim Novak of the *St. Louis Post-Dispatch*. The reporters linked a database of registered voters to other databases containing death certificates. Using these databases, they produced a list containing dozens of "dead voters." With a little old-fashioned shoe leather reporting, they were able to determine that some of these people hadn't begun to vote until after they were dead. The first of the resulting stories began like this:

> A man named Admiral Wherry, an army veteran who owned a barbecue pit and tire repair shop in East St. Louis, died more than two years ago.
>
> But that didn't stop him from voting in the Illinois Democratic primary on March 20.[6]

The story prompted immediate investigations by the U.S. Justice Department, the Illinois attorney general and the state election board.

Once you have the data in hand, joining two or more databases is simply a matter of (1) figuring out the key fields or deriving a composite key field; and (2) specifying those fields to the program you are using. Once you do these two steps, you can ask the same kinds of questions that you do with a flat-file database. The only difference is that the answers could prove much more interesting.

NOTES

1. David Milliron, personal communication, November 8, 1999.
2. Anyone who spent time in prison (the first database) also showed up in the second database. The prison records were, therefore, effectively a subset of the parole and probation database.
3. Doug Cummings, "Schools Employ Thousands with Criminal Records," *Atlanta Journal-Constitution*, November 4, 1999. Available online at <http://www.accessatlanta.com/news/1999/11/04/schools.html>.
4. The social security number is probably the best key field when it is available. Each social security number in the United States identifies one and only one person. In fact, the social security number is often referred to as an individual's federal identification number.
5. For example, a journalist might join a table of criminals to a table of school employees, but then examine only the name and address fields from the employees table. The criminals table is used only to pinpoint those school employees who are also criminals.
6. Cited in George Landau, "Ghostbusting in East St. Louis," *Uplink: The Forum for Computer-Assisted Reporting*, October 1990, 1.

I

Computer Basics

A computer is nothing more than a tool. It is an extension of the human body—in this case the brain—that allows us to perform tasks more quickly and easily and with greater power than our physical form permits. Even a simple tool like a hammer requires some training to use correctly. Any carpenter can tell you that a hammer should not be held like a club. Proper positioning of the thumb behind the shaft improves performance, allowing us to drive nails with greater strength and precision. A computer is obviously a much more complicated tool, and it requires more complicated instruction. But it is still just a tool.

Consider another intricate bit of machinery, the automobile. Sometimes we take for granted the difficulty involved in properly operating a car. After all, most of us grew up around the machines. We know they have four tires, a steering wheel, seats, a glove compartment, a rearview mirror and the like. We know they might have optional equipment, such as a CD player, air conditioning or tinted windows. We know where the gas goes, how to monitor when we need to refill the tank and more or less why we need to worry about it. What lies beneath the hood arguably makes up the most important part of an automobile, but we do not need to study internal fuel combustion or electrodynamics in order to understand how to operate one. The same is true of a computer.

This appendix concentrates on providing you with an overview of the computer. It will be necessary to become familiar with the machine's components, just as most of us know that automobiles have a transmission and cylinders even if we do not necessarily understand precisely what they do. However, my emphasis will be those aspects of computers that will help you learn how to operate them properly.

INSIDE THE COMPUTER

When many journalists look at a computer, they see a fancy video typewriter in a box. But that box contains a variety of components, often manufactured by independent companies and simply assembled by the computer maker. Imagine buying a car for which every item involved some sort of a decision. How big do you want the seats to be? What size gas tank would you prefer? Would you like two, four or eight headlights? Ironically, the only option you do not have is color. Nearly all computers come in beige.

The hardware, the physical components of the computer and the machines attached to it, represents potential. The computer can do nothing without software, programmed instructions that tell the computer what to do. The single most important piece of software on any computer is its **operating system (OS),** a group of interdependent programs that orchestrate the operation of the hardware. Unix, VMS, Windows NT and Windows 98 are all examples of operating systems. Computers manufactured by IBM initially utilized an operating system known as DOS, or disk operating system. Many users found its text-only environment cumbersome, which prompted Microsoft to create a graphical user interface to DOS called Windows. A **graphical user interface** (G-U-I or GOO-ee) is not an operating system in itself, but rather provides humans with windows, buttons and other graphical elements that make accessing software easier. GUIs make frequent use of **pull-down menus,** program interfaces that the user can pull down from a menu bar at the top of the screen, and **pop-up windows,** program interfaces that pop up in the middle of the screen. Most newer operating systems now come complete with a graphical user interface.

The Hardware

At its most basic level, a computer accepts commands or data from a user, stores the data either temporarily or semipermanently, processes it and communicates the results. Different components handle each of these functions: input, memory, secondary storage, processing and output.

Input **Input devices** accept commands or data from the user. The computer keyboard and mouse both serve as input devices. Others include scanners, pen pads or modems.

Memory and Secondary Storage Imagine that your computer is a desk. Those items that you want to have rapid access to, you keep on top of the desk. This system is like the computer's **random access memory (RAM),** which stores data electronically. The more RAM you have, the larger is the desktop on which you can temporarily keep items. Data stored electronically disappears when the power is turned off. In order to keep data more

Note: Although Microsoft's Windows I.11 and all earlier versions of the software were simply graphical user interfaces (GUIs) and not full-fledged operating systems, Windows 95 and later releases comprise operating systems as well as GUIs.

permanently, it must be stored in some other fashion, usually magnetically or optically. **Secondary storage devices** provide the capability to keep data even after power has been turned off. Think of items stored inside a desk, where there is more space, but more time is required to access them. The computer's hard drive, floppy disk drives, CD-ROM drives, magneto-optical drives and tape backup systems are all secondary storage devices.

Processing   The **central processing unit (CPU)** is the brain of the computer; it executes instructions and performs arithmetic or logical operations. In modern computers, the CPU is stored on a single silicon chip usually with some basic operating instructions stored as read-only memory (ROM). CPU speed is gauged in terms of **megahertz (MHz),** a unit of measure equal to 1 million cycles per second. The higher the number of megahertz, generally the faster the computer. Computer chip architecture also affects how fast a CPU processes instructions. Intel has set the operating instruction standard in personal computer CPUs with its 386, 486 and Pentium family of chips. Each new chip generation represents an increase in performance and capability. Because of this, a 75 MHz Pentium may actually be faster than a 100 MHz 486 chip.

Output   Output devices allow the computer to communicate processed data beyond the CPU and storage devices. The two most common output devices are the monitor and printer.

Technically, input, output and secondary storage devices are not part of the actual computer even though they may be housed in the same case. They are **peripherals,** although that term is more commonly used to refer to input, output and secondary storage devices that are external to the casing that houses the CPU.

The Software

Most software used in computer-assisted reporting falls into one of five categories: communication, spreadsheet, database, mapping and statistics.

Communication Software   **Communication software** encompasses a variety of programs designed to allow one computer to communicate with one or more other computers. Such programs might allow your computer to transmit and receive data files, browse graphical World Wide Web pages or even function as a terminal attached to some distant mainframe computer.

Spreadsheet Software   **Spreadsheet software,** sometimes referred to simply as "spreadsheets," are programs designed to perform calculations on numerical data. Spreadsheets organize data into columns and rows, much like an accountant would organize a ledger. Most journalists use the programs for rapid and repeated mathematical calculations as well as for sorting smaller electronic records. However, spreadsheets can also perform a variety of statistical and trigonometric tasks from *t*-tests to Fourier Analysis.

Database Management Software   **Database management software,** often abbreviated to "databases," comprises those programs that not only permit sorting of data, but also allow users to meaningfully filter and aggregate data. A spreadsheet can allow a user to sort a simple list of crimes alphabetically by state. A database manager can handle a larger set of data. It also grants the ability to limit that list to only those records from a certain state or to easily count the number of crimes per state.

Mapping Software   **Mapping software** allows users to take information stored in a database and depict it on a two- or even three-dimensional map. Thus, you can obtain a census database containing population figures and create a map showing the degree to which a city is racially segregated.

Statistical Software   **Statistical software** programs are designed for the application of specific statistical procedures to a variety of data. The procedures range from simple frequency analyses to advanced multiple regression diagnostics.

Distinctions among these programs sometimes blur. A good spreadsheet program can perform some database functions. It can also handle a few basic statistical procedures. A statistical package can aggregate data in ways similar to a database manager. The problem is magnified by the fact that a single group of data can be manipulated in a spreadsheet, a database manager, a mapping program or a statistical package. To solve this dilemma, return to the analogy of the computer as a tool. Each software package is also a tool. It is simply a matter of choosing the right tool for the right job. You can use the butt of a screwdriver to drive a nail, or you can use a hammer to force a screw into a board. Neither approach is particularly efficient. Likewise, you would not want to use a spreadsheet to handle database functions or a database manager to perform advanced statistical analysis.

HOW THE COMPUTER HANDLES DATA

Computers operate in a black and white world where every question has a yes/no answer. In its most basic form, each individual circuit uses pulses of electricity passing through it to symbolize yes/no, open/closed or on/off

Decimal Numbers in Binary Format	
Decimal	Binary
0	0000
1	0001
2	0010
3	0011
4	0100
5	0101
6	0110
7	0111
8	1000
9	1001

conditions. A circuit that is on passes one signal to the computer, which is usually represented with a *1*. A circuit that is off passes a different signal, which is usually represented with a *0*. Thus, computers operate in **binary,** a numerical system with only two possible values, usually represented as 0 and 1. Binary is therefore a base 2 numbering system.

We generally use a decimal, or base 10, numbering system in our day-to-day lives. One place or digit in this system can have one of 10 possible values, 0 through 9. By contrast, a **bit,** or *binary digit*, can have one of only two possible values. Therefore, it takes more binary digits to have the same data potential as a single decimal place. How many more is relatively easy to determine. Each bit has two possible values. Thus adding one bit doubles the data potential. Each additional bit doubles it again. Thus, four bits would be needed ($2 \times 2 \times 2 \times 2 = 16$) in order to handle the data potential of a single decimal.

In order to represent more complex data, computers resort to **coding**—the strings of 1s and 0s that represent various numbers, letters and symbols. Imagine a giant decoder ring with three different circles on it. The outer circle consists of an ordered list of decimal numbers from 0 to 255. The middle circle holds the binary equivalent of those numbers from 00000000 to 11111111. The inner circle holds interchangeable code equivalents for the various numbers. If we put in the EBCDIC (Extended Binary Coded Decimal Interchange Code) circle, the decimal number 80 and its binary equivalent 01010000 correspond to the character "&." Remove the EBCDIC circle and replace it with the ASCII (American Standard Code for Information Interchange) circle and you would find that 80 and 01010000 now correspond to the capital letter "P." The value assigned to any binary string depends on the code key used.

Representing all the various characters is obviously no small task. Binary strings must be assigned to the decimals 0 through 9, all letters of the alphabet

Representing Binary Data	
Term	Data Stored
bit	*a single 0 or 1*
byte	*eight bits*
kilobyte (K)	*approximately 1,000 bytes (half a typed page)*
megabyte (MB)	*approximately 1 million bytes (500 pages)*
gigabyte (GB)	*approximately 1 billion bytes (500,000 pages)*
terabyte (TB)	*approximately 1 trillion bytes (500 million pages)*

(capitals as well as lowercase), typographic symbols like periods and commas, and a variety of machine codes such as carriage returns and line feeds. Both ASCII, the coding system of personal computers, and EBCDIC, the coding system of IBM mainframes, reserve 256 different binary strings to encode data. Again, it is easy to determine how long binary strings must be to contain all those possible combinations: $2 \times 2 \times 2 \times 2 \times 2 \times 2 \times 2 \times 2$ (eight bits) = 256. The term **byte** describes the collection of eight bits representing a single character on the computer. A byte is commonly depicted in two halves. Thus, 01010000 becomes 0101 0000. It may sound a bit comical, but each half of a byte is called a **nibble,** or **nybble**—more specifically, the left nibble and the right nibble.

STRUCTURE OF THE COMPUTER

Although it is useful to understand the terminology, most of the time bits, bytes and nibbles remain behind the scenes. Just as it is easier for humans to operate with decimal rather than binary numbers, it is also much easier for us to understand computers in terms of physical structure rather than electronic. The most common and perhaps the most appropriate metaphor for computer structure is the filing cabinet. Filing cabinets store data in an organized fashion. They have drawers that contain folders, which in turn contain other folders or files.

A personal computer is like a filing cabinet. The drawers correspond to the computer's drives. Most machines have at least two disk drives: a fixed disk drive and a floppy disk drive. The **hard,** or **fixed, disk drive** is the main storage drive of the computer. It consists of a rigid, usually fixed, magnetic disk spinning inside a casing that holds electronics capable of magnetically storing data on that disk and reading data from it. On most computers, the hard drive is denoted by the letter C. Note that all computer drive designations are followed by a colon; thus, the hard disk drive is usually referred to as the C: *drive*. The **floppy disk drive** handles data from small, removable diskettes. A modern floppy disk offers approximately 1.44 megabytes of

Common Computer Drive Designations

Drive	Purpose
A:	main floppy disk drive
B:	secondary floppy disk drive
C:	main hard drive
D:	secondary hard drive or CD-ROM drive
E:	secondary storage device or CD-ROM drive
F:–Z:	other storage devices or network drives

storage space, compared with hard drives that store data well into the gigabyte range. The main floppy drive is often denoted by the letter A and therefore is generally called the A: *drive*. On computers with two floppy drives, the second drive is denoted by the letter B.

Until recently the floppy disk drives were the primary channel for transferring data to and from the computer's hard drive. Now CD-ROM (compact disc–read-only memory) drives handle most of those duties. The **CD-ROM drive** enables the computer to read information stored optically on compact discs, much the same way that stereo systems do. Newer systems also allow the computer to write information on specially prepared compact discs. These drives are often known as read/write CD-ROM drives. On computers with only one hard disk, the CD-ROM drive is usually designated with a D. On some systems, it may be designated with an E.

Additional drives, such as Zip drives, Jaz drives and SparQ drives offer larger removable disk storage, ranging from 100 megabytes for the Zip drive to a gigabyte for the Jaz and SparQ drives. Individual systems might be configured with a host of other secondary storage devices, such as magneto-optical drives and magnetic tape backup systems. In general, each storage device receives a separate drive letter on the computer in order to keep the system well organized.

In addition to physically connected storage devices, a computer may be attached to a **local area network (LAN),** a collection of interconnected computers and peripherals located within a relatively small geographic area that usually have the ability to communicate easily with one another and can often access a main network computer. Drives on the main network computer that are accessible by others on the LAN will also be designated by letters.

A filing cabinet's drawers can contain folders. The same is true on a computer. **Folders,** called **directories** in text-based operating systems, are the main component of the computer's file system, allowing users to meaningfully organize files on the computer's various drives. A disk drive can contain multiple folders. Each folder can, in turn, contain additional folders or files (Figure I.1).

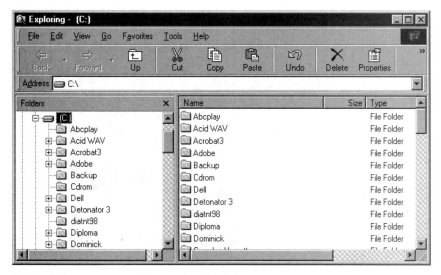

Figure I.1

A typical drive and directory file structure in Windows 98.

In computer terms, a **file** is a finite collection of bytes with a name that can be referred to in basic operations. There are two basic types of files: data files and programs. **Data files** serve as the basic mechanism for storing general data. **Programs,** occasionally referred to as **applications,** contain lists of instructions that tell the computer what to do in performing a requested operation. The type of any given file can often be inferred by the **file extension,** the portion that follows the final period in a file name. Because older DOS file extensions were limited to three digits, most files retain three-digit extensions today. The more common file extensions are .exe, .com, .bat, .txt, and .dll. The first two file extensions refer to programs, while the latter three refer to data files.

When referencing a file on the computer, we often need to state its **path,** that is, the three components of the file's location: the drive, the folder and any subfolders, and the file name including extension. Backward-leaning slashes (\) separate the drive, folder, subfolders and file name. For example, the path of your Excel spreadsheet program might look something like C:\Program_Files\Microsoft_Office\Office\Excel.exe.

SOME BASIC WINDOWS DETAILS

Most IBM-compatible computers utilize the Microsoft-manufactured operating system. Older computers use MS-DOS, often with a Windows GUI. More modern computers use a Windows operating system—Windows 95, Windows 98 or Windows NT. This section reviews some of the basic features

Some Common File Extensions

Programs

.exe	executable file
.com	command file

Data Files

.bat	batch file
.dll	dynamically linked library
.txt/.text	text file
.csv	text file using comma-separated values
.doc	MS Word file
.wpd	WordPerfect file
.xls	Excel spreadsheet file
.wk?	Lotus spreadsheet file
.dbf	dBase/FoxPro database file
.db	Paradox database file
.htm/ .html	HTML files

of Windows operating systems. Although certainly not a comprehensive guide, it should provide a few tips to enable you to manipulate and run files on your computer.

The primary component of the Windows graphical user interface is known as the **desktop,** the large interactive area you see when the Windows operating system has finished loading (Figure I.2). The desktop has several graphical icons that allow you to interact with the system. The My Computer icon allows you to see everything on your computer. The Network Neighborhood icon allows you to see other computers connected to your LAN, if you are using one. The Recycle Bin icon looks and acts like a kind of garbage can where you can drag unwanted files for disposal. You might also see other icons that represent programs or folders that store program icons. If a program has an icon on the desktop or is in a folder on the desktop, all you need to do to start the program is double-click on the icon, often referred to as "launching" the program. To double-click, simply hold your mouse over the program icon and rapidly click the left mouse button twice *without moving the mouse in any direction*.

You have a fair amount of flexibility in customizing your desktop. Clicking the right button of your mouse, called "right-clicking," opens a pop-up menu of choices: arrange icons, line up icons, and create new folders or shortcuts. A **shortcut** is an icon that allows you to access a program located elsewhere. With a little practice and your Windows reference manual, you can organize the desktop according to your specific needs or tastes.

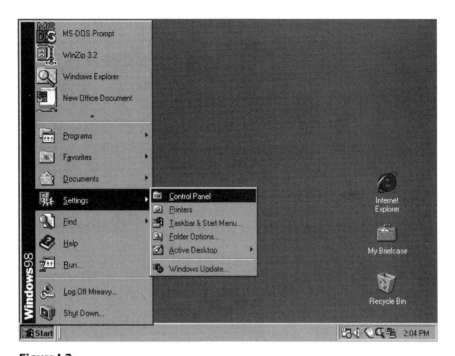

Figure I.2

A typical Windows OS desktop with the Start button activated.

In the lower left corner of the desktop is the Start button. The Start button serves as a gateway to the computer's programs. Point to the Start button with your mouse and click once on the left mouse button; a special pop-up menu called the Taskbar will appear with a variety of options. Programs lets you select from among the various applications on your machine. Documents offers a choice of the most recently used data files (i.e., word processing, graphics, etc.) that have been opened by the user. Selecting a document launches the appropriate application in which to view that document. Settings permits access to the controls and configuration information for the computer. Find allows you to search for files or folders on your computer or for a specific computer on the LAN. Help launches the Windows Help program. Run allows you to run specific programs on any drive connected to your computer. These options will be reviewed later as needed.

Arguably the most important interface program that comes with the Windows operating system is Windows Explorer, a program that allows users to view and manipulate the structure of all drives and directories on the computer. This program should not be confused with Microsoft's Internet Explorer, a World Wide Web browser that is discussed in chapter 5. To launch Windows Explorer, click on the Start button, use the mouse cursor to

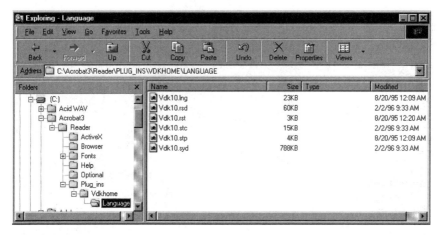

Figure I.3

Computer structure seen in the Exploring window of Windows Explorer.

highlight and click on Programs, scroll down the list until you find Windows Explorer, and click once on it.

Windows Explorer is similar to a program called File Manager that came with earlier versions of Windows. The program's purpose is to manage files on the computer. Once the program is launched, the Exploring window appears (Figure I.3). The computer's directory structure appears on the left side of the screen, with the Desktop icon at the top of the screen. Drives are listed in alphabetical order. If an icon has a plus (+) sign to its left, then you may click on that drive or directory to **expand** it, (i.e., to view the next layer of a drive or directory's contents—assuming the drive currently holds a disk). If an icon has a minus (−) sign next to it, then that drive or directory has already been expanded. You may click on the icon to **collapse** it, or temporarily close the layer to viewing. The currently expanded layer of the directory structure appears on the right side of the screen, including the size of any files in the directory and other data related to those files.

Windows Explorer enables you to easily open, copy, move and delete files or folders. It also allows you to create new folders and shortcuts. The following commands play an important part in the proper operation of Windows Explorer:

File

New creates a new folder or shortcut.
Delete removes the file or the folder and all its contents to the Recycle Bin.
Rename renames the selected file or folder.
Close exits Windows Explorer.

Edit

Undo reverses the last command given.

Cut removes the file or folder and its contents to temporary memory.

Copy places a copy of the file or folder and its contents into temporary memory.

Paste places a copy of any file or folder stored in temporary memory at the current selected location.

Select All selects and highlights the entire layer for the next command.

View

Arrange Icons sorts icons by name, type, size or date.

Options allows the user to customize various Explorer characteristics. (Note: if you want to be able to see file extensions, you must go to Options and click on the check beside "Hide MS-DOS file extensions for file types that are registered.")

Tools

Find functions like the Find command on the Start button's taskbar.

Help

Help Topics allows access to the Windows Explorer Help program.

SUMMARY

This appendix provides an overview of how computer hardware and software interact, how the computer handles data and how personal computers are structured. It also furnishes some basic information on how to find your way around a computer system. Remember that this appendix is only a very general treatment of the subject. The only way to become familiar with your system is to actually use it.

II

Tips for Writing the Computer-Assisted Reporting Story

One of the first things I said about computer-assisted reporting in this text was that computers do not change the basic duty of the journalist. They simply provide a tool that enables journalists to fulfill that duty more easily, quickly and thoroughly than before. Why, then, do you need advice on writing the computer-assisted reporting story as opposed to any other story that a journalist might do? The answer is that you don't. I just want to reinforce the notion that a computer-assisted reporting story should adhere to the same standards of journalism that other stories do. To that end, the following eight tips will help you surmount some of the obstacles that the computer can throw in the path of a good story.

CHECK YOUR FACTS

Computer-assisted reporting is often about looking for unusual patterns in the data. But when you find one, your first reaction should be one of skepticism. Ask yourself, "Is this really what I think it is?" Too often, the answer is no. Jeffrey C. Kummer of the *St. Paul Pioneer Press* recalled one such instance in his own reporting:

> We did a CAR story a few years back examining gun-related violence in Minnesota. The reporter performed what seemingly was a fairly routine analysis of death record data to determine where shooting deaths were most prevalent. The answer was not what we expected. The gun capital of Minnesota appeared to be a fairly quiet Twin Cities suburb.
>
> Once the excitement of the discovery ebbed, we went back to the data and examined the question our query posed. It turned out that we had asked the computer to count the number of gun-related deaths occurring in each city—not the cities where the shootings had taken place. A seemingly minor distinction, but an important one. The suburb that had topped our list on the first run-

through was also the home of the state's largest emergency hospital. So gunshot victims struck by bullets in Minneapolis and St. Paul were being pronounced dead once they had arrived at the suburban trauma center.[1]

Double-checking your data can save you the time and embarrassment of asking the wrong questions or, worse yet, writing the wrong story.

TAKE A STEP BACK

Too often, computer-assisted reporters feel like they are drowning in numbers. Kummer calls this feeling "CAR fatigue." Things that were once intensely interesting now seem a bit dull after you've rehashed them so many times. You need to take a step back and try to get a fresh look at the story before you start writing.

One way to step back is to prepare a written summary of your data prior to writing the story. You may recall from chapter 2 that Valerie Lilley and the team at the Peoria *Journal Star* prepared a "cheat sheet" based on their examination of the data. They then approached their own cheat sheet as if it were a press release. It made writing the story that much easier.

FOCUS ON PEOPLE

Josef Stalin once said, "One death is a tragedy. A million deaths is a statistic." Computer-assisted reporters need to keep that in mind. The computer may have made the story possible, but it is not the story itself. In most cases, the story is about people and it should be told that way. Consider this example by Patricia Callahan and Kirk Mitchell of the *Denver Post*:

> Eleven children were molested. One was forced to have sex with a dog.
> One lay injured on a bathroom floor, his face smeared with his own feces. That toddler, Miguel Arias-Baca, later died.
> They are the state's dirty little secrets.
> Foster children, wards of the state taken from abusive or neglectful relatives, suffered again in foster homes that were supposed to keep them from harm.[2]

That lead-in doesn't sound like a "computer-assisted reporting story," and that's part of what makes it a good computer-assisted reporting story. The focus is on the people, not on the numbers.

GO LIGHT ON THE NUMBERS

Although you want to establish an early focus on people, you can't communicate the scope of a problem without using numbers. Use them, but use them wisely. Too many numbers overwhelm the reader. A good rule of thumb is to use no more than three numbers in a single paragraph—that includes years and other numerical references.

PLACE NUMBERS IN CONTEXT

Numbers mean very little standing alone. They need to be placed in a context that gives them meaning. While working on a series that examined fatal shootings by police, David Ashenfelter and Joe Swickard of the *Detroit Free Press* found that Detroit officers were involved in nearly 90 fatal shootings between 1991 and 1998. To give this number more meaning, the authors used several tricks to provide context.

Provide a Frequency

Knowing how often something occurs can give it more meaning. You might also compare the frequency of an event during a given time period one year to that same period in another. Ashenfelter and Swickard looked at how many fatal shootings occurred on average each year.[3]

Detroit, with nearly 1 million residents, averaged nearly 10 fatal police shootings a year in 1990–98.

Compare It to Other Locations

A familiar way to give meaning to a figure is to compare it with the same figure in other locations. Ashenfelter and Swickard compared Detroit with New York and Los Angeles.

The Motor City rate is nearly 2 1/2 times higher than New York's rate and more than 1 1/2 times Los Angeles'—two cities sweating under the national spotlight amid scrutiny for police misconduct.

Provide a Ratio or a Rate

Readers want to know how common something is in the population. A rate or ratio presents this information. Ashenfelter and Swickard used the rate suggested by the FBI.

To make the comparison, the Free Press calculated fatal shootings on the basis of the FBI's standard measure, 100,000 residents. Detroit had a rate of 0.92 fatal shootings per 100,000 residents.

Consider All the Possibilities

Ask yourself if all your comparisons are valid, and try to discover new ways to look at the data. Despite all of Ashenfelter and Swickard's efforts, Detroit police argued that the numbers were still out of context.

Detroit Police Chief Benny Napoleon and Wayne County Prosecutor John O'Hair contend that the figures don't take into account factors that might cause Detroit's rate to be so high. They said the rates need to be viewed in the context of violent crime rather than population.

EXPLAIN YOURSELF, BUT MAKE IT SIMPLE AND QUICK

Your readers may wonder how you got your story. Don't let them. Explain your analysis, but do it simply and quickly—and preferably in the top half of the story. Consider this example from the *Bergen Record* in New Jersey. Jan Barry, Peter J. Sampson and Don Stancavish waited until the seventh paragraph before they explained the origin of their story. When they did, it was done so that readers could easily understand it:

> The Record examined more than 500 municipal, county, and school audits—
> the only public document in which this liability is disclosed—to gauge the cost
> of this benefit to New Jersey taxpayers.[4]

There is no need to say more. The reader doesn't need to know that you used FoxPro and performed 432 complicated queries. They don't need to know your SQL syntax. Just give them the basics and move on.

USE A NERD BOX FOR COMPLICATED OR CONTROVERSIAL ANALYSES

There are times when some readers will want to know every detail, from the number of records you analyzed to how you did the math, especially if the analysis is potentially controversial. But you don't want the "How We Did It" to get in the way of the story. The solution is to use a nerd box—a sidebar that explains the methodology of your study, including all the technical details as well as any assumptions that you may have made. The nerd box allows you to explain what you did and why. For example, the *New York Daily News* ran a series detailing how hundreds of New York doctors had hidden malpractice records. They created a list of the most-sued medical professionals. Their nerd box was titled "How They Were Ranked":

> The doctors, dentists and podiatrists on the Daily News' most sued list are
> ranked two ways in these profiles.
>
> The News ranking indicates where they stand in their profession based
> on the number of suits filed against them from 1988 through 1998.
> Their payment rank is based on the number of payments they made to
> patients in malpractice cases.
> The News found the number of payments and amounts in either the National Practitioner Data Bank or court records. Where the information came

from the data bank, practitioners were ranked within the state and nation for their profession.

Where the information came from court records, no ranking was possible (indicated by an asterisk).

For doctors, the ranking counts only payments of at least $30,000. All payments were counted for dentists and podiatrists.[5]

Like this one, most nerd boxes are six to ten paragraphs long. They are usually straightforward and to the point; however, more difficult analyses may require more complicated nerd boxes.

INCLUDE A SUMMARY

A summary provides the reporter with a way to get facts across more quickly and easily than a narrative does. The summary can be part of the story itself, or it can run as a sidebar. Consider this sidebar summary that accompanied an investigation of suburban politics by *Detroit News* reporters Gordon Trowbridge and Jodi Upton:

An investigation of suburban Detroit campaigns reveals:

The total suburban political war chest for last year's elections totaled $2.1 million. The amount spent per campaign often exceeded the salary paid to the officeholder.

As a group, developers, builders and others in real estate gave the most: $226,000. That group was followed by small businesses, city contractors and city employees and their unions.

Records of candidate contributions often are incomplete, inaccurate or unreadable.

Contributions here are quite high compared to communities in other states.[6]

Notice how the summary conveys a great deal of information that can be easily assimilated by the reader.

BE CONSERVATIVE

In many ways, this last tip is a corollary of the first. Even after you have checked your facts, it pays to be somewhat conservative when you release your findings. Better to understate a fact that you can hit hard later than to overstate it and be forced to run a retraction of some sort. Richard Galant, associate managing editor of *Newsday*, offers the following advice to CAR journalists:

Try to imagine all the potential counter-arguments to your central finding. Bounce it off experts. You may have to go back to the data to see if your findings and methodology are really bulletproof. Make sure your story states prominently the point of view of those who can make reasonable arguments against the central finding.[7]

Take another look at the last example under the tip titled "Place Numbers in Context." Ashenfelter and Swickard made certain to include the opposing interpretation of their data prominently in their story—the third paragraph as a matter of fact. That's the kind of journalism that Galant is talking about.

NOTES

1. Jeffrey C. Kummer, *Tactics for Writing and Editing CAR Stories*. Handout available online from Investigative Reporters and Editors <http://www.ire.org>.

2. Patricia Callahan and Kirk Mitchell, "Foster Care Too Often Fails to Keep Kids Safe," *Denver Post*, May 21, 2000. Available online at <http://www.denverpost.com/news/foster0521a.htm>.

3. The quotes provided are from David Ashenfelter and Joe Swickard, "Detroit Cops Are Deadliest in the U.S.," *Detroit Free Press*, May 15, 2000. Available online at <http://www.freep.com/news/locway/shoot15__20000515.htm>.

4. Jan Barry, Peter J. Sampson and Don Stancavish, "Public Money, Hidden Costs," *Bergen Record*, April 9, 2000. Available online at <http://www.bergen.com/news/payday09200004091.htm>.

5. "How They Were Ranked," *New York Daily News*, March 5, 2000. Available online at <http://www.nydailynews.com/manual/news/Doctors/thelist.asp>.

6. Gordon Trowbridge and Jodi Upton, "How Builders Buy Access, Influence in Local Politics," *Detroit News*, June 4, 2000. Available online at <http://www.detnews.com/specialreports/2000/campaign/lead/lead.htm>.

7. Richard Galant, *Writing the Story*. Handout available online from Investigative Reporters and Editors <http://ww.ire.org>.

GLOSSARY

absolute reference   a reference that does not change when the formula is copied from one location to another.

acquisition phase   the phase of the computer-assisted reporting process during which the data is actually obtained.

aggregates   computer functions used to create groupings of some sort.

aggregating   see **grouping.**

aglets   small programs that actually transfer themselves around the Web to actively search for data, deliver messages or communicate with other computers.

American Standard Code for Information Interchange (ASCII)   a basic set of characters used and understood by nearly every computer in the world.

anonymous FTP   a system that allows users to transfer publicly accessible files from a host computer to their local machine.

applications   see **programs.**

argument   the values that the function uses to perform a calculation.

backbone   the fast, top-level communication lines that handle most of the network's data traffic.

balanced budget   a budget in which expenditures exactly equal revenues.

baud   a channel's maximum capacity in electrical symbols per second.

binary   a numerical system with only two possible values, usually represented as 0 and 1.

bit   a binary digit; it can have one of only two possible values.

body   the actual content of an e-mail message.

bookmark   a URL that your computer stores together with the title of the page to which the URL refers.

Booleans   logical expressions that specify a set of conditions that Web documents must match in order to be deemed relevant (e.g., AND, OR, NOT).

bps rate   the speed of a modem—the number of bits per second that it can move over the line.

bridge   a piece of hardware that physically connects one LAN with another.

browser   any program that allows users to connect with a Web server, access files and display those files on the computer.

budget summary   a department-by-department breakdown of proposed revenues and expenditures.

byte   the collection of eight bits that represents a single character on the computer.

Cartesian product   sometimes called a **cross product**; the result of a faulty query that inadvertently matches every record in one table with every record in another, thus providing exaggerated results.

CD-ROM drive   the drive that enables the computer to read information stored optically on compact discs.

cell   the intersection of a column and a row within a spreadsheet.

cell address   the letter of the intersecting column followed by the number of the intersecting row in a spreadsheet.

cell reference   the cell address of the number, text or formula to be used within a formula (see **relative cell reference** and **absolute reference**).

census   a count of an entire population, usually including some numeric descriptions and characteristics of that population.

central processing unit (CPU)   the brain of the computer; it executes instructions and performs arithmetic or logical operations.

centralized approach   a method of newsroom organization in which computer-assisted reporting is confined to a specific person or group of people within the newsroom.

clauses   distinct parts of an SQL *select* statement.

client   a computer running software that requests services from a server.

coding   strings of 0s and 1s that represent various numbers, letters and symbols; used by computers to represent complex data.

collapse   to temporarily close a layer of a drive or directory's contents so that it cannot be viewed.

communication software   computer software that encompasses a variety of programs designed to allow one computer to communicate with one or more other computers.

composite key field   two or more fields used together to uniquely identify a record in much the same way as a single key field.

composition phase   the phase of the computer-assisted reporting process during which the actual writing and editing takes place.

computer-assisted reporting, or **CAR**   the use of computers to gather or analyze data for the purpose of transforming that data into information used as part of a narrative to be transmitted via a medium of mass communication.

conception phase   the phase of the computer-assisted reporting process during which the reporter generates the actual story idea.

crippleware   shareware distributed with certain key features disabled. The missing features are enabled when users pay a specific fee to the creators.

cross product   see **Cartesian product.**

data   isolated facts.

data dictionary   a reference that allows you to decode what's in a database.

data files   the basic mechanism for storing general data on the computer.

data format   the format of files produced by common spreadsheet, database or other data programs.

data mining   a process whereby reporters look at data from a number of different angles in search of patterns that suggest potential news stories.

database   a group of related data organized so that it can be accessed easily and quickly.

database management software   computer programs that not only permit sorting of data, but also allow users to meaningfully filter and aggregate data.

decentralized approach   a method of newsroom organization that emphasizes universal access to computer-assisted reporting tools.

delimited text files   files that make use of a specific symbol, usually a comma, to separate the data into columns.

demographics   vital or social statistics related to a group.

design view   the area in Microsoft Access where the user can build queries by example; sometimes called the **QBE grid.**

desktop   the large interactive area you see when the Windows operating system has finished loading.

detailed budget   revenues and expenditures broken down on a line-by-line basis.

dieware   shareware designed to stop working after a specific number of days or uses.

directories   see **folders.**

document sources   written records that are either historical (e.g., government reports) or topical (e.g., press releases, advertisements, other news stories).

domain name system (DNS)   a hierarchical scheme for converting a name to a numeric IP address.

donationware   freeware whose authors ask that users make a donation either to the authors themselves or to a designated charity.

download   the process of copying a file from the server to the client computer.

e-mail clients   programs that allow users to read, write, send, receive and manage e-mail.

examination phase   the phase of the computer-assisted reporting process during which one or more computer programs are utilized to filter, sort, group and otherwise analyze records.

expand   to view the next layer of a drive or directory's contents.

expenditures   what an organization expects to spend during the budget period.

exporting   the process of transforming a file into a format easily read by another program.

exposition phase   the phase of the computer-assisted reporting process during which the traditional telephone line and shoe leather process of journalism takes place.

field   an area of a database record where a specific bit of data is stored.

file   a finite collection of bytes with a name that can be referred to in basic operations.

file compression   the use of a computer program to temporarily shrink one or more files.

file extension   the portion of a file name that follows the final period.

file transfer protocol (FTP)   a set of rules governing the transfer of files between two computers using TCP/IP.

fixed-column format   a format that physically lines data up into columns, with each column representing a single character; sometimes called **fixed-width format.**

fixed-width format   see **fixed-column format.**

flat-file database   see **nonrelational database.**

floppy disk drive   the disk drive on the computer that handles data from small, removable diskettes.

folders   the main component of the computer's file system; they allow users to meaningfully organize files on the computer's various drives.

form   a series of boxes and buttons that allows the user to enter letters, numbers and other information.

formula   an equation that describes a calculation and defines the numbers, text or other formula to be used in that calculation.

freeware   software distributed free of charge. Users can obtain a copy via the Internet and use it as long as they desire.

functions   predefined formulas that perform calculations in a spreadsheet based on information provided by the user.

generic text files   files that lack the formatting codes that some programs put in. As a result, they generally take up less space. Perhaps more important, generic text files can be read by virtually any commercially available program.

graphical user interface   a computer interface that provides humans with windows, buttons and other graphical elements that make accessing computer software easier.

group by   an SQL clause that tells the computer to group aggregates together by a specific field.

grouping   performing a variety of mathematical functions on a specific field or fields; sometimes referred to as **aggregating.**

hard, or **fixed, disk drive**   the main storage drive of the computer; it consists of a rigid, usually fixed, magnetic disk spinning inside a casing that holds electronics capable of magnetically storing data on that disk and reading data from it.

hardware   the physical components of the computer and the machines attached to it.

having   an SQL clause used for filtering aggregates.

header   the first few lines of an e-mail message, those that handle information regarding the source, destination and contents of the message.

header row   a row within a spreadsheet—generally Row 1—that contains column descriptions.

home page   a Web site's front or opening page, which often acts both as a gateway and as a tool for organizing the site's contents.

host   a computer running software that provides services to clients.

hub   a piece of hardware that serves as a common wiring point, like the hub of a wheel.

hypertext   a kind of "super" text consisting of traditional, linear text together with links to other documents or to other places within the same document.

Hypertext Markup Language, or **HTML**   a specialized code that uses hidden tags to format documents that will be read by Web browsers.

hypertext transfer protocol, or **HTTP**   a formal set of rules that allows computers to exchange Web documents.

importing   bringing a file of a different format into the program you are using.

information   one or more facts placed in a context that gives them meaning.

input devices   computer components that accept commands or data from the user.

Internet   a global network of computer networks utilizing a common language to communicate with one another.

Internet protocol   the formal set of rules that govern how electronic messages are broken into packets, routed and reassembled.

Internet service provider (ISP)   a business that concentrates on connecting its subscribers directly to the Internet.

interviewing the data   the critical thinking process involved in pulling a story out of a spreadsheet or database.

IP address   a series of four numbers, separated by periods, that uniquely identifies every computer connected to the Internet.

Java applets   small applications that are downloaded from the server and run on a user's computer.

key field   a field that uniquely identifies each record in a table, usually so that it can be cross-referenced with another table or tables.

keywords   words that the search engine attempts to match in documents within its database.

links   highlighted words or graphics that allow users to jump from one hypertext document to another referenced by the link.

list owner   the person responsible for administering a mailing list.

local area network, or **LAN**   a collection of interconnected computers located within a relatively small geographic area.

location phase   the phase of the computer-assisted reporting process during which the appropriate data is located.

log-in ID   see **user name.**

log-on process   passing a user name and password to another computer in order to identify the user and gain access to the system.

long form   a census form that contains all the questions of the **short form** as well as 58 items about social and economic factors such as income, occupation and schooling; sometimes called the sample questionnaire.

mailing list   an electronic discussion group consisting of computer users who register their addresses with a server that facilitates the exchange of e-mail on a specific subject or subjects.

mainframes very large and expensive computers designed to be used by hundreds or thousands of users either simultaneously or in batches.

mapping software computer software that allows users to take information stored in a database and depict it on a two- or even three-dimensional map.

measurement error mistakes resulting from the way census study subjects are counted or measured.

megahertz (MHz) a unit of measure equal to 1 million cycles per second.

metasearch engine a search engine that takes requests from users, sends those requests out to one or more other search engines and organizes the responses into a single, readable report.

microcomputers see **personal computers.**

microprocessor a tiny silicon chip containing miniaturized circuits that comprise most of the computer's functions in a fraction of the space.

MIME, or **multipurpose Internet mail extensions** the current standard for transferring multimedia e-mail messages, binary attachments and other nontext data.

modem a piece of hardware that allows a computer to send and receive signals over a telephone line.

nagware shareware that displays an annoying screen urging users to register the software. The screen often requires that users hit extra keys or simply wait a few seconds in order to get the program to run properly.

nerd box a sidebar that explains the methodology of your study, including all the technical details as well as any assumptions that you may have made.

netiquette a loose code stipulating acceptable behavior for communication on the Internet.

network interface card a circuit board installed in the computer with ports for wires that physically connect it with the rest of the network.

nibble, or **nybble** half of a byte.

nonrelational database a single, stand-alone table of data, sometimes called a **flat-file database.**

online service provider (OSP) a business that concentrates on connecting its subscribers to a variety of services located on its own site.

operating system (OS) a group of interdependent programs that orchestrate the operation of computer hardware.

optical character recognition (OCR) software programs that enable the user to transform a picture of text into a word processing document.

output devices components that allow the computer to communicate processed data beyond the CPU and storage devices.

packets small pieces of data that include an origin and destination.

parsing a process of placing text into appropriate columns.

password a series of characters that helps ensure that people other than the registered user cannot use his or her account.

path the three components of a file's location, that is, the drive, the folder and any subfolders, and the file name including extension.

people source   any individual or individuals who might provide journalists with a story idea, from family and friends to government officials and whistle-blowers.

per capita figure   a figure representing the number of people or items for each unit of a population.

percent difference   the point difference between two numbers expressed as a percentage of the expected (first) value.

peripherals   input, output and secondary storage devices that are external to the casing that houses the CPU.

personal computers, or **PCs**   desktop-sized computers designed to be purchased by individuals or small businesses.

PINE (Program for Internet News and E-mail)   the most common host-based e-mail client.

point difference   the number of points separating two percentages.

population   any defined group of people or things.

pop-up windows   computer program interfaces that pop up in the middle of the screen.

port   a logical channel associated with each program on a host computer.

Portable Document Format, or **PDF**   a universal file format intended to allow users to distribute, over the Internet and Web, documents that retain their original format.

Post Office Protocol (POP or **POP3)**   a set of rules governing the exchange of electronic messages between a client and a server.

precision journalism   the use of social science techniques, particularly quantitative methods such as surveys, as an aid in reporting the news.

programs   lists of instructions that tell the computer what to do in performing a requested operation.

projected revenues and expenditures   the proposed budget for the coming year.

pull-down menus   computer program interfaces that the user can pull down from a menu bar at the top of the screen.

QBE grid   see **design view.**

query   a formal request for information from a database.

Query by Example   a query language in which you use your mouse to build a query by selecting from various options on the screen; often referred to as QBE.

random access memory (RAM)   that part of the computer that stores data electronically.

range   a block of cells within a spreadsheet.

ratio   a comparison that states the number of units of one thing for each unit of another.

record   a collection of individual data items pertaining to one entry in the database.

record layout   a listing of the names of all fields contained in a database, along with some information about those fields.

redact   to delete fields or records from a database, usually for the purpose of protecting the privacy of the individuals whose data is contained within the database.

relational database   a collection of two or more tables that are intended to be used in conjunction with each other.

relative cell reference   a cell reference that points to other data in relation to the cell in which the reference is located (see **absolute reference**).

revenues   what an organization expects to collect during the budget period.

router   a piece of hardware that sends data in the general direction of its destination.

sample   a fragment selected from a population.

sampling error   differences between the sample and the population that are due to simple chance.

scanner   a piece of computer hardware, looking much like a copier, that takes a picture of something and transforms it into a computer file.

search engine   a program that allows interaction with a searchable database of Web pages, a database that usually contains each page's title, URL and a brief excerpt or description.

searchable database   a collection of related data that can be searched according to one or more criteria.

secondary storage devices   computer devices that provide the capability to keep data even after power has been turned off.

second-level domain   in a URL, the shorthand name for the organization operating the computer.

select query   in SQL, a query that allows the user to choose which data from a table should be displayed and the manner in which it should be displayed.

self-extracting file   an executable program that decompresses and extracts files from the attached archive.

server   a computer that runs software that provides some type of service to other computers able to connect with it.

shareware   software distributed free of charge, but with the idea that users who decide to keep the program will pay a specific fee to register it. Users registering the software frequently receive technical support and other benefits.

shell account   an interface that allows the user to input text commands in order to access the server's programs.

short form   a census form that contains a limited number of basic questions about race, gender, housing and so on that are administered to every person and household in the United States; sometimes called the 100 percent questionnaire.

shortcut   an icon that allows you to access a program located elsewhere.

signature   a short text file tacked onto the end of all outgoing messages, usually providing details about the sender and his or her company.

simple mail transfer protocol (SMTP)   a set of rules governing the exchange of electronic messages between servers.

software   programmed instructions that tell the computer what to do.

sorting   the term used for ordering items within a spreadsheet, either alphabetically or numerically, in ascending or descending order.

specialized search engines   search engines that gather information for their databases by crawling the Web, much like larger engines do; however, specialized engines crawl only a limited number of sites either within a specific region or that deal with a specific topic.

spiders   programs that connect to Web pages and download the text to a database.

spreadsheet   a two-dimensional file comprised of columns and rows that is used to facilitate mathematical and other operations.

spreadsheet software   computer programs designed to perform calculations on numerical data.

statistical software   computer programs designed for the application of specific statistical procedures to a variety of data.

Structured Query Language (SQL)   the industry-standard query language used by most database management programs.

TCP/IP (transmission control protocol/Internet protocol)   the standard set of rules that all networks use to communicate over the Internet.

telnet   a protocol that allows a user to create a text-based link to a remote host and utilize its programs.

third-level domain   in a URL, the portion that represents a subdomain within the organization.

thread   single online discussion consisting of the initial message and all subsequent replies.

top-level domain   in a URL, the two- or three-digit extension that represents all those computers operated by organizations of a specific type.

transformation phase   the phase of the computer-assisted reporting process during which the data is moved to a usable storage medium, usually CDs or floppy disks, and translated into a readable format.

uniform resource locator, or **URL**   the precise access address for a Web page.

upload   the process of copying a file from the client computer to the server.

user name, or **log-in ID**   an identification for individual users or types of users to a computer system.

UUdecode   the program that translates UUencoded ASCII files back into binary data.

UUencode   an older, Unix-based program used to translate binary data into ASCII format.

Web directory   a table of contents for the Web that usually allows users to either browse through categories or conduct a subject-oriented search of its Web page database.

Web page   an HTML document placed on a Web server.

Web sites   collections of related Web pages.

webmaster   the person who creates or maintains the Web site.

wildcard   a character that matches all characters or groups of characters, rather than a single character, when doing a search comparison.

Windows Explorer   the program that allows you to interact with your computer's various drives, directories and files.

Winsock   a Microsoft Windows–compatible program that allows the computer to utilize TCP/IP.

WinZip   a Windows-based program that allows users to compress files and add them to an archive as well as decompress files and extract them from an archive.

wizards   utilities within a program that guide users through potentially difficult tasks in that program.

World Wide Web   a subsegment of the Internet that allows users to exchange graphical images, sound and hypertext.

ZIP file   a compressed archive, that is, a file that contains one or more other files in compressed format.

INDEX

9-track tape, magnetic tape, 4
Adams, Pat, 12, 14
aglets, 73
aggregates, 153–158, 166–168
AltaVista, 65, 66
America Online, 20, 21, 25–26, 27
Anders, Bob, 134, 145n
Anderson, Mark, 19
ARPANET, 22–23
ASCII, 124, 127, 190
Ashenfelter, David, 200, 203, 203n
Ashkinaze, Carole, 34
Atlanta Journal-Constitution, 5, 175, 177, 185n

bankruptcy, 10–16
Barlett, Don, 4
Barry, Jan, 201, 203n
Bergen Record, 201, 203n
Bibo, Terry, 15
binary, 190
Booleans, 66–68
bps rate, 27
Brimeyer, Jack, 15
Broken Pledges: The Deadly Rites of Hazing, 48
Brooks, Larry, 15
budget
  as public records, 90
  balanced, 88
  detailed, 91
  examining over time, 101
  example of, 89
  expenditures defined, 88
  in-depth analysis of, 98–102
  narrative, 101–102
  projections, 89
  revenues defined, 88
  summary, 91
  using a spreadsheet to examine, 89–102
Bureau of Labor Statistics, 25
byte, 191

Callahan, Christopher, 60
Callahan, Patricia, 199, 203n
campaign finance data, 140–141
Capps, Kalleen, 9, 11, 121
Cartesian product, 180
CBS, 3

Census Bureau
  Census 2000, 119
  data, 5, 109–111, 115, 116–119, 119n, 126
  FTP site, 76
  terms used by, 116–118
  Web site, 25, 70, 73, 108, 109
Centers for Disease Control and Prevention, 127
Central Intelligence Agency, 20
central processing unit (CPU), 188
client-server relationship, 28
Clinton, Bill, 20, 21
Compuserve, 19, 27
Congress, 15
computer-assisted reporting (CAR)
  acquisition phase, 11–13
  and elections, 3
  centralized approach, 16
  composition phase, 15–16
  conception phase, 10–11
  decentralized approach, 16–17
  definition, 2
  examination phase, 13–14
  exposition phase, 14
  investigative projects using, 18
  location phase, 11
  process, 10–16
  publishing data, 21
  short stories using, 18, 47
  transformation phase, 13
  writing the CAR story, 21, 141–143, 198–203
Cronkite, Walter, 4
Cummings, Doug, 185n
cross product, 180

Daily Times, 48
Dallas Morning News, 21
data
  ASCII, 124, 127
  definition, 2
  delimited, 124
  demographic, 107
  downloading, 74, 122
  exporting, 122
  fixed-column, 124
  fixed-width, 124

Pennsylvania Women's Press Association, 62
Peoria Journal Star, 10–16, 33, 199
personal computers, 5
Philadelphia Daily News, 133
Philadelphia Inquirer, 4, 21
POP, 35
Postal Service, 48
Poynter Institute, 58
precision journalism, 4

QEQ approach, 140, 141
queries
  broken down, 143–144
  case sensitivity in, 149
  definition, 139
  in action, 141–143
  in QBE, 147, 161–171, 173
  in SQL, 147–152, 154, 156, 158–159,
    161–164, 167–169, 173
  QEQ approach to building, 140
  questions to ask when creating, 159–160
  select, 139, 147, 148–150
query by example (QBE), 147, 161–171, 173,
  182–184

Rapid City Journal, 19
random access memory (RAM), 187
record layout, 136–137
redacting fields, 178
Reid, Whitelaw, 1, 7n
Reisner, Neil, 60–61, 64
Remington Rand, 3
Reuters, 48
Roberts, Janet, 146, 166
Robinson, Brian, 35
Robinson, John, 4
Ryerson Institute for Computer-Assisted
  Reporting in Canada, 58

Sampson, Peter, 201, 203n
San Diego Union-Tribune, 47
San Jose Mercury News, 21
scanner, 121
Schalben, Arville, 2, 7n
Schneider, Joseph, 47
Schwartz, George E., 48
Shelbyville News, 102
select statement, 148–150
shell account, 28
shortcut, 194
Siegel, Jules, 33
SMTP, 35
Social Security Administration, 176
Society of Professional Journalists, 66

software, 5, 188–189
sources
  document, 10
  people, 10
South, Jeff, 58
specialized search engines, 69–70
spiders, 65–66
spreadsheets
  absolute references in, 109
  calculating difference in, 93
  calculating per capita figures in, 112–115
  calculating percent change in, 94–96
  calculating percent of total in, 108–109
  calculating ratios in, 115–116
  cell references, 87
  cells, 85
  columns, 85
  copying cell formulas in, 93
  definition, 85
  examining a budget with, 89–102
  examples of, 84
  formatting, 92
  formulas, 87–88, 93–96
  functions, 105–106, 118
  handling negatives in, 94
  header row, 85
  locating and obtaining, 121
  news stories using, 13, 104
  percentage and point differences in, 110
  performing basic calculations with, 85–88
  physical limitations of, 85, 104
  sorting in, 96–98
  range, 106
  relative cell referencing, 88
  row, 85
  uses for, 136
  worksheets, 85
St. Louis Post-Dispatch, 21, 184
St. Paul Pioneer Press, 198
Stancavish, Don, 201, 203n
Steele, James, 4
Stevens Point Journal, 35
structured query language (SQL), 147–152,
  154, 156, 158–159, 161–164, 167–169,
  173, 179–182, 201
Sweet, Jonathan, 35
Swickard, Joe, 200, 203, 203n

TCP/IP, 23, 74
telephone-assisted reporting, 2
television, 6, 9, 11, 12, 21, 33, 34, 46, 47, 57,
  73, 115
telnet, 28, 75
threads, 39